War Memorial Park

Trevor Harkin
2007

War Memorial Park Publications

War Memorial Park

First Edition 2007

Published by War Memorial Park Publications

ISBN: 978-184426-448-3

Printed by Printondemand-worldwide Ltd

For a copy of this publication e-mail trevor_harkin@hotmail.com

In association with

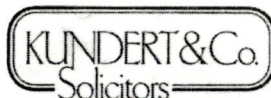

KUNDERT&Co.
Solicitors

In Memory of

Royal Inniskilling Fusiliers

Lance Corporal 14679 Daniel Doherty
Died 1st July 1916

Corporal 14680 James Doherty
Died 16th August 1917

Company Quartermaster Sergeant 5758 John Doherty MM
Died 22nd March 1918

Contents

The War Memorial by George Shaw

Preface

In 2004 on a visit to the War Memorial Park I noted the details of a memorial plaque dedicated to a Private F. Grant. Having researched my own family tree, I researched Private Grant's details via the Commonwealth War Grave Commission and on subsequent visits to the War Memorial Park noted the names on all the plaques. I added all these details to a web page and launched www.warmemorialpark.co.uk.

Local appeals were made and relatives of the deceased came forward with information, this enthusiasm combined with the number of hits the website received inspired me to research further. On the journey I released my first book *'Bablake School and the Great War'*, this is my second book produced to be available on the 80th Anniversary of Earl Haig dedicating the cenotaph at the War Memorial Park.

Trevor Harkin

Acknowledgments

Researching and compiling this book would not have been possible without the support of my wife, Emma and children Molly and Toby allowing me to indulge in this passion.

George Shaw for producing the drawing on the front cover and permitting its reproduction. The Commonwealth War Grave Commission (CWGC) Head Office in particular Maureen Annetts and Julie Somay, were fundamental in helping with the complex searches and background information whilst their UK Office assisted with grave location in the UK. The CWGC have also permitted reproduction of the map of the Somme and the campaign maps of the Ypres Salient. The work of the equivalent bodies in Australia and Canada also needs to be recognized. Photographs of Private Ernest Lumbert have been uploaded to the Canadian web page. Foe those commemorated in Tyne Cot Cemetery, research has been shared with the Passchendaele project. Information has also been shared with Susan Tall, author of *'Kenilworth and the Great War'* and Bill Smith author of *'Armstrong Siddeley Motors – The Cars, The Company and the people in definitive detail'* and Peter Burden, author of *'The Lion and the Stars a History of Bablake School'*.

Researching the content of this book would have been impossible without the assistance of Bablake School, in particular Terry Patchett, Robert Dougall, Chris Mellers and the late John Lawrence, who all offered encouragement and information throughout the period of research.

The men commemorated enlisted with a number of different Regiments and thanks need to be expressed to the following curators and archivists.

Alastair Massie from the National Army Museum, Jacqueline Minchinton from Northampton County Council, Matthew Buck, Curator Kings Regiment Liverpool Museums, Bryan Johnson Curator of the Warwickshire Yeomanry Museum, David Baynham and Stephanie Bennett from the Royal Regiment of Fusiliers (Royal Warwickshire), Mike Marr and Dino Lemonofides, Oxfordshire and Buckinghamshire Light Infantry Museum, Mick Wilkes from the Worcestershire and Sherwood Foresters` Regiment, Celia Green and Martin Everett from the Royal Regiment of Wales Museum, Colonel (Retd) I. H. McCausland of Royal Green Jackets, Alan Readman, West Sussex Records Office, Major (Retd) T. W. Stipling and Barry Yelland Duke of Cornwall's Light Infantry Museum, Tony Sprason, Lancashire Fusiliers' Museum, Martin Everett and Brian Owen, Regimental Museum of the Royal Welsh, Major C. M. J Deedes, Light Infantry Office, Geoffrey J. Crump, Cheshire Military Museum, Louis Scully, Worcestershire Regiment, Rachel Holmes, Royal Hampshire Regiment Museum, Major Douglas Farrington,

Lancashire Regiment, Lieutenant Colonel George Latham, Seaforth Highlanders and finally Stuart Eastwood, Border Regiment.

Thanks also to the following individuals and institutions who assisted. Dr. Robin Darwall-Smith, Magdalen College, Presidents and Fellows of Magdalen College, Mr. Michael Riordan, St. John's and the Queen's Colleges, Jackie Tarrant-Barton, Old Etonian Association, Julie Wakefield, Museum of the Royal Pharmaceutical Society, Alan Nutt, Chairman, Coventry No 3 Branch (GEC) Royal British Legion, Valerie Bedford and David Fletcher, Tank Museum, Rolls Royce Heritage Trust, Parkside Branch, Miss Anna Sander, Lonsdale Curator of Archives and Manuscripts, Balliol College, Jo Draper, Lyme Regis Museum, Douglas Mathieson and Derek Oliver, National Library of Scotland, John Moreland and Rusty MacLean, Rugby School, Vicky Harrison, York Minster, Rob Phillips, King Henry VIII School Library and Nigel Lutt Bedfordshire and Luton Archives and Records Section.

In the research, I came across a number of individuals who are working on projects which have relevance to those commemorated. In particular, information has been shared with the following and I thank them for their input and permission to use pictures and material. Rob Phillips, King Henry VIII School, Terry Reeves, Local War Memorials, Patrick Casey, Clifton Rugby Club, Andrew and Liz McDonald, Second Lieutenant Cheshire, Mandy Breculli, Foleshill Congregational Church, Stephen Pearson, Western Front Association, Stockport, Alex Revell for information on those killed in the RAF, Rod Evans for information on the men with a Birmingham connection and Chris Baker webmaster and author of the Long, Long Trail: The story of the British Army in the Great War.

The records maintained by Coventry Local Studies Library and the City Archives have been essential in adding information to the details of the fallen and those who served and their permission to use pictures and photographs is gratefully acknowledged. The St. Barbara's Church, Queen's Road Church, Holy Trinity, the Royal Warwicks Club, The Earlsdon Working Mens Club and St. John's Church all supplied information about their memorials.

Thanks to the following for publicity, Sheila Adams from 'The Earlsdon Echo', Tom Cooke, BBC CWR, Cheryl Liddle, Coventry University Alumni Association, Cathy Clapison, Coventry Council, Mike and Vivien Mattocks from the Coventry Family History Society, The Coventry Telegraph, Mercia FM, Warwickshire Life, Marion Thomas for displaying a poster in the café in the park and Christopher Jones from Kundert & Co. Solicitors for association with this project.

3

Neil Clark for access to his pictorial databases on officers who died in the Great War. Mick Baker for donating an entire series of *'The Great War...I Was There'*. Diana Fisher for the indexing work on local service men, Kay Dunkley, Coventry Family History Society, Brian Cornelius, Tim Parsons, David Hughes and Roydan Buckler for an insight into medal collecting and Lee Lindon for access to the material on Captain Pridmore and Private Faulks. Sue Wilson for assistance with intricacies of Microsoft Word, Nigel Hoare for access to his WW1 books, Alexander Hoare for assistance with promotional materials, Dave Lewis from Culture and Leisure and Mark Percival, GIS Manager, Coventry City Council, Simon Potter from Upfront Publishing, Ron Herdman, Chairman, Friends of the War Memorial Park, and finally proof readers Dave Howlin and Terry Patchett.

In numerous cases I have been contacted directly by the families of the Fallen and I thank them for their assistance. Colin Irving (Gunner Herbert Charles Collingbourne), Rebecca Baker (Gunner Alfred George Middleton), Robert Clarke (Lance Corporal Victor Leslie Clarke), Father Michael Gamble (Private William Stagg), Daphne Plummer (Private Arthur Lewin Marshall Bull), Terry Patchett (Trooper William Ivens Patchett), Jill and Trevor Paginton (Lance Corporal Sydney James Riley), Maxine Spencer (Private Eric Keppell Purnell) , Andrew Bell (Private Walter Frank Francis), Mrs Julie Stevenson (Private Lawrence Cecil Cox), Lynne and Nigel Page (Gunner Frederick George Page), Mr R. Barnett (Sapper William Joseph Barnett), Mrs Vera Bench (Bench family), Malcolm Bennett (Bench family), Bertram Rawlins (Son of Private Bert Rawlins), Alan Turner (Private William Simmons), Peter Tomlinson (Private Ernest Edward Waring), Mr. Ken Olorenshaw (Private Percy Elliman), Victoria Constance Hutt (Daughter of Arthur Hutt VC), Graham Williams (Arthur Hutt VC), Mr. Richards (Captain Joseph Arthur Richards), Mr. John Greenhill (Second Lieutenant Joseph Arthur Edwards) and Michael Smith (Private Edward Walter Newbold).

To those who remain anonymous but were cajoled into helping by those mentioned above, I also express my thanks.

The Evidence

Throughout this book various resources have been compiled to build a history of the men commemorated in the War Memorial Park. The commemorative plaques were the main source of information. The original plaques typically show initial(s), surname, rank, regiment or ship and year of insertion. In isolated cases replacement plaques show forenames and date of death.

The plaque of Private H. H. Harper

Over time some of the plaques have been lost, to identify these plaques the records of the Coventry City archives have been utilised. A search of the archives revealed several plaque lists, the most relevant being a Park Attendant's log book which although undated appears to be written just after World War 2. No records could be found prior to this as it is thought they were either destroyed deliberately or due to the air raids of World War 2. Therefore any plaques which have disappeared prior to this log cannot be accounted for as evidence no longer exists, plaques were placed in the park from 1925 to 1937.

To supplement this material, information was also obtained from the Commonwealth War Grave Commission. The Commission's official cut off date for a death to be counted as war related is the 31st August 1921, this date is determined by *'The Termination of the Present War (Definition) Act'*. Some of the men commemorated in the Park died after the 31st August 1921, these are not formally documented as war related. About one third of the Commission's records show no details for next of kin. This is because not all the "Final Verification" forms sent to the last known address of a casualty's next of kin were returned.

Other sources have been consulted: *'Soldiers who died in the Great War'*, *'Canadian Overseas Expeditionary Force Attestation Papers'*, *'The National Archives of Australia'* , and the *'City of Coventry: Roll of the Fallen'*. The last, published in 1927, includes the names of 2600 soldiers who fell and were either born, employed or resided in Coventry. Detail on each entry varies but typically covers name, rank, regiment, former regiment, address, birth details, occupation and in some cases employer. It is estimated that over 35,000 soldiers from Coventry served during the Great War.

For those who fell from Bablake School, material from the Bablake Archives was fundamental for underpinning this project: The 'Bablake School Magazine' known as *'The Wheatleyan'* and the 'Admission records' were used. For former pupils from King Henry VIII School, issues of 'The Coventrian' were referenced. The local employee magazines of the time have also been searched for relevant details as well as the local papers, *'The Coventry Graphic'* and *'The Coventry Herald'*. Family information has been obtained from the 1901 census.

The *'Battalion War Diaries'* in some cases have also been acquired. Privates were generally not mentioned; the diaries` entries vary in length dependent on the operations that day. In some cases the date wounds were received has been verified, in the remainder the action the Battalion was involved in on the day or just prior to the date has been included. Museum and local councils have also started their own databases and material has been taken from these sources. In numerous cases I have been contacted by members of the family and the information was received gratefully.

It is important to note, however, that the cross- referencing of material has indicated anomalies, in particular order of forenames, middle names, rank, spelling, address etc. In the case of names I have gone with the majority. Material also came from the National Archives in terms of Medal Index Cards (MIC) and the Records of Seamanship. *'The London Gazette'* has been used for citations and dates of commission. Each piece of evidence from the above sources adds to the picture of those commemorated. If the individuals are mentioned on other war memorials throughout the city, I have also noted this but my database is still ongoing.

The Impact of the Great War on Coventry

From the assassination of Archduke Franz Ferdinand on 28th June 1914, it took only five weeks for Europe to slide from a state of peace to a state of war. Britain was bound by treaty to aid Belgium and thus declared war against Germany on the 4th August 1914. It was not until the closing week of July that the Coventry public realized the probability of War. It was traditional for the citizens of Coventry to go on holiday over the Bank holiday weekend and people left Coventry for their holidays as usual. The 7th Battalion, Warwickshire Territorials left for their annual camp at Ryhl.

On Sunday, (August 2nd) British cabinet councils were held and newspapers keen to portray the latest events published editions in the morning, afternoon and night. The bank holiday was rather a time of scuttling back home and the citizens of Coventry returned in their thousands in the coming week. Tuesday found banks still closed, with intimation that they would re-open on Friday. The British Government delivered its ultimatum to Germany. Notice was given to reserves, sailors and soldiers in the City to report at depots and stations one night, and the men departed early the next morning. The Territorials came back from Ryhl to be sent to Weymouth for duty and Colonel Wyley called for volunteers to raise a second battalion, and men quickly responded.

The army at this point comprised of less then 500,000 men including some 250,000 reservists. Lord Kitchener, the newly appointed Secretary of State for War, was not convinced that this number was sufficient and believed that at least 1,000,000 men would be required. Conscription was not an option, instead a new army of volunteers would be raised. Two days after war was declared, Parliament sanctioned an increase in strength and Kitchener issued his first 'call to arms'. This was for 100,000 volunteers, aged between 19 and 30, at least 1.6m (5'3") tall and with a chest size greater than 86cm (34 inches). The advertisement that appeared in *'The Coventry Graphic'* is shown on the following page:

YOUR KING & COUNTRY NEED YOU.

A CALL TO ARMS.

An addition of 100,000 men to his Majesty's regular Army are immediately necessary in the present grave National emergency.

Lord Kitchener is confident that this appeal will be at once responded to by all those who have the safety of our Empire at heart.

TERMS OF SERVICE.

General service for a period of three years or until the war is concluded.

Age of enlistment between 19 and 30.

HOW TO JOIN.

Full information can be obtained at any post office in the kingdom, or at any military depot.

GOD SAVE THE KING!

This prompted scenes in Coventry that were repeated across the whole country. In mid-August 1916 *'The Coventry Graphic'* reported *"Remarkable scenes have been witnessed outside the recruiting office in Coventry this week, crowds of men waiting to join the army. The prospective applicants have had a trying time in the hot sunshine and many waited for hours before being admitted. Better accommodation would have been much appreciated. Writing to the Graphic a reader who tried to enlist said "I have waited six hours this week trying to get into the army. Such delay does not encourage one's patriotism".*

Brisk recruiting in Coventry

The Editorial of *'The Coventry Graphic'* was quite vocal and on the 21st August 1916 stated *"The remarkable increase in recruiting in Coventry this week is gratifying in more ways than one. This war is not a kid glove-fight and the sudden swelling in the numbers of men offering themselves for service is not the result of chance. The appearance of crowds of men outside the recruiting office was largely a consequence of powerful persuasion exerted at the principal works. And the reason for this is not far to seek. The mere trickle of recruits received from the city and district, which has a large population of single young men, made it imperative for someone to take action in order that Coventry should contribute something like its proper quota to the new army. Two things were obvious (1) that there were plenty of young men willing to serve the country if encouraged and guided towards making a definitive decision; and (2) that in the matter of recruiting the city had little or no lead".*

Elaborating on the 'powerful persuasion' the article continued that *"some medium more stirring then printers ink was needed to awaken the young manhood of the country to a sense of its responsibilities. Actual local leadership is vitally necessary for concerted effort to be achieved. This has been forthcoming in many towns, but in Coventry it has been conspicuous by its absence. We had the men willing to enlist, we had residents willing to take part in encouraging them, but a blight seemed to fall over the whole business. Small wonder then the large works realising that procrastination was fraught with deadly danger to the nation and all its industries, adopted measures to stimulate recruiting. Some one had to take the matter up and leaders of local industry stepped into the breach which urgently required to be filled".*

This caused an increase in queues at the recruiting office and a long queue was formed outside the Masonic Hall. In numerous cases prospective applicants detached themselves from the crowd and went off disgusted at the delay and at the end of the afternoon were told to return the following day. This in consequence caused loud complaints, some men walked to local villages to enlist and beat the queues in Coventry. The number of recruits from Coventry placed in the Royal Engineers was considerable as the special mechanical knowledge possessed by the men was very suitable for work in the Engineers and also local Regiments were very popular. By the 21st August, 350 men had successfully enlisted as only a proportion of the applicants were deemed suitable.

It was also suggested that *"these brave fellows were accompanied to the station – as in other towns – by a band or some other token of the City's recognition; but the way in which they have been allowed to depart without a civic farewell is a reflection on those who might easily have organised a demonstration which would show the recruits that the city is indeed proud of them. At present they go away silently without sign or indication that the city appreciates their patriotism or values their services, and though they are going to face whatever dangers fate has in store for them, they have been denied the send off which falls to the lot of a football team departing to play a cup tie"*.

By the Middle of August England became the asylum of Belgians driven from their homes, and Coventry took in some hundreds. The refugees first of all lodged at Whitley Abbey under the care of the local committee.

In the case of the Siddeley Deasy works the employees were told to go and enlist and do their patriotic duty and a large proportion of employees volunteered, however on the receipt of a large order from the Government for 150 lorries attempts were made to call the men back. It was quickly realised that men with key skills would be required until appropriate replacements could be found. This prompted the firms like Rudge Whitworth to issue means of identification for war workers. In addition to the War Badge supplied for every employee on War Work they were also furnished with a Certification Card. Both sides are shown on the following page.

WAR OFFICE

21st October, 1914.

Gentlemen,

I wish you to impress upon those employed by your Company the importance of the Government work upon which they are engaged. I fully appreciate the efforts which the employes are making, and the quality of the work turned out. I trust that everything will be done to assist the Military Authorities by pushing on all orders, as rapidly as possible.

I should like all engaged by your Company to know that it is fully recognised that they, in carrying out the great work of supplying Munitions of War, are doing their duty for their King and Country equally with those who have joined the Army for Active Service in the field.

Yours very truly,

Kitchener

Messrs. Rudge-Whitworth, Ltd.,
Coventry.

This is to Certify that

....

is engaged in the manufacture of Stores, Equipment, and Munitions of War, and therefore he is unable to Serve his Country in any other manner.

For RUDGE-WHITWORTH, LTD.,

W. G. BLATCH,

Secretary.

This Ticket must be given up on leaving the Firm's service.

Rudge Certificate

Female workers were employed to continue production as men went off to the front and in some cases, as in the one below, men came out of retirement. For the first time, women were also employed as policewomen, post women, telegraph messenger girls and tram women. The shops and public schools were nearly all staffed by women. In the summer of 1914, some 200,000 women were employed in munitions work by the last month of the war this was 947,000.

An article for 'The Coventry Graphic' entitled 'Doing his bit at 80!. Coventry's Oldest Munition Worker' stated that one of the proudest men in Coventry was Mr. John Walmsley an employee of the Coventry Movement Co. Ltd who was engaged on munition work and possessed a war badge at the age of 80. How he came to be employed at war work was related in a letter from the firm, who wrote:" *Some three months ago Walmsley applied to us for a job on munition work, and although we were doubtful of giving him a start thinking that a man of his age was too old to work in a factory among machinery, we did put him on, and he has since proved himself to be a wonderful old Coventry Citizen and one we feel proud to employ*".

Walmsley was 80 the previous October; and he had been a Freeman of the City for 59 years, and was entitled to payment from the Freemen Seniority Fund. He was in receipt of the old age pension, but this, of course, he had to give up in order to enter again on regular work. Walmsley was working from 7.30am to 8.45pm. He had lived at the same house for upwards of 50 years and was reported to be in the best of health and spirit.

A Coventry Pals Battalion was not formed as in the case of the Accrington Pals who recruited 1,000 men in ten days. Evidence shows that the men from Coventry enlisted with friends, neighbours, colleagues and family members. The local papers covered patriotic families that enlisted together and on one occasion asked *'"Which was the most patriotic street in Coventry ?"*. Where possible pictures were shown of the families or colleagues from particular works who had enlisted together. Firms were requested to maintain a 'Roll of Honour' and former employees of the firms requested to inform the firms if they enlisted. An example of the campaign is shown below.

The
ROLL of HONOUR

IS
YOUR
NAME
on a
ROLL
of
HONOUR
?

IF YOUR NAME goes down on your firm's Roll of Honour, it also goes on that mighty Scroll which records the names of all who have rallied round the Flag.

There is room for your name on the Roll of Honour.

Ask your employer to keep your position open for you. Tell him that you are going to the help of the Empire. Every patriotic employer is assisting his men to enlist, and he'll do the right thing by you.

Tell him NOW——

Your King and Country Want you——TO-DAY.

At any Post Office you can obtain the address of the nearest Recruiting Officer.

GOD SAVE THE KING.

The citizens of Coventry were not just confined to enlisting and munitions work, all sorts of committees for all kinds of war work were formed. These included the relief of men, women and children whose relatives were in the forces. Work was organized with the Red Cross, funds for prisoners of war and others were opened and supported. Members of the Clergy went as chaplains to the Navy and Army, others to work in factories, some doctors took duty in the field and at Home Stations, and those who remained here shared the work of absent colleagues. There were large bodies of citizens who did voluntary work, connected with recruiting, tribunals, pensions and billeting. Work was undertaken in addition to normal working hours.

The Ministry of Munitions was formed in May 1915 and extensive orders for munitions were placed in Coventry, spending over £40,500,000. The factories in Coventry produced big ordnance, quick firing guns, aeroplanes and parts, machine tools, shells, small arms, ammunition, motor vehicles of all kinds, cycles, tanks, ambulance trailers, aircraft engines, gun and submarine parts, bombs, incendiary bullets and drop forgings. Production continued throughout the day and night requiring 30,000 men, women and girls to be drafted into Coventry.
Statistics coming from the National Filling factory stated that the following were supplied from Coventry;
Fuses filled 19,940,000
Grenades filled 9,880,000
Detonators filled 31,060,000

To accommodate the workers, six hundred houses were quickly put up in Stoke Heath and Holbrooks. The situation was improved with workers sharing accommodation sharing occupation between night and day. Over 16,000 people came into Coventry daily by Railway train and went out at evening or morning to Birmingham, Leamington, Warwick, Rugby, Bedworth, Nuneaton and Atherstone and the surrounding villages.

Aerial warfare did not seriously affect Coventry. No actual damage took place through air raids, but the city was the object of at least two attacks. On January 31st 1917, German raiders skirted the city and passed to South Staffordshire, where much damage was done. On April 12th 1918 the raiders dropped bombs in the grounds of Whitley Abbey and on Baginton sewage farm. The guns at Keresley and Wyken Grange came into action and the powerful searchlights were used. Aeroplanes went up from Radford Ground to meet the raiders, who however passed to the south west and avoided an engagement.

There were three Royal visits to the city during the war – King George V came in 1915; the Queen and Princess Mary in 1917 and Princess Victoria in 1917. The citizens of Coventry experienced food shortages and rationing was introduced in the Autumn of 1917. Coventry hospital had 140 civilian beds at the outbreak of war; at the end there were 160 civil and 180 military beds. The hospital treated 2,497 wounded soldiers. Seventeen convoys came into the City. Forty five members of the motor transports section responsible for moving the wounded in Warwickshire removed 6250 cases and covered 17,250 miles.

In almost all factories, funds for the relief of dependents of those who were serving, were commenced and over £100,000 had been subscribed when hostilities ceased. An example of this comes from Siddeley Deasy Co. Ltd. In December 1914, Mr. W. Ridgeway, a shop steward, approached Mr. Siddeley to grant permission to do something for the shop mates who had enlisted and for wounded soldiers. A Committee was formed and employees asked to agree to the following deductions from their wages

Earnings up to 20/- weekly..................2d per week
    From 20/- to 30/-....................3d per week
    From 30/- to 40/-....................4d per week
    Over 40/-............................3d in the £ per week

In September 1916 it was agreed that 10% should go to a Benevolent Fund. By January 1918 a new structure came into place with the contributions being halved, this being due to the large number of new employees. The Benevolent Fund would now receive 25%. By 18th November 1918 the fund had received £15067 18s 4d. 'The Employee Quarterly' shows that the fund was closed in December 1918 and *"it will now be our duty to devise a plan by means of which the surplus of £4000 can be used to the best advantage of the widows and children of our men who have fallen, for the men who have been disabled at war and for those who have had the good fortune to return home"*.

In 1924, *'The Employees Quarterly'* reported that a historical event took place on the 1st July 1924 when the War relief Fund made it's final payment to an old lady who had charge of her grandchild, whose father was killed in the war and a few weeks afterwards lost his mother. A huge sum was invested in a Fund for children who lost their fathers for them to draw out at the age of 21. The first child drew an amount of £37 on the 11th July 1925 and the last £42 on December 14th 1939.

It was estimated that over 35,000 men from Coventry enlisted and over 2,600 fell during the conflict. *'The Coventry Graphic'* for the 15th November 1918, stated *"having lasted four years and three months and a few days, the Great War has arrived at its penultimate stage, and the proceedings that followed the receipt of the intelligence of signing the Armistice are only the forerunner of that greater demonstration which will occur when peace is an established fact. We were all heartily sick and fed-up with the war and the sailors and soldiers more so then the civilian population...But few of our soldiers and sailors will spend Yuletide at home, their happiness will be enhanced in the knowledge that every day brings them nearer to the time when their King and country will have no further claim upon them in respect of active service"*.

On the 8th October 1919, the Town Clerk, George Sutton wrote the following letter to '*The Coventry Graphic*', appealing to ex-service men: '*The City Council, on behalf of the citizens are desirous of presenting a small souvenir to Coventry sailors, soldiers and airmen who served in the War, as an expression of the City's appreciation of the courage and devotion they displayed, and of the victorious issue to which, by their aid, the War was brought. In order that the necessary list may be compiled, all men who joined the Forces from Coventry are invited, as soon as possible, to send a postcard or letter addressed to the Town Clerk, Council House, Coventry, stating their name and present address, the unit with which they served, their rank, and the date when they left Coventry, to join the forces'*.

Two months later, on the 20th December 1919, one of the local firms, Rudge Whitworth threw a work's party for returning soldiers. The number that had joined was 444, the number of employees that were demobilized and returned to work was 141, the number of men that had died was 35. During the war the works had send out 3,854 parcels totalling £3,027 to service men. In weight this was 6,675 lbs, including 5,882 tins of fruit etc, 3,783 pairs of socks and 966 woollen articles. The fund had paid $6,805 to the wives of 229 married men and in total raised £12,842.

Some of the Returned Soldiers

Lost Four Sons: The Bench Brothers

During the Great War, patriotism was at an all time high and some of the families in Coventry were bereaved of one or two sons. These men were also nephews, husband and fathers to those that had been left behind. Coventry sons died in the Battle of Jutland, Mesopotamia, Palestine, Italy, Greece and many other places.

At the dedication of the War Memorial, Eliza Bench was one of the key dignitaries meeting Earl Haig and Arthur Hutt VC. As she had lost four sons, the biggest direct loss to a Coventry family she symbolised the losses of Coventry and sacrificial motherhood, and played a pivotal role in the dedication ceremony.

Joseph and Eliza Bench had seven children. Six sons, Charles William, Joseph, Ernest William, Thomas William , Thomas and Harry Noel. Their only daughter was called Alice.

The details of the brothers are below:

On the extreme left is Private Arthur Bench, 1st Battalion, middle left, Sergeant Ernest Bench, 2nd Battalion, middle right, Lance Corporal Charles Bench 11th Battalion, and far right is Sergeant Joseph Bench, 3rd Battalion. At this stage all the brothers were in the Royal Warwickshire Regiment.

Sergeant **Ernest William Bench**, 2nd Battalion, Royal Warwickshire Regiment was killed in action at Loos on the 25th September 1915. He was born on the 5th January 1889 at Warwick and resided at 93 Broad Street. Ernest is buried in Cabaret Rouge British Cemetery. 'The Coventry Graphic' reported *"after serving all through the campaign with the 2nd Battalion, Corporal Bench son of Mrs. Bench Broad Street, Coventry has been killed in action. His cousin who is in the same Battalion said that Corporal Bench was wounded and placed in the transport to be taken to the dressing station, but he got away and returned to the thick of the fighting. He was a very popular Non Commissioned Officer and will be much missed"*.

Sergeant **Joseph Bench**, 1st Battalion Royal Warwickshire Regiment was killed in action in France on the 11th April 1917. He was born on the 21st December 1891 at Warwick and resided at 26 Station Street East. He was a soldier by profession, has no known grave and is commemorated on the Arras Memorial .

Sergeant **Charles William Bench**, 1st Battalion, Royal Warwickshire Regiment was killed in action at Ypres, 23rd July 1917. Charles was born on the 1st January 1879 at Warwick and resided with his parents and brothers at 93 Broad Street. He enlisted at the outbreak of war and prior to this was employed as a spinner.

'The Coventry Graphic' stated that *"Mrs Bench of Broad Street, Coventry has received news of the death of Sergeant Charles William Bench. This makes the third son who has been killed in action. All three had the rank of Sergeant. Two more brothers are still serving. In a letter conveying to the relatives the sad news of the death of Sergeant C. W. Bench deceased Company's Captain says "It is with the deepest regret that I write to report the death of your son. He met his death like the very gallant soldier he was whilst manning the parapet. He did not suffer and was killed almost instantaneously. Knowing of your numerous losses, I put him in the second line this time instead of the first, it being a safer place, but as fate decreed, he was our first casualty. He is a great loss to his regiment, to me and to his numerous friends".* Sergeant Charles Bench is buried in Crump Trench British Cemetery, Fampoux.

Sergeant Charles William Bench Memorial Plaque

By the end of the war, Eliza would have received four 'Notifications of Death', the one shown is for Sergeant Charles William Bench.

No. ....
(If replying, please
quote above No.)

ARMY FORM B. 104—82.

Record Office,

191

Madam

It is my painful duty to inform you that a report has been received from the War Office notifying the death of :—

(No.) *6266* (Rank) *Sergeant*

(Name) *Charles William Bench*

(Regiment) *1 Royal Warwicks Regt*

which occurred *with the Exp.dy Force France*

on the *23rd July 1917*

The report is to the effect that he *was killed in action*

By His Majesty's command I am to forward the enclosed message of sympathy from Their Gracious Majesties the King and Queen. I am at the same time to express the regret of the Army Council at the soldier's death in his Country's service.

I am to add that any information that may be received as to the soldier's burial will be communicated to you in due course. A separate leaflet dealing more fully with this subject is enclosed.

I am,

Madam

Your obedient Servant,

Capt for *B* *Lew*
Officer in charge of Records
i/c Infantry Records
No. 7 D............. P.T.O.

8307. Wt. 15148/M 1365. 175M. 2/17. R. & L., Ltd.

Notification of Death In Service

G v R 1

HE whom this scroll commemorates was numbered among those who, at the call of King and Country, left all that was dear to them, endured hardness, faced danger, and finally passed out of the sight of men by the path of duty and self-sacrifice, giving up their own lives that others might live in freedom.
Let those who come after see to it that his name be not forgotten.

Serjt. Charles William Bench
Royal Warwickshire Regt.

Memorial Scroll

The last casualty from the family was **Private Thomas Bench**, 2/8th Battalion, Worcestershire Regiment who died aged 37 on the 15th November 1917. He was the husband of Hannah and they resided at 48 Chapel Street, Rugby. He was born in Warwick on the 27th June 1880, employed as a house decorator he originally enlisted with the Hampshire Regiment, prior. After his training he was drafted, with about sixty three other men into the 2/8th Battalion, Worcestershire Regiment.

19

All of these men trained together, so Thomas was with friends when he joined the Worcesters. This was about August 1917, sadly he was not to live very much longer. At least one in five of Thomas's draft died before the war ended. Private Bench is buried in Brown's Copse Cemetery, Roeux.

By the time Harry Noel enlisted in September 1918 he had already lost four of his brothers. They had been killed in action between the 25th September 1915 and the 15th November 1917. Harry Noel did not see active service as he was demobilised in March 1919. It is known that Alice worked locally in a munitions factory.

The Demobilisation Certificate of Harry Noel Bench

In addition to the Bench brothers , the family also had nephews that served in the Royal Navy. Regrettably the names of those pictured below have been lost over time and it interesting to observe that a pin badge of the Royal Warwickshire Regiment can be seen on the brother in the middle.

A Family Picture of three of the Brothers with Cousins

The circumstances of how Eliza Bench was invited to the Dedication are not known, however the death of all her sons are recorded in the Roll of the Fallen and appeared in the local papers. During the ceremony, Eliza Bench proudly displayed the twelve campaign medals sent to her on the death of her sons. Her husband, Joseph Bench was not permitted to accompany his wife during the ceremony as many families only received one ticket. Each ticket permitted entrance to one person only and these were mainly used by the mothers and wife's of the deceased.

The picture on the following page shows the moment of Eliza Bench meeting Earl Haig.

Eliza Bench and Arthur Hutt (Inset) Meeting Earl Haig

6266 SERJEANT
C. W. BENCH
ROYAL WARWICKSHIRE REGT.
23RD JULY 1917

After attending the War Memorial dedication, Mrs Eliza Bench received a letter from Coventry Corporation (shown on the following page) thanking her for her attendance at the Ceremony on what must have been to her a *very trying occasion'*. Unfortunately Eliza Bench did not have the opportunity to visit her son's graves. The headstone of Sergeant C. W. Bench is shown on the left. The brothers are commemorated in St. Mary's Church in Warwick

COUNCIL HOUSE,
COVENTRY

12th October, 1927.

Dear Mrs. Bench,

     I wish to express my thanks to you for the part you took on Saturday last in the ceremony of unveiling the War Memorial. The entrance of Corporal Hutt V.C. and yourself into the Chamber of Silence, at the time when the Field Marshal and I myself entered it, is agreed by all to have been one of the most impressive moments in a memorable ceremony, and I know the sympathy of the vast company in the War Memorial Park went out to you. I should like to express my appreciation of the great sacrifice you made in the Country's cause, and my thanks for your participation in what must have been to you a very trying occasion.

Yours sincerely,

Fred Lee

Mayor.

Mrs. E. Bench,
93, Broad Street,
COVENTRY.

Letter Received by Mrs. Bench

The Common: A Brief History

The land and estate around Stivichall were originally owned by the Bishop's of Coventry and Lichfield, ownership then changed to Thomas Fisher in 1547. A further sale of the majority of land took place sixteen years later, when Thomas and Arthur Gregory made a purchase. The remainder of the land, not owned by the Gregory Family was itself sold in 1619 to a Clement Fisher, and retained by his family until the eighteenth century.

On April 9th 1838, the first main railway line to Coventry was opened and proved so popular that two years later, plans were drawn up to connect Coventry with Warwick and Leamington. In 1842, a descendant of John and Arthur Gregory, also called Arthur Gregory bought the land kept from his ancestors from the descendants of Clement Fisher. This land would later become the park.

One of the most significant events in the vicinity of Stivichall was the addition of Coats of Arms Bridge in 1844. The bridge went over Cock's Lane now known as Coat of Arms Bridge Road and required the London and North Western Railway to purchase seven and half acres of land plus two cottages from the Gregory family. For this they were charged £8,000 and Arthur Gregory insisted that his coat of arms be displayed on the east side of the bridge and on the west side the coat of arms of the Hood family, his wife's maiden name.

Coat of Arm's Bridge

When Coventry Corporation purchased the land from the Gregory family, they also purchased an additional amount of land known as 'The Grove', this was at the junction of Leamington Road and Kenilworth Road and came with a former Toll House (pictured below).

The Grove, Kenilworth Road, Coventry.

The Grove

The Toll House saw a variety of uses eventually being demolished by the Council in the 1960's. Plaques can be observed around the area of the Grove, these are not allocated to ex-service men but Citizens of Coventry being honoured by their families.

An Early Postcard

Pictured above are children playing on Styvechale Common at the turn of the century. The road in the background was citied as being Earlsdon Avenue. The picture was taken prior to the hedgerows being inserted and the road running horizontally is Kenilworth Road previously known as Long Lane.

The Need for Remembrance

During the First World War Coventry was an important centre for the manufacture of munitions and few other towns or cities gave such a large proportion of their men to the fighting forces. The Council determined that it was necessary to raise enough funds to erect a fitting memorial to the men of Coventry who courageously gave their lives for their country. The then Mayor (Councillor J. I. Bates) , early in 1919, invited ladies and gentlemen representing all classes of the community to form a Town's Committee. Many suggestions as to the form of the memorial were brought before the Town's Committee, but after carefully considering them all, the committee came unanimously to the conclusion that no scheme was so appropriate or offered such great advantage, both from the point of view of the present and the future, as that for a Memorial Park at Stivichall, together with the acquisition of full public rights over Stivichall Common.

The Honourable A. F. Gregory, Lord of the Manor of Stivichall, gave an option to the committee to purchase the freehold land and the manorial right over Stivichall common for the sum of £31,000. He returned £2000 as his contribution to the scheme, thus reducing the net price to £29,000. At a Council meeting of March 1919, the proposal to pursue this option was first discussed and concurred. The local press immediately supported the decision.

The editorial of 'The Coventry Graphic' dated March 28th 1919 and entitled 'Coventry's War Memorial' stated the following *"Coventry's war memorial scheme is one that should appeal to the general body of citizens. In respect of open spaces, the city perhaps is much better off than many other Midland industrial centres, but an addition to the number should be welcomed by everyone. The idea is to purchase 120 acres of land at Stivichall, and the rights of Stivichall Common from the Honourable A. Gregory at a cost of £31000, the land to be converted to park and the common left in its present wild state. Our opinion is that the scheme is an ideal one and ought easily to be carried through by voluntary effort. During the past four years the amount of money that has been amassed by Coventry firms has been enormous; and remembering that the same is directly the outcome of the war, those who have handled the huge amounts should foot the account for the permanent memorial. Colonel Wyley has generously given the fund a send off with £1000 and there are certainly many other firms and private individuals connected with the city who could do as much, or more, without missing the amount"*. An appeal was launched to raise the remaining £29,000. It was quite common to decorate a tram, in order to raise the required funds a tram was decorated.

The Government decided that Saturday the 19th July 1919, a day of peace would be celebrated and Coventry joined in the celebrations. In Coventry the celebrations began with over 4,000 boys from the elementary school singing on the Friday Evening at 8.00pm. On Saturday the combined Sunday schools represented the British Nations and allies massed in Pool Meadow at 9.45am to the 1st verse only of the National Anthem followed by hymns " God Bless Our Native land", "God the all merciful" and "All people that on earth do dwell".

At 3.00pm a Pageant gathered at the Barracks square before also marching around the City. In the evening at 10.00pm a simultaneous hour long grand firework display was held at Spencer Park, Radford recreation ground and Stoke Green.
Unfortunately after the peace celebrations ended riots broke out in the City Centre as it was though that some of the larger shops were German owned. Dunn's next to the King's Head hotel and several other shops in Broadgate and Cross Cheaping had windows broken. The riots came to an end after three nights when the crowd was repeatedly charged by the police. As crowds were then prevented from assembling in Broadgate after 9.00pm on following evenings, further violence did not occur.

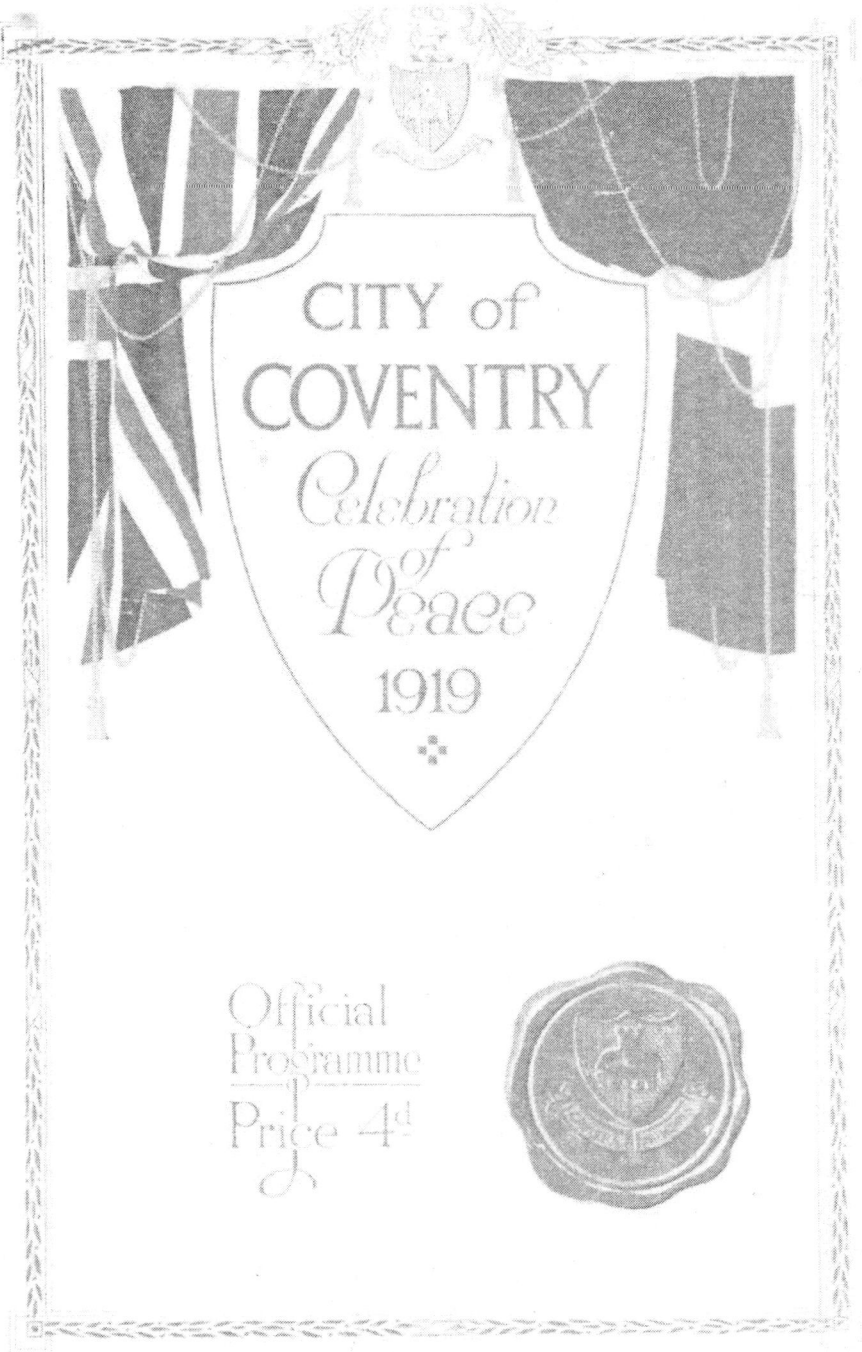

CITY of
COVENTRY
Celebration
of
Peace
1919

Official
Programme
Price 4d

As the relatives, colleagues and friends of the Fallen came to terms with their loss War Memorials began to be erected in places of Worship and places of work. In some cases these memorials were free standing or *'Rolls of Honour'*. The Editorial of *'The Coventry Graphic'* was again very vocal on this issue and on August 19th 1919 stated *"Permanent war memorial schemes in Coventry and the surrounding neighbourhood do not appear to be making that health and popular progress we should like to see, and probably one reason is that the form some of them are to assume does not appeal to the tastes of the people generally. A big lot of money is still required before the Coventry scheme can materialise, and the experience is the same in many other districts. The fact of the matter is, the wishes of the men who have done the fighting have not been considered to the extent they deserve, and in instances brought directly to our notice the form of memorial suggested does not in the slightest degree appeal to ex-service men. As things are today- the high cost of everything and the labour unrest- to some extent place war memorials " out of court", as it were, and many of the schemes look like becoming belated efforts"*.

Alderman W.H Grant was chairman of the committee charged with the erection of a fitting tribute to the Foleshill men who had given their lives in the war. The Foleshill War memorial was unveiled on the 21st September 1919. It had been presented through the generosity of Mr. W. T. Henderson, a local businessman, a striking white cenotaph being thirty feet high and he ensured ex-servicemen were employed in its construction.

A picture of the Unveiling of the Foleshill War Memorial

A postcard of the memorial shows the intricate details involved in it's construction and represents all the forces involved in 'The Great War'. The memorial was not inscribed with the names of all those who fell from Foleshill. A fine two colour souvenir programme was printed for the tea and entertainment arranged for the dependents of the men who fell in the Great War. It bore a picture of the memorial on the front cover. The inscription read "Foleshill Public Memorial. Erected to the memory of our glorious heroes who fell in the Great War". The memorial was of a temporary nature and it was hoped that it would be replaced by something of a permanent character.

IN MEMORY OF THE FALLEN OF FOLESHILL.
Memorial presented by W. J. Henderson, Esq.

A Postcard of the Foleshill Memorial

King George's private secretary wired *"The King is interested to hear that today, discharged sailors and soldiers of the Foleshill district are paying honour to their heroic comrades who have fallen in giving their country a victorious peace. His Majesty hopes that the bereaved may be consoled and encouraged by the knowledge that their loved ones did not die in vain"*. There were also messages from Field Marshall Lord Haig, Admiral Lord Beatty and the Bishop of Coventry. Estimates suggest 10,000 people attended the ceremony.

On the 12th October 1919 the ex-service men of Coventry, desiring to commemorate the sacrifice of their comrades who gave their lives in the Great War provided a temporary cenotaph, which by permission of the corporation was erected in Spencer Park in the Dalton Road corner. David Spencer a Coventry Draper and wool merchant had presented the land for the park in 1882, six years before his death.

Unveiling of Cenotaph Spencer Park 12.10.19

The Cenotaph was simple in design and character. The ceremony in 1919 marked Coventry's first attempt at a memorial to it's dead from the First World War. Despite being performed in very poor weather the ceremony was reportedly attended by thousands who gathered after a procession from Pool Meadow. The Heads of the procession collected the sword and the Mace bearers on the way past the Council house. The Mayor performed the unveiling ceremony, although he referred to the cenotaph, not unkindly, as *"quite a homemade affair"*. It was constructed of wood in the form of an obelisk surmounted by a cross painted in black and white. It had been designed, built and paid for by discharged soldiers. It would appear a larger memorial had not been planned at this stage as it was hoped that the wooden cenotaph would simply be replaced by an identical stone one.

Estimates suggest 10,000 people attended and the Mayor (Councillor Bates) in his course of address remarked *"that although they had many monuments in Coventry, none would be more appreciated by the citizens, not only at the present time, but in the years to come"*. The service was conducted by Canon Littlewood (inset).

Five days after the dedication *'The Coventry Graphic'* dated October 17th 1919 referred to the ceremony in *'The Editorial'*: "*What would otherwise have been a most impressive ceremony was spoilt somewhat by the heavy rain. I refer to the Drumhead Memorial service on Sunday afternoon, and the unveiling of a temporary cenotaph in memory of our fallen heroes. The event was on similar lines to that which took place at Foleshill some few weeks ago, various organisations assembling at Pool Meadow, and marching in procession to Spencer Park, where the service was held. The rain did not mar the enthusiasm of those taking part, although it is safe to assume that the attendance would not have been so large but for the beautiful autumn sunshine that prevailed earlier in the afternoon. The whole arrangements were carried out by the local branches of the discharged and demobilised sailors and soldiers federation, who even bore the expenses of the erection of the war memorial, and the thanks of all Coventry citizens are due to this organisation.*

With regard to the design of the cenotaph itself, without belittling the efforts of the federation concerned, in any way, I hardly think it is so imposing as the one at Foleshill. Of course it has to be remembered that this was the gift of a Foleshill resident, but one would have thought that the City of Coventry possessed plenty of public spirited men who would have followed this worthy example. Again, I should have liked to have seen Coventry first in the field. Very few people knew of last Sundays arrangements until the week previous, and it appeared to an outsider that the whole affair was rushed through, simply following the lines of our Foleshill neighbours. This may not be the case as I know the preliminary arrangements to an occasion such as this are always extensive, but I would have preferred Coventry to have struck out on some bolder lines, distinct altogether from those that characterised the Foleshill ceremony. However, no doubt my wishes will be gratified when the real event takes place – I refer to the opening of the new memorial park at Stivichall-and in the meantime we ought to be thankful to the sailors and soldiers federation for providing the temporary cenotaph at Spencer Park".

On December 20th 1919, the Radford Village War Memorial was unveiled by Councillor C. Vernon Pugh in the presence of a large assembly, including members of the Radford War Memorial Committee. The memorial is an obelisk, 2' wide and 8' 6" high, on the sides bronze panels bear the names of those who served and a crucifix next to seventeen names denotes the names of the fallen. The memorial was actually a generous gift from Councillor Pugh.

The picture on the following page shows the dedication, with the Mayor and the Bishop of Coventry in attendance.

Dedication of the Radford War Memorial

The appeal to raise the £29,000 required to purchase the land from the Gregory family was in fact a total of £31,562 8s. 9d was raised by public subscription. The purchase was completed and the land formally handed over to the Corporation (to be held by them on behalf of the citizens) on the 26th October, 1920 before Mr. Bates laid down office. The main entrance was proposed to be at the Grove and in December 1920, 256 avenue trees were planted on the sides of Kenilworth road.

Roll of the Fallen

At the start of 1924, the mammoth task of compiling the 'Roll of the Fallen' was given to the City Librarian, Charles Nowell. The details from the initial pages of the Roll of the Fallen are replicated below:

For the purpose of compiling this roll the term "Coventry men" has been held to include those born in Coventry, together with those who at any time lived or were employed in the City. The following details have been inserted wherever possible: name, Rank, regiment or Ship; Place and date of birth; residence and occupation; date of enlistment; date of death and place of burial; details of service decorations awarded. This record was compiled at the invitation of the City Council of Coventry, by Charles Nowell, City Librarian and printed by W. W. Curtis Ltd, Cheylesmore Press, Coventry, September, 1927.

Foreword

The citizens of Coventry as a lasting tribute to those who fell in the Great War 1914 –1918, have provided (by subscription) the War Memorial and the beautiful Park in which it is erected. In the Memorial itself, is placed this Roll of the Fallen, so that those who follow may be ever reminded of the sacrifice they so nobly made, together with the consequent grief borne by those who mourned them.

Although great care has been taken in the compilation of this record, it cannot possibly be a complete roll of those who fell, and arrangements have been made to include any additional names, which may be received later, in the official copy to be enshrined in the Memorial, and in those copies available for public inspection in St. Mary's Hall and in the Gulson Library.

This civic roll of honour, therefore is record of 2587 Coventry men who fell in the great war of 1914-1918 a record of men who gave us their all for us. How our hearts throb with emotion at the price paid, yet with what pride do we recall devotion, their valour, their sacrifice even unto death; perpetuating the glorious traditions characteristic of the British nation wherever liberty and freedom has been assailed.

What of the future and the inheritances placed in our care and custody by these brave heroes ?, "never again", should be our watchword. It should be the duty of those who are their successors to work and labour, with all earnestness, to make the future happier, more peaceful and more joyful.

So may our destiny be along the surer paths of Peace, may we be spared the terrors and sufferings of war endured by those we lovingly cherish and ever remember.

May their memories and sacrifices be the precursor of an everlasting Peace and the brotherhood of mankind.

Coventry has taken a prominent part in many events which have shaped the history of England, but no chapter of its annals is finer then that containing this glorious but tragic record. Therefore let those who follow after see that its glory remains undimmed, and that this sacrifice is ever held in proud and grateful remembrance

>Their glorious name shall be adored,
>Great with love and great their worth;
>Their fame shall purify the earth,
>And honour be their dear Reward.
>
>Alderman Fred Lee, Mayor

A supplement was added to the Roll of the Fallen shortly after it was published adding an additional thirteen names, bringing the total to 2,600. Cross referencing databases and local papers against the Roll of the Fallen reveals that the true total is higher then 2,600.

'The Coventry Herald' stated *"The Roll of the Fallen, is witness indeed to the share of Coventry in the grim struggle which saw many thousands leave the city to take part in the war. It is a grievous loss – no less the 2,587 men in their prime, having years of usefulness before them, to whom, in numerous instances no doubt, life was very precious and widening in all its allure: plenty of sons whose parents have never ceased to mourn them, not a few heads of families whose widows and children still feel the loss"*.

Paying for the Plaques

The initial concept to plant a memorial tree and associated plaque originated in 1922 when a request was made by the Stoneleigh Lodge of the Ancient Order of Druids to plant a tree commemorating its fiftieth anniversary. The request was granted and the landscape changed with the introduction of an oak tree.

The War Memorial committee in February 1923, considered as an agenda item the planting of trees by the citizens in memory of fallen relatives. The tree would be accompanied by a plaque suitably inscribed. At the meeting, Councillor Friswell stated *"that the cost would be 25s inclusive"* and in the course of the discussion it was suggested that the trees should form the avenue along the main walk. The Chairman of the Baths and parks committee (Councillor Friswell) and Mr G. W. Pridmore were appointed to form a sub committee to go into the details.

In the following years the sub committee, received applications payment for the trees. Two years after the scheme was approved, in 1925, 109 trees were planted in the park forming an avenue from the main entrance at the Grove to the memorial. These were followed by a further 26 in 1926 and 46 in 1927. By October 1927, 181 Copper beech memorial trees had been planted by Coventry citizens in memory of individual men and more trees were planned for the following autumn. The remaining plaques were planted from 1928 to 1937 until they aligned all the avenues and an area identified by the rose garden. The plaques are not laid out in either an alphabetical order or linked by regiment and it is thought that allocation was possibly done on a ballot basis.

Several families lost more then one relative and they may have had to pay an additional amount, three plaques and one tree as in the case of the Warner family. If this was the case it set the philosophy adopted for the plaques inserted after World War 2.   Several men also have two plaques each they are Private Alfred Garnett Bentley, Private Harold Hubert Harper, Private Herbert William Harper, Captain Harold Jackson and Gunner Frederick George Page.

1914 — THIS 1918
TREE
WAS PLANTED TO THE MEMORY OF
GNR. F. G. PAGE
10TH BDE. R. FIELD ARTILLERY
1927

During research the evidence suggests that the Siddeley Deasy Co. Ltd War Fund was used to pay for plaques to the Fallen from the company, as the names on the companies *'Roll of Honour'* exactly aligns with 26 men who have plaques in the park. This does not appear to by the case for any other employer.

The surnames of those involved in the War Memorial Committee also appear as in the case of Captain Percy Malin Pridmore, who's uncle was a former Mayor and Colonel Wyley who had generously donated £2,000 towards the scheme. It is not known is he was asked to pay an extra 25s for his son's plaque, Lieutenant William Reginald Fitzthomas Wyley.

Ascertaining who paid for the remainder of the individual plaques is only possible in a number of isolated cases as the information has been retained by the descendants of the Fallen. Betram Rawlins is able to inform us that his father's plaque was paid for by his sister, Gloria. The mothers of Private Edward Walter Newbold, Lance Corporal Victor Leslie Clarke and Gunner Herbert Charles Collingbourne were fundamental in ensuring that plaques were obtained to commemorate their sons. The relatives of Sapper William Joseph Barnett cannot figure out how the family found the money to pay for the plaque.

During research many of the families who contacted me, did not know that their relatives had a plaque in the park or the location of the plaque. As one of the examples, the early records from the archives show that two brothers had plaques in the same location, Private John Bartlett and Private Henry Bartlett. Henry's plaque went missing prior to 1961 and only John's remains.

Plaques were not only erected to the memory of individual men but also to specific groups of men. Two off these were to the men of the 1/7th Battalion and the 2/7th Battalion, Royal Warwickshire Regiment and they read *"This tree was planted to the glorious memory of the officers, N.C. Officers and men of the 1/7th Battalion, Royal Warwickshire Regiment who fell in the Great War (1914 -1918) from the 7th Battalion Royal Warwickshire regiment, Old Comrades Association"*.

Plaques to various 'Brethren' also proved popular, and there are plaques for *"Our Fallen Brethren by the Grand Independent Order of Loyal Caledonian Corks, Coventry District"*, *"The Fallen Brethren A.O.F Court Earl Leofric"*, *"Brethren of Sir William Thrasher Lodge, 2844"* and finally to the *"Elder Brethren by Toc H, Coventry Branch"*.

Sir William Thrasher Lodge

St. John's Ambulance Brigade also dedicated a plaque to the Fallen members of the Coventry Branch.

St. John's Ambulance

A collective plaque was also erected to the Tramway men who fell from Coventry Corporation, it is presumed that this plaque was paid for by their colleagues. It is known that sixteen men died from Tramways Department and they are also commemorated on a memorial in the Council House.

The Opening Ceremony

City of
Coventry.

CAMERA PRINCIPIS

Souvenir
Programme

Official Opening & Dedication
of the War Memorial Park.
Saturday, July 9th, 1921.

By His Worship the Mayor (COUNCILLOR W. H. GRANT),
and the BISHOP OF COVENTRY.

PRICE SIXPENCE.

The park was dedicated and officially declared open on the 9th July, 1921. The official programme explained the role of the Memorial committee and the acquisition of the full public rights over Stivichall Common. Under two headings ' A Memorial to Coventry Heroes' and 'Laying Out The Park' the programme provided some insight into the future of the Park.

A Memorial to Coventry Heroes

At some suitable spot in the Park it is intended to place a monument or appropriate memorial to the brave men in whose memory the scheme has been undertaken. Exactly what form this will take has not yet been decided, though various suggestions have been made. It may be taken for granted, however that such a memorial, of a character worthy of it's purpose, will be provided in or about the park, and that the names of the honoured dead will be recorded thereon for the admiration and reverence of posterity.

Laying Out The Park

The main area of the Park will be made available as playing fields, the need for which, in an expanding City like Coventry, is only too well known. There will be ample space for cricket, football, hockey, tennis and other games, and these facilities will prove of the greatest value in the healthy development of the young people of the city. A children's playground can easily be provided and a small portion of the park can also be laid out and beautified as garden and flower beds, among which the older people will find pleasure in walking. A suggestion has been made that an open air bath may be provided. Whether this will be possible will depend, of course on the funds available and on obtaining a sufficient supply of water on the site, but the idea is an excellent one and will if possible be carried out.

VIEW OF STIVICHALL COMMON.

PLAN OF MEMORIAL PARK.

A Plan of the Park as it appeared in the Programme

'*The Coventry Herald*' reported the opening under the heading and sub-headings '*Coventry's War Memorial Official: Opening of the park at Stivichall. Impressive and historical opening. Witnessed by huge assembly*'.

The Procession

A procession from the Barrack Square was the opening spectacle of the day, and even the great heat did not restrain the citizens from lining the route and going in their thousands to the ceremony. Promptly at 2.15pm, the procession from Barrack Square was met at the bottom of Hertford Street by the Mayor and Corporation. The procession proceeded in a dignified manner through the centre of the town. The Bishop and the Sub-Dean joined en route. The procession was of a representative character, the order being as follows; Detachment of "Mounted Police", the 4th Battalion, Royal Warwickshire Regiment A detachment of Yeomanry, half a detachment of ex-service men, the Chief Constable and his staff, the Mayor and Corporation, Ministers of the churches, Salvation Army, Justices of the Peace, ex-service men, Special Constables, 2nd Cadet Battalion Royal Warwickshire Regiment, Cadet Battalion Catholic Cadet Corps, Boy Scouts, British Red Cross, St Johns Ambulance, British Red Cross VAD, Coventry District Nursing Association, Girl Guides, Salvation Army Lifesaving Girls and pupils representing secondary and elementary schools. On each side of the Mayor and Corporation marched a guard of honour of twenty five ex-service men.

The procession marched to the accompaniment of the Territorial Band and to fully appreciate it's impressiveness, one had only to stand in Warwick Road where the whole length of the pageant could be viewed. The progress of the assembly was witnessed by a great concourse of people who lined the whole of the route.

At The Park

The opening and Dedication Ceremonies

Entering the park in a blaze of tropical sun, with the thermometer at 140 degrees in the open, the visitors walked on the parched grass the brown of which was covered by the leaves of the trees scattered about. Proceeding down a gentle declivity, one came to the enclosure and platform which lent a dash of colour to the scene, with the railway lines in the background glittering like molten silver under the pitiless sun. The platform, with standing for about 80 people was bright with tri-coloured draperies and mattock in gold on a royal purple background, surmounted by the word "Remembrance" standing out in bold lettering worked in white flowers on a scarlet background. This in turn was surmounted by a crown worked in palm leaves and red flowers, with a Union Jack stirring lazily in a slight breeze on a flagstaff over all.

Remembrance

The platform was surrounded by a special enclosure for seating over 400 widows and parents of the Fallen, and also for the disabled, together with close upon 800 guests of the Mayor and Mayoress. Outside the enclosure, there was an assembly of well over 20,000 people, the scene upon the arrival of the procession being a memorable one as well as one of historical interest for future generations through the agency of the photographers present. The various parts of the procession filed in and took up their positions quietly and smoothly, the bright scarlet of the robes worn by the Mayor and Aldermen, and the blue of the councillors, varying with the Bishops rich attire in completing the picture as they took up their positions on the platform in front of which the City Chamberlain, the Sword and Mace Bearer, and the Town Crier with their old world robes and caps. The ex-service men's organisations were represented on the platform by officials from several local branches: Messrs J. P. Martin, J. H. Barnes, I. L. Shaffir, G. Walker, W. Newbold, C. J. Wareham, H. A. Jackson, D. Callow DCM and J. Ball.

When all had taken up their positions, the proceedings opened up with a verse of the National Anthem, followed immediately by the singing of Healey Poster's "*My Country 'tis of Thee*" by a choir of 3000 children. With Mr John Potter as conductor and A. F. Collingbourne as assistant, the singing, accompanied by a band of the 7th Warwicks, was beautiful in the extreme, the voices blending very effectively with the band music, which had been arranged by Mr Charles Bronson, the musical director at the Coventry Opera House.

The Mayor's Address

The Mayor, in formally opening the Park, said *"it was in glorious memory of the brave men of Coventry who made the supreme sacrifice in the Great War, and to those who, equally willing to face death, came through the inferno, many of them broken and maimed, and to all who played their part in the great struggle. To their glorious memory, the Park had been purchased by their grateful fellow citizens as a tribute to be handed down and enjoyed for all time by those who followed. It would be difficult to imagine a more fitting tribute that could be in a more picturesque setting. In the heart of leafy Warwickshire amid sylvan surroundings is the centre of Shakespeare's England, and astride, in part with common lands, a great historic highway along which Kings, Queens and armies had marched in peace and war, it would serve alike the purpose as a memorial to the living and the dead. It was nothing less than an inspiration which prompted its acquisition, and they owed a debt of gratitude to those who initiated the scheme and carried it to a successful term. The £31,000 representing the purchase price was made up by the widow's rites, the splendid contribution of the workers, the tradesmen, the manufacturers and others while the vendor generously reduced the burden by returning £2,000 of the purchase price; others who he regretted were not with them were equally generous"*.

Proceeding, the Mayor paid tribute to the Town Clerk (Mr G. Sutton), upon whom the burden of the scheme fell, and passed on to review the share taken by Coventry in the Great War. The City furnished the ranks with 35,000 men who answered the call.

Preparing for the Dedication and Unveiling

After the official opening of the Park, the next stages of development could be deployed. *'The Coventry Herald'* dated October 12th 1923 and headlined *'City War Memorial; The Scheme Explained'* detailed the work that was required in the War Memorial Park and agreed by the Coventry War Memorial General Committee and Sub-Committees. The Chairman explained at the Committee that the Sub-Committees had met the previous evening to try and push forward the lay-out of the Memorial Park. The plan submitted showed that the park itself was 120 acres in extent, in addition to which there was an additional 62 acres of common land, making a total area of 182 acres.

It was the wish of the council that they should do something to find work for the unemployed during the winter and as a scheme for improving the Memorial Park had been hanging about for some time it was their duty to push it forward. Several schemes had been presented for consideration and the one before them on that occasion was the only one which they felt would find work for any reasonable number of unemployed. If that plan met with the approval of the meeting it would be passed on to the Baths and Parks committee to carry out.

The scheme before the committee was 38 acres of the park to be laid out as ornamental ground, to include bowling greens, tennis courts, bandstand etc. The principal entrance to the park at a point near the Grove, with a connecting road to the main Warwick Road. From the entrance a main walk, laid out about 20 feet in width and 230 yards in length. Trees planted on each side of the walk, leading through the centre of an ornamental portion.

At the end of the Avenue, it was suggested, there should be erected a monument to the fallen. This monument would be placed on the summit of the first ridge, so that people proceeding along the main walk will have a view of the monument on the summit. A portion of the ground between the Kenilworth and Stoneleigh Roads would be laid out in ornamental beds, shrubberies etc with walks in various parts. In addition it was proposed to make three bowling greens and 48 tennis courts, together with a pavilion, these would be placed on a site near the Kenilworth Road, in close proximity to the tennis courts.

A band-stand would be erected on a site adjacent to the position of the present temporary bandstand. A second access would be made on the Kenilworth Road to the portion of the park it is intended to lay out, and a further entrance would be added on the same road, opposite Earlsdon Avenue. It was intended to leave the grove as it is for the present, with the exception that a road will be made through from the Warwick Road to the park. The remainder of the park will not be interfered with.

The probable cost was also discussed and this required collaboration between the Baths and Parks and War Memorial sub-committees. These stated that they had considered plans for a suggested layout of a portion of the War Memorial Park near the Grove entrance, the plan having been prepared by the City Engineer and approved by the Baths and Parks Committee. Illustrations of memorials erected in other towns had been presented and the following were elected as a sub-committee to interview a representative of local architects, with a view to designs and estimates of cost being submitted to the War Memorial Committee:-
The Mayor Ald. Pridmore, Councillor Friswell, Councillor Ivens and the City Engineer.

The Chairman pointed out that a sum of between £3,000 to £5,000 would have to be raised for the purpose. Mr. Tickner, Head of the local society of Architects stated that the Society were willing to submit designs without conforming to conditions laid down by the Royal Institute of British Architects. In the sub Committee considerable discussions took place on the question of the advisability of having the names of the fallen on the monument and it was generally realised that it would be a most difficult matter to secure all the names. Alderman Pridmore suggested that the names might be inscribed on parchment placed in a cavity on the monument.

The town clerk mentioned that at a previous meeting there was a recommendation that the Baths and Parks Committee should have prepared, if possible the names of the fallen citizens to be inscribed on the memorial. Mr. Hayward finally moved that "*as the result of the difficulty of getting a correct list of citizens who have fallen, the committee is of the opinion that it is not desirable to put any names on the war memorial to be erected in the park, and the committee further recommend that a book containing the names shall be provided and kept in the library*". This was seconded by Alderman Pridmore and agreed to.

Considering the cost of the monument, Mr. Hayward thought that there would be difficulty in getting a big subscription list and he was of the opinion that the expenditure of £3000 was sufficient. Mr G. W. Pridmore thought £5000 the least they should spend; a £3000 memorial would be a "laughing stock". It was agreed to base the cost of the monument at £5000.

It was decided that the Coventry Society of Architects should arrange for competitive designs with estimate of costs, and also to invite non-members of the Society to submit designs. At the outset it was suggested that Mr. G. A. Steane should be appointed a member of the general committee as representing the Coventry Society of Architects but:

Mr. Steane said it gave his Society great pleasure to co-operate with the committee and they appreciated it very much. They were anxious to do all they could for the scheme so that the work done should be a credit to the city and all concerned. The architects felt that this was a competition, and any help they gave would have to be unofficial, and therefore it would not be advisable to be represented on that committee. It would be better if the City Engineer acted as a link between the architects and the committee.

Members of the committee now had the scheme explained to them by the City Engineer (Mr J. E. Swindhurst), and many questions were asked as to the layout.
Ald. Pridmore: Supposing we had an agricultural show ?
The City Engineer: It would occupy practically the same space as previously
Mr .E. Hayward: What area do you suppose utilising ? About 38 acres
Mr. E. V. Dodd: About a quarter of the park
Replying to further questions the City Engineer said there were 23 football pitches in use at the present time, and the carrying out of the present scheme would mean the loss of five of these pitches. There would be 48 tennis courts and the levelling of these would provide work for the unemployed. The question of providing a crown bowling green and hard tennis courts would all depend on the amount of money available. Provision was made in the plan for three bowling greens.

Mr. Nettleton asked that in view of the possibility of better trade and with more money available, would it be possible to convert the proposed bandstand into a concert hall, so that provision could be made for the public in wet weather ?
The City Engineer; There is room for anything; it is all a question of money. There is no reason why that should not be done in the future. The thing to be considered now is the right lay-out; the Park will go on improving for the next 50 years and it will be a beautiful place some day.

Further the City Engineer said the land around the bandstand would be left as grassland. It was hoped to have a children's corner in another portion of the park.
Mr. Nettleton proposed that the scheme be approved by the committee, stating that the sub-committee came to the conclusion that it was worthy of the City Engineer and worthy of the City. Mr. G. W. Pridmore seconded and the resolution was unanimously carried. Mr. E. V. Dodd: Shall we get anything from the unemployment grants Committee for the work ? The City Engineer: I do not see why we should not.

At a later meeting of the joint sub-committee Messrs G. A. Steane (President), T. F. Tickner and H. Whiteman (Secretary) attended on behalf of the Coventry Society of Architects, The Chairman explained the views of the joint sub-committee in regard to the suggested memorial and stated that the conference had been arranged with a view to the Coventry architects, submitting competitive schemes for a memorial.

In November 1923, Coventry Architects were invited to submit competitive designs for a monument in the War Memorial Park. Mr W. Haywood LRIBA of Birmingham was appointed by the President of the Royal Institute of British Architects to act as assessor, and he awarded the first place to the design submitted by the Mr. T. F. Tickner, FRIBA and the second place to the design submitted by Mr. T. R. J. Meakin LRIBA.

Another fund was launched in 1924 for the erection of a monument. In this year the competition winner Mr. T. F. Tickner died and on his death his practice was taken over by Messrs T. R. J. Meakin who had come second but were advised to follow the late Mr. Tickner's design. The contractor chosen was Mr J. G. Gray of Coventry. Also in 1924 the mammoth task of compiling the Roll of the Fallen was given to the City Librarian, Charles Nowell.

In September 1924 an appeal to the public for £5000 for the purpose of the monument was issued by the Major (Alderman W. H. Grant). The amount actually raised was £5350 13s 3d. The total amount received from citizens in the appeals of 1919-1920 and 1924-1925 was £36,913 2s 0d

On January 14th 1927, 'The Coventry Herald' reported that "*The Baths and Parks Committee of the Coventry City Council have decided that sixty men be engaged through the Labour Exchange , preference to be given to ex-service men to work in the War Memorial Park. Thirty of the men are to work on Monday, Tuesday and Wednesday and thirty on Thursday, Friday and Saturday alternately. The wages to be paid to the men will be the gardener's rate viz 1s 7d per hour and the working hours will be from 9.00am till 4.00pm from Monday to Friday and 9.00am till noon on Saturday*".

.In August 1927, the monument was completed. It was built of white Portland stone and stood 87' high, encircled by eight steps. Four feet above the top are two shelves on which flowers can be placed. The Chamber of Silence is 12' 6" square and 18' 6" high having two doors and a white marble floor. Wrought iron gates were also erected to the entrance to the park and the pillars supporting the gates were constructed from stones of the old city wall.

PARK GATES AND WAR MEMORIAL, COVENTRY.

The Park Gates

A week prior to the War Memorial unveiling the Mayor Fred Lee wrote to the local papers with the following communication addressed to 'Manufacturers and Tradesmen and other employers of ex-service men':

Dear Sirs,

As far as you possibly can allow your ex-service men employees to leave work not later than 11.30am on Saturday, October 8th so that they may take part in the ex-service men's parade which is arranged. There will be such great numbers making their way to the War Memorial Park and the ex-service men's parade itself be such a large one, that it is essential for the parade to leave Pool Meadow not later than 1.30pm so that the men may be in their allotted positions in the War Memorial Park not later than 2.15pm.

Unless however the men leave work by 11.30am it will in many cases be impossible for them to get their lunch and reach the Pool Meadow in time. I am sure that having regard to the unique character of the occasion, this appeal will be generously responded to by the employers of Coventry.

I am sir, yours faithfully.

The route which had been revised slightly was from Pool Meadow to the War Memorial Park via Priory Street, Ford Street, Hales Street, Burges, Cross Cheaping, Broadgate, Hertford Street, Warwick Road to the main entrance.

The ex-service men's Association were also making their own arrangements, and in the last week of September the ex-Yeoman in the weekly meeting held in the 'Sir Colin Campbell' decided to attend. Branch members were asked to parade at Holy Trinity School, Ford Street at 1.00pm, wearing medals and black tie. The names of those who would be attending were requested to forward their names to the Branch Secretary. The Stoke ex-service men's club were also encouraging those who were no longer in any association but anxious to attend to join them at the club premises and also in the parade. Ex-service men of the South Midland Howitzer Brigade were asked to parade under their old officers, ex-members of the RAF were requested to contribute to defray the cost of a wreath

It was estimated that 4,000 men would take part in this parade and according to military authorities, decorations VC, DCM, MM etc should come first, beginning at the middle and top left side of coat. Then follows service medals in the order which they were awarded those for the Great War being 1914 Star, 1914-1915 Star, General Service Medal and Victory Medal.

Three days prior to the unveiling the Town Clerk, Frederick Smith reminded all *'that the War Memorial Park on Saturday the 8th will be opened for the entrance of Ticket Holders and the Public at 1.00pm and will be closed at 6.00pm. On Sunday the 9th the Chamber of Silence will be open from 10.30am to 12.30pm and from 2.30pm to 5.30pm. The Council House will be closed at 11.30am on Saturday the 8th October'.* The Postmaster of Coventry also announced the 3.30pm town delivery and the 2.30pm town collection would be suspended. Letters could be arranged for by collection from the Sorting office. In the park workmen had been busy until 1.00am and for more then a fortnight the work of buildings, barricades, platforms, seats, amplifiers and microphones had taken place.

The Memorial Prepared for the Unveiling

'The Coventry Herald' ranked the forthcoming dedication as one of the main events in local life since Coventry became a City and it would be a day long remembered. On the day a dedication and order of ceremony would be available at 3d. per copy to members of the public. This booklet containing sixteen pages will be free to ex-service men and the relatives of the Fallen.

Arrangements for Earl Haig were meticulously laid out. On Arrival from Euston, he will be received by the Mayor and Town Clerk, inspect a guard of honour of the 7th Battalion, Royal Warwickshire Regiment and proceed by car to the Council House, On arrival here, he was to inspect another Guard of Honour of the 1st Battalion, Royal Warwickshire Regiment and then have dinner with the Mayor.

Leaving the council House at 2.40pm to get to the park for further inspection of the British Legion's Guard Of Honour and then a detachment of the Warwickshire Yeomanry. The Mayor would then present Mrs E. Bench who lost four sons and

Corporal Arthur Hutt VC who would accompany the Earl into the Chamber of Silence where he would place the Roll of Honour in a carved oak cabinet.

The service would start at 3.00pm and finish forty five minutes later, the hymns being specified as " O, God our help in ages past", The Son of God goes forth to war" and finally " Now thank we are all our God". During service, prayers would be said by the Bishop and after the opening prayer and hymn, the Mayor was to address the assembly and the Earl Haig to unveil the memorial to the following words "To the glory of God and to the memory of the men of Coventry who laid down their lives in the Great War, I unveil this memorial in the name of the Father, and of the Son and of the Holy Ghost". At the close the last post would be played , with a moments silence, followed by the 'Reveille' and one verse of the National Anthem. Wreaths would then be placed and Earl Haig would address the ex-service men in a marquee and thanks accorded by the Mayor to the Field Marshall for his kindness in visiting Coventry.

After the park, Earl Haig would return to the Council House having tea in St. Mary's Hall where the guests of the Mayor would be entertained. Departure would be at 6.30pm for the Railway Station with the Mayor and Town Clerk to catch the train leaving Coventry at 6.42pm.

In the great effort of which the ceremony of the 8th October 1927 will mark the culmination of the willing help received from all classes of the citizens, but it is felt by the War Memorial Committee that the services of the following should receive special mention in the local press: Alderman W. H. Grant for his zealous chairmanship of the War Memorial committee; Councillor W. Ivens and R. Perkins, previous chairmen of the Baths and Parks committee; the Editors of the "*Midland Daily Telegraph*", "*Coventry Standard*" and "*Coventry Herald*"; Mr. George Sutton (Hon. Secretary 1919-1924) and Mr. Frederick Smith (Hon. Secretary 1924-1927); Mr W. J. Wall and Mr J. Heritage Peters, for services in connection with the raising of funds; Mr. F. H. Harrod who organised the parade of ex-service men; Mr. J. E. Swindlehurst, Mr. E. H. Ford, Mr. Harry Lord, Mr. Sydney Larkin, Mr. G. Tough and Mr. W. J. Cattell.

The Memorial Dedication and Unveiling

844

ENTRANCE BY GATE **C**

COVENTRY WAR MEMORIAL

Unveiling and Dedication by
FIELD-MARSHAL EARL HAIG

Saturday, 8th October, 1927, at 3 p.m.

This Ticket admits ONE PERSON ONLY to the Enclosure
indicated " **PINK** " on the Plan.

*Ticket Holders are advised to be in their places not later
than 2.15 p.m.*

FOR PLAN SEE OTHER SIDE

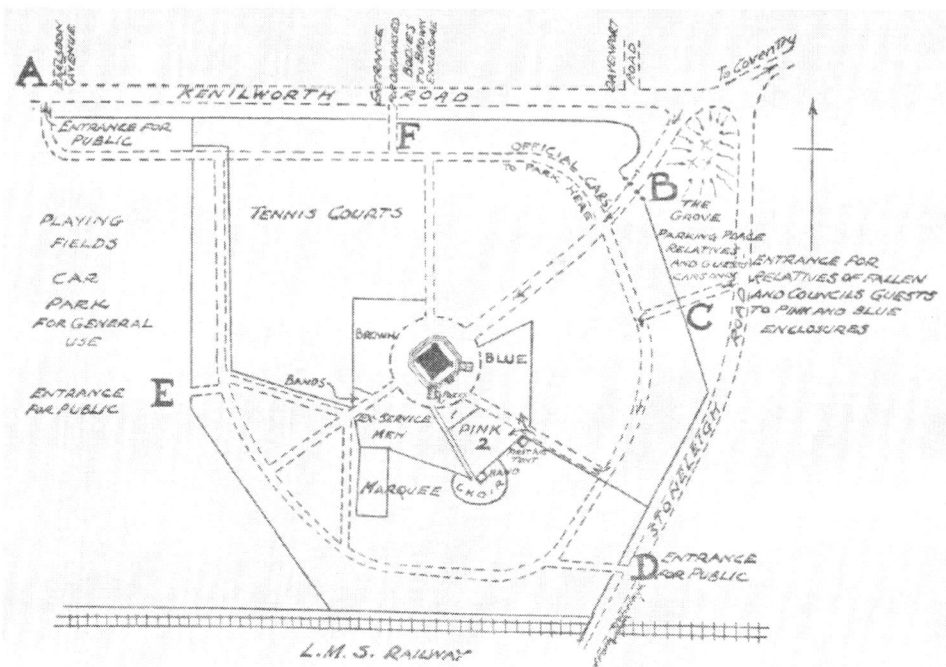

A Ticket for the Dedication

On the 8th October 1927, Earl Haig arrived on the express train at Coventry station as per the plan and was greeted by a small party of officials from the Council. Shortly after this he inspected a Guard of Honour and was driven to the Council House for lunch.

Field Marshal Haig inspecting a Guard of Honour

The route was lined by a large crowd and he received enthusiastic cheers from sightseers as he drove by. Whilst Earl Haig was having lunch, the 4,000 ex-service men in the parade left Pool Meadow at 1.30pm to make their way to the War Memorial Park. As requested they wore their medals showing a fine display, many of the men taking part also showed signs of the physical scars of war. The first photograph on the following page shows the men from Siddeley Deasy awaiting the start of the parade. The second was taken from the steps of the War Memorial and shows the ex-service men proceeding past the memorial having come from the gates of the park.

Ex-service men from the Parkside and Whitley Works

Ex-service men on parade

'The Coventry Herald' stated *"A pleasant sun brightened the remarkable scene, a splash of colour from the robes of the Alderman contrasted with the white stone of the memorial, the green turf and the bronze yellow tint of the trees. A stir from the direction of the main entrance, with words of command and rifles grounded. Earl Haig and the entourage walked passed the guard of honour and he had a word for many of them including those that had been maimed. There were privileged places for the relatives of the dead and ex-service men catered for. The widow of the late Mr. T. F. Tickner was amongst those present".*

Earl Haig with the Mayor

Waiting for Earl Haig on the platform was a proud Corporal Hutt VC and by his side Mrs Bench wearing twelve medals belonging to her four dead sons. As Earl Haig approached a hush fell over the crowd and the service commenced and eye witnesses suggest 'the scene was one never to be forgotten'. *'The Coventry Herald'* reporter commented on the vast crowd of 50,000 people who seemed dwarfed by the Memorial, so impregnated with meaning and embedded in a typical English setting. The service started with the singing of the grand old hymn " *O' God our help in ages past"* and the crowd sang with eagerness.

The sacred keynote of the service was struck in prayer by the Bishop of Coventry *"We remember before thee, the great company of our brothers who left their homes and all that they held dear and laid down their lives for their country. In thankfulness and hope we commend their souls to thy gracious keeping and we beseech thee to grant that as we raise this memorial, so may we walk worthy of their fellowship".*

It was the turn of the Mayor who expressed his thanks to Earl Haig for unveiling the war memorial and that this was not the moment to commemorate him, but as the years had passed it brought in an ever clearer light that ensured his name was always remembered with gratitude and pride by his fellow countrymen. The Mayor continued it was unnecessary for him to detain the assembly with details of the memorial but stated " *No memorial no matter how ample it may be could be adequate to the great sacrifice which had been made by those who today were in all our thoughts". After dwelling on the heritage of Coventry and thanking the crowd, The Mayor was reminded of the following words:*

Others, I doubt not, if not we
The issue of their toils shall see
Young Children gather as their own
The harvest that the dead have sown
The dead, forgotten and unknown"

In addition the Mayor ended with the words " *No, not forgotten and not unknown. For as long as this monument shall stand, they will remain enshrined in the hearts and minds of Citizens of Coventry".* Field Marshall Earl Haig then proceeded to unveil the memorial and his full address is replicated below:

Mr. Mayor, Ladies and Gentlemen,
We are met on an occasion of sad memories, but one on which pride and gratitude are mingled with sadness. Pride that in their country's hour of need the men of this city and district did not shirk their duty. Gratitude for the unswerving loyalty and unselfish devotion which, for our sakes and for the salvation of all that we hold dearest, carried them unflinching to their gallant end. I am very glad to see so good a number of ex-service men here today. It is indeed only right and proper that they, above all others, should join prominently and in force in the tribute which Coventry today is paying to the memory of her dead. The long list of names inscribed upon the Roll of Honour which it will shortly be my duty to deposit in the Chamber of Silence are names of your own comrades, of men who fought beside you, with whom you shared, the good and the evil fortunes of war. You, above all others, know the nature of the fullness of the sacrifice they made.

Men from this city, whether in the Warwickshire Yeomanry or the Royal Warwickshire Regiment, show the whole course of the war, from start to finish. They did not at first form part of my command, but the work of the 1st Battalion as part of the 10th Infantry Brigade in the first Battle of Le Cateau in 1914 has gone down in history to the lasting glory of Warwickshire men. Men of the same fine regiment, Regulars and Territorials, took part with the 4th and 61st Divisions in the preparatory engagement on the 1st November 1918, which cleared the way for the final battle of the war.

Warwickshire Men's Record

Regulars and Territorials, Infantry and Yeomanry and Artillerymen too – Warwickshire men, Coventry men went through the war from the first day to the last. The price demanded was a heavy one, and those who were spared to come back from the furnace of the fighting front will never forget the comrades upon whom it fell to pay the price. But I am glad for other reasons to see so strong a muster of ex-service men at this Memorial service. It is nine years now, or very nearly, since the conclusion of the fighting, and nine years is a substantial portion of a man's working life. But it is not enough to dim the memory of the war or the friendships formed. It should not be enough to make any ex-service man forget the duty he owes in other ex-service men, or the sense of brotherhood which amid the tremendous experiences of the war knit all service men together.

Many men came out of the war with little enough to equip them for the peace conditions into which they had to enter. All through the past nine years there has been urgent need for ex-service men to stand together, to recall and strengthen their old friendships and to co-operate as an organised body to assist those of their number who for one reason or another failed to find a place for themselves in the bitter competition of civilian life.

Example of the Ex-service men

Much help has been given, as I gratefully acknowledge, by men and women in all parts of the country who have been glad of the opportunity when the war was ended to acknowledge in practical fashion the debt they owe to those who bore the burden of the fighting. Yet the need has been and still is very great, and without the example of comradeship, goodwill and solidarity which ex-service men as a whole have shown to the whole country in their dealings with each other and in confronting the peace time difficulties, I do not think that the response of the general public to their appeals for consideration and assistance would have been so great or that their needs would have been met to the extent that they are being met today.

By coming together by forming the British Legion, by organising the relief committee, their employment centres and social clubs: in a word, by setting an example of self-help inspired by a sense of comradeship and of duty one towards another ex-service men leave performed a signal service to themselves, and, as I believe, to their fellow countrymen. They have been a steadying influence in a period of exceptional stress and strain and difficulty, and have maintained of their own volition a spirit of discipline, patriotism and public service the value of which has been and is incalculable.

The Finest tribute to the dead

I want this great ex-service movement to go on inspired by the same motives, governed by the same sense of public service and private generosity. I want it not merely to keep alive among ex-service men themselves the comradeship of the old army, the comradeship which bridged differences of rank and education, yet acknowledged the claims of discipline and duty, but to carry that comradeship into the dealings one with another of all British citizens, and above all those of the younger generation, until it becomes part of the life of the whole nation.

Ex-service men at the Dedication

I can conceive of no finer tribute to the memory of our dead than the achievement of such a work as that. This splendid monument which you have erected to commemorate for ever the supreme sacrifice of your own friends and relatives, and those other monuments which have risen in almost very town and village in these islands, are no blatant exaltations of militarism, no altars to the Gods of War. They are the expression of our reverence and our gratitude towards those who set the welfare and safety of their fellow countrymen and women far above their own pain and suffering and counted the duties of citizenship of more value than their own lives.

It is to a constant recollection of our duty of British men and women, heirs of a splendid past, and trustees, we hope, for a long and honourable future, that this Memorial calls us. It is an example of the courage with which duty should be undertaken of the price at which, if need be, duty must be carried out. It reminds us that duty, courage and self-sacrifice are the foundations upon which comradeship is built.

To the glory of God and to the memory of the men of Coventry who laid down their lives in the Great War, I unveil this Memorial in the name of the Father and of the Son and of the Holy Ghost.

As the Field Marshall pulled the cord, this released the Union jack which uncovered the doors of the Chamber of Silence. The Guard of Honour stood to attention, Earl Haig saluted the memorial and the assembly stood bow headed prior to singing *"The Son of God goes forth to war"*.

Field Marshall Earl Haig Unveiling the Memorial

Proceedings continued and the Roll Of Honour and key of the Chamber of Silence were passed to Earl Haig. He opened the door, nearby were Corporal Hutt VC, the embellishment of valour and Mrs. E. Bench, the symbol of sacrificial motherhood.

Field Marshall Earl Haig Receiving the key from T. Meakin, Architect

The Roll of Honour was placed in a carved oak cabinet, after this tense moment, a prayer was said followed by a hymn. To end the ceremony, the Royal Warwickshire Regimental band sounded the *'Last Post'*, and a minute's silence followed prior to official wreaths being placed, including one by Earl Haig.

A Floral Tribute

The crowd were then permitted to gain entrance to the Chamber of Silence and Earl Haig went to address the ex-service men in a marquee. Those in attendance at this event sung ' For he's a jolly good fellow' on his arrival. The policy and the Charter of the Legion along with the plans for assisting the unemployed were discussed. Earl Haig then went for tea in St. Mary's Hall with guests of the Mayor and returned to London.

Following on from the dedication, Earl Haig expressed his pleasure to the splendid turnout of the British Legion Guard of Honour and to convey his appreciations, throughout the day he also spoke to the Mayor stating "*He has unveiled many memorials but he had never seen such a splendid organisation as that which awaited him at Coventry. Everything had worked out as the timetable and the whole display was one which filled him with admiration. The Earl asked the Mayor to convey to the Town Clerk and all who assisted with the preparations, his appreciation of the reception accorded to him by the wonderful multitude which gathered. When I saw such discipline, I thought 'The Heart of England is still there'*".

Pilgrimage to the War Memorial

Earl Haig wrote in his diary "*Open Coventry War memorial arriving 1.10pm departing 6.42pm*" and the dedication of the War Memorial also appeared in 'The Times' on the 10th October 1917. The Siddeley Deasy 'Employees Quarterly' included an article on the War Memorial unveiling written by C. D. Siddeley stating "*This memorable event should not be allowed to pass without expressing my thanks at the privilege of being asked to take charge of the parade of ex-service men from the Parkside and Whitley Works. The muster, approximately 250 strong, was very well turned out, and I am happy to know, both from my own observations and reports, that there was certainly not a smarter unit than ours. At the same time we can take credit to ourselves as being practically the only unit which realised it was a ceremonial parade, with the resultant discipline as to smoking on the march. In addition, an expression of appreciation, in which I believe all ranks will join, is due to the individual shop representatives under the chairmanship of Mr. Woodford, who organised and had the whole thing cut and dried, so that when it came to those of us who were parading, doing our little bit towards making the day a success, everything was quite easy".*

Reviews of the dedication the following week concluded that *"The monument Coventry has erected will be more powerful than words spoken or written. It will be a perpetual reminder of an obligation and a duty that no one worthy the name of an Englishman would seek to evade".*

CITY OF COVENTRY

ORDER OF CEREMONIAL
AT THE UNVEILING AND DEDICATION
OF THE

COVENTRY
WAR MEMORIAL

BY

FIELD-MARSHAL EARL HAIG
K.T., O.M., G.C.B., K.C.I.E., G.C.V.O.

ON

SATURDAY, 8th OCTOBER, 1927,
AT 3 P.M.

THIS MEMORIAL IS ERECTED BY THE CITIZENS
OF COVENTRY IN GRATEFUL REMEMBRANCE
OF THE 2,587 MEN OF COVENTRY WHO LAID
DOWN THEIR LIVES IN THE GREAT WAR.

The Future of the Memorial

After the dedication, questions were immediately raised as to the future of the Memorial. The Chamber of Silence was to be opened every afternoon and during the morning and afternoon on Sundays, comments were made on the lights which proved so successful for illustrating the Memorial during the evening of the dedication. In response to this a suggestion was taken up for the memorial to be prepared with permanent lighting that was harmonious with its design and beauty. The flood lighting installed for the dedication from the eight arc lamps would be maintained until after Armistice Sunday.

Another interesting policy which was adopted, was a new Mayoral duty. Every Sunday the Mayor who would now be the custodian of the Chamber of Silence key would open the doors and turn one page in the Roll Of Honour. At a set hour every week it was hoped the Mayor would be accompanied by relatives of the Fallen and this would be *'one of his most pleasing of duties'*.

The Bishop of Coventry wrote of the future *"the question now remains as to what is to be done to secure that the Tower of Remembrance shall be a living force in our community and not just a striking feature of the landscape, closed and silent. The Memorial undoubtedly should be a living reality in the years to come, and it would serve a useful purpose if people's opinions on the subject could be ascertained"*.

Concluding, *'The Coventry Herald'* reiterated *"the monument is the people's own tribute to their heroic fellow citizens, and that they should have frequent access to it. Though raised to the glory of the dead, it is no dead monument. It has a message for all time, and it will come home more deeply if the people not viewing it from a distance are able to move about it freely and intimately"*.

After the City's War memorial had been unveiled by the late Field Marshall Earl Haig on the 8th October 1927, the cenotaph placed in Spencer Park was removed. For eight years it served as symbol of the remembrance and regard of the ex-service men for their comrades, and it was the goal of many pilgrimages and tributes. It was thought appropriate by the Council to mark the spot it occupied by the planting of a memorial tree. The tree selected was an oak, grown from an acorn gathered at Verdun after the repulse by the French of the great German attack in 1916. The service was led by Councillor Perkins (Chairman of the Baths and Parks Committee) and the initial hymn was *'Onward, Christian soldiers'*.

Today a small stone acts as a reminder of the Cenotaph unveiled on 12th October 1919 and this can still be seen in the Dalton Road corner of the park.

The Plaque in Spencer Park

The Death of Earl Haig

Field Marshall Earl Haig died on the 29th January 1928, aged 66, from heart failure. He was given a state funeral on the 3rd February 1928. Crowds lined the streets as his body was moved from St Columba's Church to Westminster Abbey. After the service at the Abbey, the procession proceeded to Waterloo Station for the journey to Edinburgh where his body laid in state for three days at St Giles Cathedral. He was buried at Dryburgh Abbey.

The Plaque in the Chamber of Silence

A tablet to his memory (shown above) was unveiled in the Chamber of Silence on the 11th November 1928. A tree was also planted in his memory by C. L. Hayward of the British Legion (shown below). Countess Haig visited the Memorial Park on the 27th January 1929 and on her death she was buried next to her husband.

Died at Home

Of those commemorated in the War Memorial Park thirteen are classified as dying at home, this means they are buried in cemeteries within the UK. Nine casualties are buried within the boundaries of Coventry; seven in London road, one in Radford and one in Foleshill. The remaining four men are buried in different locations; Bath, Belfast, Gosport and London. The last date of death officially recognised by the Commonwealth War Grave Commission (CWGC) is the 31st August 1921, this aligns with the *'Termination of War Act'*. Veterans who died after this date are commemorated in the War Memorial Park, the death of Reginald Frederick Henry Gibbens a wheeler with the Royal Field Artillery who died on the 29th March 1925 falls into this category.

London Road Cemetery

As casualty's began to return from the front, it prompted the following suggestion from a concerned citizen who wrote to the Editor of *'The Coventry Graphic'*, the letter appearing under the headline *'A Hero's Portion at the Cemetery'*.

"Sir,

Would it be out of place to suggest that the corporation should set aside a piece of ground in Coventry Cemetery as a Heroes portion in which free internment could be made of soldiers who died on returning to their native city. It seems rather grim to suggest this, but the fact has to be faced that many soldiers may return broken in the war and perhaps so injured that their enfeebled constitution will hardly enable them long to survive. I understand that this concession has already been made at several places, and I read that the Northampton Council has set aside a portion of the civic cemetery for this purpose.

The City should surely relieve the relatives of the dead heroes of the necessity of paying for graves; indeed the City should deem it an honour to grant them a last resting place, upon which future generations could not look unmoved. I would go as far as to suggest that all Coventry men serving with the colours should be able to claim a last resting place in this portion no matter how long they live after the war; for they are all heroes and should be remembered as such to the end of their days-and after".

This suggestion was not adopted, Coventry Cemetery officially contains ninety four burials of the First World War and they are spread in locations throughout the grounds.

The first casualty to be buried in London Road Cemetery and commemorated in the Park is Private **Horace Jesse Ellis,** (23291) 10th Battalion, Royal Berkshire Regiment who died on the 12th October 1917 aged 26. The Royal Berkshire Regiment raised thirteen Battalions during the war and lost 6,688 men. Horace was born on the 19th March 1891 at Banbury, he resided at 3c. 7h Bayley Lane and prior to enlisting in March 1916 was employed as a labourer with Siddeley Deasy. He is buried in Plot no 19 square 193.

The Plaque of Private Ellis

Four months later on the 8th February 1918, Second Lieutenant **Frederick George Smith,** Royal Flying Corps was buried. Frederick aged 20, met his death whilst flying near Basingstoke. Born on the 15th November 1897 at Kingston-upon-Hull, he was the only son of Henry and Alice Smith residing with them at 14 Gloucester Street, Coventry. Frederick attended Rugby School from 1912 to 1913 and after leaving Rugby School he entered the service of the British Thompson Houston Company in Coventry employed as an Engineer. Frederick remained at the firm until he enlisted in July 1917, receiving his commission as a Second Lieutenant in the RFC in October 1917. At his interment in Coventry Cemetery Dr. David (Headmaster of Rugby School) and Canon Robin officiated, tributes of sympathy were received by his parents from friends in all parts of England. His headstone reads *"through time death glorious to life eternal"* and his name is inscribed on a British Thompson

Houston memorial along with thirteen of his colleagues. This memorial is located in the Royal Warwicks Club, Coventry, in addition to this his name is on the stained glass in St. John's Church. Second Lieutenant Frederick George Smith is pictured on the left as he appeared in *'The Coventry Graphic'*.

One week after the armistice Second Lieutenant **Jack Garside**, Royal Air Force, formerly Oxfordshire and Buckinghamshire Light Infantry, was killed aged 21 whilst flying at Brancaster, Norfolk on the 18th November 1918, after serving with them for exactly one month. Born the 19th June 1897 at Cleckheaton, he was the son of George and Sylvia Garside and resided with his parents at 47a Widdrington Road, Coventry. An engineer, Jack enlisted in October 1915 and served as Private 5542 with the 2/4th Battalion in France until he was discharged on the 18th October 1918 having been granted a commission with the RAF. In similar circumstances to Lieutenant Smith, Jack worked at British Thompson Houston and his name is inscribed on the works memorial in the Royal Warwicks club. He has a CWGC headstone and is front of this is placed a vase with the insignia of the RAF and the word 'Jack'.

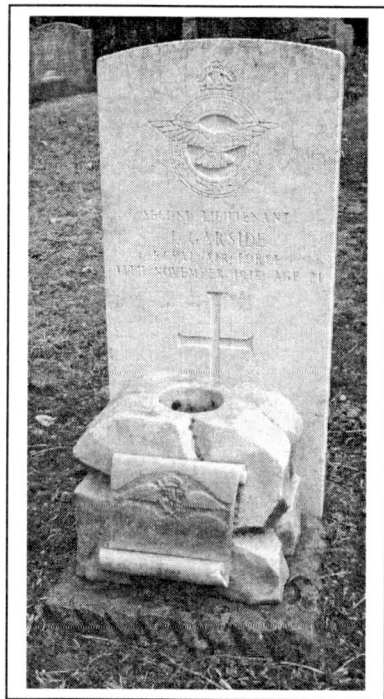

Private **Charles Wilfred Roe,** 4th Battalion, Devonshire Regiment died at home on the 7th March 1919, aged 19. Charles was born on the 25th February 1900 in Arden Street, Earlsdon. At the time of his death he resided at 12 Meadow Street, Coventry. Charles enlisted in August 1918 as a Private and prior to this was employed as a turner. In addition to being commemorated in the War Memorial Park, the Cathedral Church of St. Peter's in Exeter contains a memorial plaque to all the men from the Devonshire Regiment who died in the Great War.

Lance Corporal **Austin Timmins,** 778th Mortar Trench Company (Salonika), Royal Army Service Corps died at home aged 38 on the 16th August 1919. He was invalided from Salonica probably having contracted malaria. This campaign was considered by many to be a 'side-show'; the Allied army stationed there were known back home as the "Gardeners of Salonika" owing to the perceived lack of activity.

In reality the forces had to cope with extremes in temperature and malaria. Cases of malaria increased as the infected men were compelled to stay in Macedonia due to the threat of submarine attack under evacuation. In 1917 63,396 out of a strength of about 100,000 men were affected by the disease; by 1918 evacuations were again possible and many men would suffer relapses for years to come. In total the British forces suffered over 160,000 cases of malaria out of a total of over 500,000 non-battle casualties. Austin was born on the 18th March 1881 at Bridgnorth, Shropshire the son of Richard Timmins of Bridgnorth. Austin was married to Agnes Jane residing at 118 Stoney Stanton Road, Coventry. He was employed as a warehouseman prior to enlisting in August 1916.

Private **John Harold William Hastings,** Royal Army Service Corps (Motor Transport) died at home on the 19th October 1919. Despite dying prior to the end of the *'Termination of war act'*, his death is not recognized by the Commonwealth War Grave Commission. John was born on the 18th May 1894 at Oxford and resided in Coventry employed as a motor driver. He served just over four years, enlisting in September 1915. John was buried on October the 24th 1919 in Plot No. 11 Square 196 and resided at 51 Hastings Road and his plaque was one of the last plaque to go into the War Memorial Park.

One of the last Plaques

Wheeler **Reginald Frederick Henry Gibbens,** 91st Brigade, Royal Field Artillery died at home on the 29th March 1925. His name did not appear in the original *'City of Coventry: Roll of the Fallen'* but was added along with thirteen other names in a supplement. Reginald was buried on the 2nd April in Plot No. 200 Square 120. He resided at 6 Huntingdon Road although the death register lists he died at 4 Ludlow Road. Reginald was born on the 2nd February 1895 at Keresley and was employed as a motor body builder prior to enlisting in September 1914.

Foleshill Congregational Burial Ground.

There are two casualties of the Great War buried in this cemetery both of whom were treated at military hospital prior to their deaths. The first casualty is Gunner **Walter Williams Atkins** who has a plaque in the War Memorial Park and was treated at a Military Hospital in Bovington Camp, the other being Foleshill born Private Percy Kelley, Royal Air Force who died from pneumonia at Endell street military hospital on the 27th November 1918. Private Kelley does not have a plaque in the War Memorial Park.

Old and New Headstones

Gunner Atkins, Machine Gun Corps (tanks) died on the 9th February 1917 and was buried on the 15th February 1917. His plaque shows he was in the 19th Company, G Battery. Walter was born on the 4th August 1895 at 57 Henley Road, Bell Green, the son of Mr W. Atkins of the same address. An Engineer he enlisted in March 1916. Walter probably died as a result of an injury/illness which had taken place at Bovington rather than having been shipped back from France as a result of an injury/illness. In this latter case Walter would have been treated at a larger hospital. The left picture above shows Walter's old headstone. This reads "Our *dear beloved and only son. Heavy Section Machine Gun Corps (HSMGC) who after serving with the tanks in France died at Bovington Camp, Dorset*". Gunner Atkins original headstone was replaced by one from the CWGC in 2002 that has the insignia of the Tank Corps as opposed to the Machine Gun Corps.

Officers Receiving Lessons in the Use of Tanks

At the outbreak of war in August 1914 the tactical use of machine guns was unappreciated by the British Military. After a year of warfare the need was recognised and the Machine Gun Corps was authorized in October 1915. The Heavy Section was formed in March 1916, becoming the heavy branch in November of that year. Men of this branch were amongst the members of the tank crews when they first saw action during the battle of the Somme in September 1916 at Flers. In July 1917 the heavy branch separated from the MGC to become the Tank Corps.

When Gunner Atkins was in France with the tanks then it would be either A, B, C or D Companies, the last two companies saw action on the 15th September 1916 but his name does not appear on the crew lists though they are not complete. A Company saw a bit of action towards the end of the year and B Company saw none. Men were posted back to Bovington because of their experience when Earl Haig ordered a massive expansion of the tank force.

Radford Cemetery

According to the CWGC this cemetery contains only four graves of the Great War: Private Maurice Green , Lieutenant Henry Phillip Walter Laughton (RAF), Private HFV Manning and Surgeon Lieutenant Howard William Pickup. Also buried here but not officially recognised is Gunner **Horace Rupert Whitmill** , 3/1 SMH Brigade, Royal Field Artillery who died at home 17th February 1921. Horace was born on the 1st October 1897 at Kenilworth, resided at 72 Northfield Road and was employed as a shop assistant until enlisting in May 1915.

Belfast City Cemetery

Private **William Webb**, Prince Albert's Somerset Light Infantry died in Belfast at the Military Hospital on the 19th July 1918. He was born at Fulham, Middlesex and employed by Siddeley Deasy Motors Ltd enlisting in Kenilworth. William is buried in Belfast Cemetery; the names of the fallen in this cemetery are commemorated on a Screen Wall. William's name also appears on the St. Nicholas Memorial in Kenilworth along with those 138 other men from the community.

Haslar Royal Navy Cemetery, Gosport

Acting Engine Room Artificer 4th Class, **Edward James Geater** was attached to the training depot HMS Victory II and died age 22 on the 10th September 1918. He was the son of Captain and Mrs Geater of 32 Waveley Road, Coventry and was born on the 23rd July 1896 at Fort Chambray, Gozo on the Maltese Islands. A fitter he enlisted in June 1918. A year after his death *The Coventry Graphic* printed the following *"In memoriam; In proud and loving memory of E. J. Geater beloved eldest son of Captain and Mrs Geater, who died doing his duty 10th September 1918, aged 22 years. Sadly missed but never forgotten by his Mother, Father, brother and sisters".*

Gosport was a significant sea port and Naval depot, with many government factories and installations based there. In addition to the Haslar Naval Hospital, the Royal Naval Cemetery was installed at the depot. This contains 763 Great War graves, two are unidentified.

Bath (Locksbrook) Cemetery

Cadet **Hubert Arthur Morley,** No. 7 Squadron No. 7 Observers, School of Aeronautics, RAF died at Bath aged 18 on the 27th October 1918. A war hospital was situated nearby and in Bath (Locksbrook) Cemetery there are forty four graves directly related to casualties from the hospital. He was son of Arthur and Annie S. Morley, 67, Far Gosford Street, Coventry. Whilst his father was employed as a cycle works time keeper, Hubert was an engineer's apprentice. Enlisting in June 1918, he had completed five months with the RAF at the time of his death. A pupil at Bablake School he is commemorated on the school memorial.

Kensal Green (All Souls) Cemetery, London

Private **Frederick Cecil Abel,** 9th Battalion, Cheshire Regiment (formerly 21887 Royal Warwickshire Regiment) died of wounds received at Messines Ridge aged 19 on the 20th June 1917. Frederick was the son of Sidney and Mary Eliza Abel of 92 Widdrington Road, Coventry. He was born on the 5th February 1898 at Hassocks, Sussex, enlisted in October 1916 and was previously employed as a loom builder.

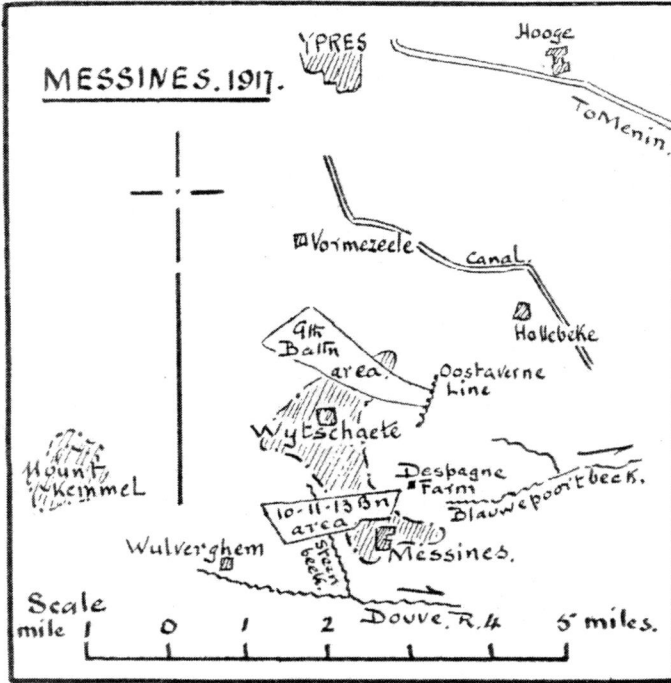

Map Showing the Battalion Position at Messines

On the 1st June 1917 instructions were received by the Battalion that they would take part in an offensive against the Wytschaete – Messines ridge. The following days were spent preparing for the attack. On the 6th June the men were fed a hot meal and the Battalion strength going into action was 20 officers and 650 other ranks. In between 2.15am and 2.45am the men had reached the assembly position and were given a tot of rum prior to zero hour at 3.10am. At zero hour the mines went off and the barrage opened up, the Battalion systematically achieved objectives. At 7.50am casualties were estimated at 100. The number of casualties by the 8th June had become clearer: 34 men had died of wounds and 120 men were wounded. The clearing of the battlefield had also commenced and captures included machine guns which were sent to Battalion Headquarters; no casualties were reported on either the 9th or 10th of June.

Frederick is buried in Kensal Green (All Souls) Cemetery, London. A screen wall records the names of casualties whose graves could not be individually marked. This cemetery contains two members of the Cheshire Regiment who died during the war. Frederick's brother, Sidney Arthur Abel also died in the week prior to the Battle of the Somme on the 26th June 1916 and has a plaque in the War Memorial Park. The 9th Battalion lost 713 Warrant Officers, NCO's and Privates during the Great War.

The War at Sea

Seven of the men commemorated in the War Memorial Park died at sea. The first was Stoker 1st Class Herbert Charles Wilkins who died on the 26th November 1914 and the final death was Paymaster Edward Leslie Peirson, Royal Naval Reserve who was killed in an explosion on HMS Vanguard at Scapa Flow on the 9th July 1917.

HMS Bulwark

On the 26th November 1914, HMS Bulwark was anchored off Sheerness Harbour in Kent; at 7:53am a massive internal explosion caused the ship to sink instantly. Over 700 officers and men were lost with only a handful of survivors, the internal explosion was probably caused by mishandling of ammunition or poor storage of cordite charges, some of which were twelve years old. HMS Bulwark was commissioned at Devonport, Plymouth on 18th March 1907 and from the outbreak of War she carried out Channel patrol duty. On board HMS Bulwark when she exploded was Stoker 1st Class **Herbert Charles Wilkins** from Coventry, who died aged 25 as a result of the explosion. His body was not recovered and he is commemorated on the Portsmouth Naval Memorial. Also known to have perished in this disaster was Ordinary Seaman, Frederick Thomas Adkins aged 18 from Stoneleigh and Ordinary Seaman Arthur Reynold Pears aged 22 of 49 Coronation Road, Coventry.

The only plaque for HMS Bulwark

HMS Formidable

The first battleship to be sunk in the war was HMS Formidable. She was sunk on New Year's Day 1915 whilst on exercises and channel patrol off Portland Bill. HMS Formidable was struck by the first torpedo at 2.25am from U-24 commanded by Captain Lieutenant Rudolph Schneider. The torpedo hit the number one boiler, port side which caused the ship to list heavily to the starboard as the ship started to flood. At 3.15am, a second torpedo from U-24 hit the portside, ninety minutes later she capsized and sank in 180 feet of water, 37 miles off the Devon Coast.

The 15,250 tons Battleship was launched in 1898 and first commissioned in 1901. HMS Formidable had a full complement of about 750 men; initially there were approximately 200 survivors. Bad weather including thirty foot waves contributed to the high loss of life and the ship.

Accounts from the survivors of HMS Formidable provide some insight into the events that occurred on the ship in the final hours. *"There was no panic, the men waiting calmly for the lifeboats to be lowered many of the boats were smashed as they were lowered into the water, killing all occupants, or else were swamped with water or men and sank. One pinnace with seventy men on board was picked up by the trawler Provident, 15 miles off Berry Head. The second pinnace took off another seventy men. This boat was soon half-filled with water as the men desperately bailed - with boots, caps, even a blanket, anything that came to hand. One seaman apparently sat over a hole in the boat from the time they started away to the time of rescue. The enormous swell sometimes at 30ft was terrifying, but morale was kept up by any means, humour, singing, even bullying. Petty Officer Bing admitted punching men who wanted to give up".*

The survivors unanimously agreed they owed their lives to Leading Seaman Carroll, who continued to cheer and inspire. Dawn broke out of sight of land; a liner and eleven other craft were spotted by the survivors, but the pounding seas and huge waves hid the pinnace. Night came with more relentless gales. On land, blackout restrictions were in force, and there are two explanations for the seamen seeing light from the shore. Petty Officer Bing saw a red light seven miles away which could have been the Lyme harbour light. The other explanation from J. H. Taplin, another survivor, was that a sudden bright light shone out three miles off, which may have been from the Assembly Rooms cinema in Lyme Regis. The machine had broken down and the operator examining it shone the lamp through the window for a second or two.

As the pinnace approached the shore it was first seen at Lyme by Miss Gwen Harding and her parents walking home along Marine Parade after dining out with friends. She had glimpsed the outline of a boat, her mother confirmed her suspicions and the alarm was raised. Of the seventy one men in the pinnace, forty eight were brought ashore alive, six were found to be dead on arrival, fourteen died during the twenty two hours the men had fought for survival and were buried at sea, and three died after landing. The landlady of the Pilot Boat Inn, Mrs. Atkins, took many survivors in and the pub became rescue headquarters. Many of the townsfolk brought food and blankets. Others took men into their homes to rest and recuperate, while those needing medical aid were sent to hospital. The dead were placed in the entrance to the cinema and subsequently buried in Lyme Regis Cemetery.

Captain Loxley, his second-in-command, Commander Ballard, and the signaller stayed at their posts throughout and eventually went down with the ship in true naval tradition. One of those on board was **Edward Wallace Maxwell** who was part of the Carpenters crew; his body was not recovered and he is commemorated on the Chatham Naval Memorial which commemorates 8,515 sailors of the First World War. Edward was aged 38 and served under the name of William Leigh, he was known locally as 'Wally'.

A Plaque also showing a 'Nickname'

HMS Arabis
The next sailor to lose his life and be commemorated in the War Memorial Park is **James William Randall,** a leading stoker on board HMS Arabis. This ship was torpedoed by German destroyers off Dogger Bank in the North Sea on the 11th February 1916. HMS Arabis was in service as a mine sweeper and providing escort duties; she was launched on the 6th November 1915.

Shortly before midnight on the evening of the 10th February 1916, a German Flotilla consisting of eight groups of three to four torpedo boats proceeded in line abreast with the light cruiser Pillau. The three groups on the right wing sighted four darkened ships which they took for light cruisers. However, they were minesweeping sloops of the new 'Flower' class of 1,270 tons, a speed of 17 knots, and armed with two four inch guns. Nineteen torpedoes were launched at them but only HMS Arabis was hit. She remained and fired vigorously but sank after more hits. The other sloops got away, and boats of the Flotilla saved the Commanding Officer and thirty members of the crew of HMS Arabis. Leading Stoker Randall died in this encounter.

The Sons of John William and Mary Ann Randall

The three sons of John William and Mary Ann Randall of 23 Stratford Street, Stoke, Coventry appeared in *'The Coventry Herald'* under the heading 'Three heroic Stoke brothers'. James on the left, George Frederick in the middle and Bombardier Ernest Randall on the right. George and Ernest were in the Royal Field Artillery.

James was born on the 6th December 1891 at Finedon, Northants and is commemorated on the Plymouth Naval Memorial, which commemorates 7,251 sailors of the First World War. George Frederick Randall died on the 5th May 1917 at the Western Front and also has a plaque in the War Memorial Park whilst Ernest survived the war.

HMS Queen Mary
The Battle of Jutland on the 31st May 1916 was the biggest naval battle of the First World War and a major face-off between Sir John Jellicoe Commander in Chief of the Grand Fleet, Admiral Sir David Beatty and German High seas commander Admiral Reinhard Scheer.

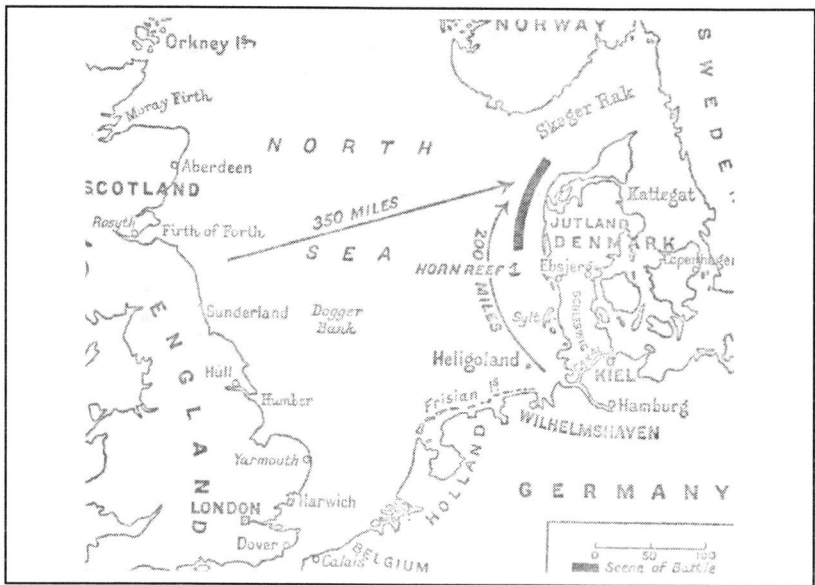

Scene of the Battle of Jutland

HMS Queen Mary was built by Palmers and launched in 1912; she had taken part in Heligoland Bight, the Battle of Dogger Bank and the Battle of Jutland. During the Battle of Jutland, after receiving direct hits from the German ships Seydlitz and Derfflinger, the Queen Mary blew up with the loss of 1,266 crew, with only nine survivors.

The Battle of Jutland started at 3.30pm and lasted for approximately eighty minutes. The Germans had the advantage, for the British ships were silhouetted against the western sky making ideal targets and shortly after 4.20pm HMS Queen Mary was hit. German shooting was indeed very good, with the crews impeccably drilled, their range finding better and the shells better quality. When German shells hit they penetrated and exploded. When a salvo of shells hit the HMS Queen Mary she suddenly blew up: the vulnerability of British ships being exposed as one of the shells penetrated the magazine causing a massive explosion. In total the British lost fourteen ships in the Battle of Jutland, with both sides citing a victory.

Earl Haig's Diary from Saturday June 3rd 1916 concludes *"News of the action by our fleet of Jutland was received today. It confirms what was in a German wireless message yesterday: fourteen British ships sunk but German losses also very great, and doubtless more severe in proportion to their much smaller strength. General opinion on the message received is that we have not won a great victory at sea so we are a little disappointed".*

Two sailors from Coventry with plaques in the Park were on board HMS Queen Mary when she sank, Gunner 1st Class Charles John Jones and Engine Room Artificer 3rd Class James Moss Hewitt. HMS Queen Mary had been built by Palmers and launched in 1912.

Charles John Jones was born the 23rd of June 1881 in Spencer Street and resided at 44c. 1h. Gosford Street. He received his early education at St. Michael's Church School, and gained a scholarship tenable at Bablake which he attended for three and a half years. Charles was a sailor by profession: he had seen nineteen years of service, going straight into the Navy from Bablake at the age of 16. The *'Registers of Seamen's Services'* show he served on a variety of ships from 11th November 1900. He was passed educationally for Petty Officer on the 3rd March 1908 and then seamanship on the 6th November 1911 and promoted to rank of acting Gunner on the 14th March 1913 at which point his record ends.

At the outbreak of war he was on a torpedo boat but was transferred to the battle cruiser in November 1914. This was his second engagement as he had also taken part in the Battle of Dogger Bank, 24th January 1915, which saw a British tactical victory, though they failed to capitalise fully on the advantage of faster ships. In this encounter Warrant Officer Jones broke one of his fingers.

Two pictures of 1st Class Gunner C. J. Jones

Only a few months before his death he paid a visit to his mother who lived at 296 Swan Lane. Charles was a married man and just before the war was engaged in the training of naval cadets. His name appeared in the Admiralty list of officers who lost their lives during the sinking of the HMS Queen Mary and on the Bablake School Memorial.

James Hewitt as the son of Eliza Mary Hewitt of 35 Moor Street, Earlsdon, Coventry and was born on the 22nd November 1891 at 61 Warwick Street. James is commemorated on St. John's and St. Barbara's Memorials. Both men are commemorated on the Portsmouth Naval Memorial along with 9,665 sailors of the First World War.

HMS Ghurka
Stoker 1st Class **Rowland Whitehouse** was serving on HMS Ghurka when she was sunk by a mine in the English Channel on the 8th February 1917 with a heavy loss of life, over nine years after her launch on the 29th April 1907. Rowland was born on the 15th January 1880 at Pelsall, Staffordshire, the son of Abraham and Ann

Allsop Whitehouse of Heath End, Pelsall. His occupation was a blacksmith, and prior to enlisting he was a reservist. Rowland resided at Beech Cottage, Red Lane and is also commemorated on the Portsmouth Naval Memorial.

HMS Pheasant

Second Class **Wireman Horace James Cantrill** aged 19 also lost his life in a mine explosion. HMS Pheasant was sunk off the Orkneys on the 1st March 1917. Horace lost his life with all eighty five members of the crew. He was born on the 19th July 1897 at Foleshill, residing at 172 Cross Road with his parents John Pearson and Elizabeth. Horace enlisted in February 1915 and had served just over two years, being previously employed as an electrician. Horace is commemorated on the Portsmouth Naval Memorial. HMS Pheasant lay undiscovered until the late 1990's when she was successfully found at a depth of eighty four metres in a bespoke mission called Operation Pheasant Hunt.

HT Transylvania

Lance Corporal **Frederick Henry Barrett,** 905th Motor Transport Company, Army Service Corps was killed aged 32 whilst bound for Egypt in the Hired Transport Transylvania. On the 4th May 1917, the Transylvania was proceeding to Salonika with reinforcements, when she was torpedoed and sunk by a submarine off Cape Vado, a few kilometres south of Savona, Italy. Over 400 lives were lost. Frederick was the son of S. A. and W. Barrett and the husband of R. M. Barrett, of Annandale, 17 Meriden Street, Coventry.

Frederick was born on the 20th August 1884 at Northampton, and employed as a florist and fruiterer until enlisting in August 1916. The 85 bodies (including Frederick's) recovered at Savona were buried two days later in a special plot in the town cemetery. Those whose bodies could not be found are commemorated on the Savona Memorial. The name F. Barrett also appears in St. John's Church.

HMS Vanguard

The last casualty to die at sea and commemorated in the War Memorial Park is Assistant Paymaster **Edward Leslie Peirson,** Royal Naval Reserve. He was killed in an explosion on HMS Vanguard at Scapa Flow, age 26, on the 9th July 1917. Edward was the son of Sidney and Edith and he resided with his parents at 12 Park Road. He was born on the 7th February 1891 and received his education at King Henry VIII School, Coventry and then Heidelberg College, Germany. A chartered accountant by profession.

HMS Vanguard was built by Vickers at Barrow and launched in April 1909 and joined the Royal Navy at Devonport in October 1910. She saw all her service in the Home Fleet and at the outbreak of war she formed part of the 1st Battle Squadron at Scapa Flow. HMS Vanguard took part in the Battle of Jutland on the 31st May 1916 but did not suffer any damage or casualties. On the 2nd June 1916, Edward wrote to his former school. His letter appearing in *'The Coventrian'*:

"At last we have had an action, and I am glad to say, our ship came through without being hit, although shells were flying about short of us, between our masts, over the forecastle, and astern of us. I was at my new action station, which is an important role; but it had one disadvantage, which was, that I could see nothing of what was going on, as I should have been able to do so if I had stuck to my old one. You may be surprised when I tell you that I felt quite cool under fire, not a bit excited, or nervy even. It might just have been a practise shooting, so far as I was concerned.......the fact that I had to set a good example may have had something to do with it, but if we had got hit badly, things might have been different.

I cannot say much about the action, because no one at present on board knows anything like all that happened, and I do not know how much of what I know I may safely tell you. Any how, I think we took a good toll on the Germans. Many a German body with cork waistcoat on we passed floating about, although I did not see them myself. Zepps were also seen, but I saw pratically nothing of the action myself. This ship was present for about two hours of the action, I should say, and I know for a fact that we registered several hits against enemy cruisers and destroyers. I suppose it is the biggest naval action the world has ever seen; certainly more ships and men were opposed to one another than ever before.

Needless to say, I did not get much rest during the last three days. Last night I had a middle, the night before I snatched about an hour's uneasy rest at my action station in my clothes and appreciated my bath this morning. I may perhaps be able to tell you more next time I write, but at the present moment I am extremely busy. I have just had to type the Captain's report on this action. I am longing to look at a newspaper to see what took place generally.

One piece of good news for you. I have learnt that by my correcting our range at my plotting table and transmitting it to the Gunnery Department Commander we were able to hit an enemy cruiser, and there is little doubt she went to the bottom. At any rate, she was in a very disabled state in the mist. Everyone, including the 'Guns' is very delighted, and so am I, because I had very little practice at the new toy (once before only); and further, the officer who did the work before I took it over had never done anything of the sort before, even in practise firing.

We also hit a light cruiser and a destroyer and drove off a torpedo boat attack, with no loss to ourselves. Furthermore I understand that so far as the Battle Fleet was concerned, we were in the hottest part of the line, and were very lucky not to get hit. The only pity was, that it came on very misty, and when the Germans saw our Battle Fleet they soon packed up and made off in the mist".

At approximately 10.00pm on the 9th July 1917 a huge explosion occurred on HMS Vanguard. An investigation showed this was probably caused by spontaneous ignition of her cordite, initially sabotage was expected as the explosion resembled that of HMS Natal suffered in Cromaty Firth in 1915. From her complement of 823, approximately 804 men were killed. The final resting place of HMS Vanguard is at a depth of 34 metres just north of Flotta. In the 1960's and 70's some salvage was carried out, but since 1982 she has been declared a war grave. Edward was a member of the Queen's Road Church and is commemorated on a stained glass memorial in the church, on the Chatham Naval Memorial and in King Henry VIII School. His obituary also appeared in *'The Coventrian'.*

"He entered the School in the Preparatory Department and left when Head of the School in 1905, after gaining many prizes, including the Junior and Senior Butterworth. His name will be known to most for his energy in helping to found the Old Boys' Club, of which he was Honorary Secretary until he joined the Navy.

After leaving School he went to Heidelberg College, where he passed the Matriculation Examination for London University. He then became articled to his father, Mr. Sidney T. Peirson and while a student contributed prize essays on professional subjects; he won his first prizes at the Test Examination of the Midlands District, and at the Final Examination of the Institute of Chartered Accountants he gained the first place in Honours, together with the Institute prize value £10 10s., the Sir William Peat Gold Medal and about £40 in money.

In addition to his professional work, he lectured on Advanced Bookkeeping at the Technical Institute, till soon after the outbreak of war he volunteered for active service, and was appointed Assistant Paymaster on HMS Eclipse, a light cruiser, which was paid off three or four months later. His next appointment was to HMS Vanguard, a super Dreadnought of over 20,000 tons. In addition to his immediate duties of his office, he became successively range finder, spotter, and head of the plotting table, work of paramount importance. His accuracy enabled the gunnery officer to do good execution on enemy ships at the Battle of Jutland. He was highly complimented on his work, and one of the senior officers wrote that "he was gaining distinction by his able management of fire control" and "was one of the busiest officers on the ship and had made himself indispensable on the Vanguard".

The War in The Air

Private **Francis Daulman Cox,** 22nd Squadron, Royal Flying Corps (attached from the 28th Battalion, London Regiment, Artists' Rifles) died of wounds at the Canadian General Hospital, France age 24 on the 26th November 1916. He was the eldest son of Walter James and Mary Jane Cox of 4 Coundon Street, Coventry and born in 1892. He received part of his education at Bablake School which he attended from 1902 – 1907. In London he joined the Artists' Rifles in October 1915 and went through training in the London district and in France, later he was attached to the Flying Squadron.

Private Cox was flying as an observer in FE 2b 6950 of No. 22 Squadron, Royal Flying Corps flown by Second Lieutenant M. R. Helliwell when he was mortally wounded on the 26th November 1916. Second Lieutenant Helliwell was also wounded in the action, the controls of 6950 were so damaged the plane crash landed near Pozières. A victory was credited to Lieutenant Hans von Keudell of Jasta 1. This was the ninth of his twelve victories he achieved before being shot down by Sopwith Pups of No. 46 Squadron on the 15th February 1917. Private Cox is buried in Etaples Military Cemetery and appears on the Bablake School Memorial.

Captain **Harold Jackson,** 41st Squadron, Royal Flying Corps died of wounds received during the Battle of Messines age 21 on the 7th June 1917. He was the brother of Mr. F. H. Jackson of Fairhaven, Palmerston Road, Coventry and the son of Mr. F. T. Jackson of The Spring, Stoke, Coventry. Harold was born in 1897 at Stoke Green and resided in Coventry. He was employed as an apprentice in an engineering works and enlisted in 1915.

Soon after the outbreak of war he joined the Ruffy-Beauman School of flying, at Hendon and there obtained his pilot's certificate. Captain Jackson was then granted a commission in the 13th Battalion, Royal Warwickshire Regiment transferring to the RFC three months later. On the 1st October 1916, Captain Jackson flew out to France and was promoted Captain and Flight Commander in March 1917. On the day of his death he was miles over German lines when he sustained a direct hit by a high explosive. Although his foot was blown off and his arm practically severed at the shoulder he brought his machine back. He died at the dressing station shortly afterwards and is buried in Chester Farm Cemetery, Zillebeke.

Jackson is the fifth man from the left of the pilots (second row) wearing a forage cap. '*The Coventry Graphic*' after the end of the war stated a memorial was placed in Stoke Church (by members of the Jackson family) to the late Mr. and Mrs. Jackson and their youngest son Harold Jackson who was killed on June 17th 1917. This memorial could not be found, his name appears on the family grave in St. Michaels Cemetery, Stoke, Coventy with the words "*In memory of Captain Harold Jackson, RFC, died during the Battle of Messines 7th June 1917*" and is inscribed on the memorial in the front porch.

Second Lieutenant, **Kenneth Purnell Barford**, 2nd Squadron, Royal Flying Corps was reported missing in the Somme area aged 19 on the 27th March 1918. He was the son of Henry Widowson Barford and Mary Barford and resided with them at The Bungalow, Kenilworth Road, Coventry. Kenneth was born in 1899 at Coventry and educated at King Henry VIII prior to Elstow School in Bedford. He gave up his studies and was gazetted in August 1917, subsequently qualifying as an observer in December 1917.

The start of the German offensive of the 21st March 1918 saw the role of the RFC squadrons change dramatically. Instead of aerial reconnaissance Kenneth became involved in bombing raids and disrupting the enemy's advance. Six days after the start of the offensive Kenneth and his pilot Lieutenant Edward Smart were shot down whilst carrying out a low level bombing sortie by Manfred Von Richthofen, (the Red Baron). Their plane becoming his 72nd victim and one of the victims he claimed on this date.

Having left their base at Hesdigneul, near Bethune at 3.20pm, in conditions of poor visibility they were flying their Armstrong Whitworth FK8 B288 without fighter protection having become separated from the rest of the squadron. Their plane was shot down by the Red Baron after firing approximately 100 shots into their aircraft south of the river Somme, just west of the village of Foucaucourt and about 10 miles from Albert.

Smart and Barford are remembered on the Arras Flying Services Memorial; in addition Kenneth's name appears on a plaque in Holy Trinity Church, Henry VIII School and on a memorial plaque for Elstow School in the church of St. Mary and St. Helen in Bedford. The plaque in Holy Trinity reads *"The sanctuary candlesticks of this church were given to the Glory of God in loving memory of Lieutenant Kenneth Purnell Barford by his parents. He was reported missing March 27th 1918 in the sector Bray sur Somme. Aged 19 years"*.

The Red Baron was that notorious that shortly after his death on the 21st April 1918, the following article under the headline *'A Famous Aviator'* appeared in *'The Coventry Graphic'*:

"Coventry interest in aeroplanes and airmen must be our excuse for referring in this week's Topics to the death of the famous German aviator, Baron Von Richthofen whose record showed the conquest of nearly one hundred opponents. The airman's record is said to surpass even those of Boelcke and Immelmann, and it may be news to our readers that several men belonging to Coventry and the neighbourhood had occasionally engaged all three of the German pilots who have been named in the foregoing. Baron von Richtofen was a brother of Lieutenant von Richtofen another intrepid airman, who was responsible for the death of Captain Ball VC ".

Corporal **Reginald Arthur Lucas** DSM Royal Air Force was officially lost at sea, presumed drowned aged 21 on the 27th April 1918. He was born on the 8th August 1896 in Coventry and resided at 6 Gordon Street with his parents, Thomas Henry and Fanny Francis. His sister also resided at this address. A mechanic, Reginald gave up this trade and enlisted in 1915.

In 1917 Corporal Lucas was decorated with the DSM for sinking a German submarine on the 22nd September 1917. Corporal Lucas was onboard a Curtiss H-12 flown by Flight Sub-Lieutenants N. A. Magor and C. E. S. Lusk, with CPO E. A. Boyd. The submarine was originally identified as UB-72 but later research identified the submarine as UB-32. The sinking of the U-Boat was reported as *'Possibly sunk by bombs dropped from RNAS aircraft at 5145N 0205E. 24 dead (all hands lost)'*. UB32 was commissioned on the 22nd July 1915 and was responsible for the loss of 22 ships sunk with a further three damaged.

On the 25th April 1918, Corporal R. A. Lucas DSM was killed in action while flying in Curtiss H-12 8677, from Felixstowe, together with Captain Norman Ansley Magor DSC, J. G. Stathearn DSM, and Ensign S. Potter, US Navy. The Curtiss was shot down in an action with aircraft from SFL I and a victory credited to Oblt zur See Friedrich Christiansen. This was his sixth victory out of an eventual thirteen.

'The Coventry Graphic' reported Corporal Lucas's death stating *'at the time of his death he was engaged with seven enemy aeroplanes'*. He is commemorated on the Hollybrook Memorial, Southampton. This memorial commemorates by name almost 1,900 service men and women of the Commonwealth land and air forces whose graves are not known, many of whom were lost in transports or other vessels torpedoed or mined in home waters. The memorial also bears the names of those who were lost or buried at sea, or who died at home but whose bodies could not be recovered for burial. Among those commemorated on the Hollybrook Memorial is Field Marshall Lord Kitchener, Secretary of State for War, who died when the battle cruiser HMS Hampshire was mined and sunk off Scapa Flow on the 5th June 1916.

Second Lieutenant **Charles Fletcher,** 7th Squadron, Royal Air Force died of wounds aged 22 on the 19th September 1918. He was the son of Charles Joseph and Ann Fletcher and born on the 21st March 1896 at Coventry. He was married to Ann and lived at 60 Summerland Place, The Butts, Coventry. He was employed as a draughtsman and enlisted in April 1918.

Charles was mortally wounded when flying as observer in RE 8 C2530 of No. 7 Squadron RAF, flown by Second Lieutenant H. M. Matthews when the aeroplane was shot down (probably by ground fire) on the 28th September 1918. The airmen were on a contact air patrol over the Houthulst sector, and had left Proven aerodrome at 7.15am. C2530 was one of four aircraft from No. 7 Squadron that suffered combat damage on the 28th. Charles died of his wounds on the 29th September and is buried in Haringhe (Bandaghem) Military Cemetery.

Second Lieutenant **Evan Llewellyn Howells,** 23rd Squadron, Royal Air Force died aged 19. He was born on the 31st July 1899 at Coventry and resided at Haynstone, Stoke Park with his parents Evan and Florence. Evan attended King Henry VIII after which he became a builder's pupil, until enlisting in January 1917 with the RFC.

He qualified as an observer on August 7th, and went onto become a pilot joining the 23rd squadron in France on September 30th 1918. At 9.00am on October the 23rd, Second Lieutenant Howells took off as part of an offensive patrol. At 10.20am his machine was involved in a collision and his aircraft was seen crashing to the ground. He is buried in Ovillers Communal Cemetery and listed on the memorial at King Henry VIII School.

Lieutenant **Ernest Harold Masters,** 45th Squadron, Royal Air Force was accidentally killed whilst flying at Duisans, near Arras aged 19 on the 24th December 1918. He had previously been awarded a Croix De Guerre with Palm whilst in France. He was the son of George and Fanny Masters of 176 Humber Avenue, Coventry and born on the 25th January 1899 at Langley, Birmingham. He resided in Coventry at 1 Swan Lane and was employed as an engineer until enlisted in May, 1917. He is buried in Duisans British Cemetery.

Lieutenant **Ernest Charles Robinson,** 10th Squadron, Royal Air Force died age 30 on the 20th January 1919. He was the son of Thomas and Ann Robinson and husband of Ethel Gertrude Robinson of 28 Starley Road, Coventry. Ernest was born on the 2nd April 1888 at Stafford and employed as an Engineer, enlisting at the outbreak of war. He is buried at Lille Southern Cemetery, *'The Coventry Graphic'* stated he died of pleurisy (inflammation of the membrane enclosing lungs) and prior to the war he worked at Siddeley Deasy. On his wife's family plot in London Road Cemetery a crucifix is dedicated to the memory of Lieutenant Ernest Charles Robinson, this reads *"In loving memory of my dear Husband Lieut. Ernest Charles Robinson who died on January 20th 1919 aged 30 years. Interred in the communal cemetery at Lille, France. Thy will be done"*.

Iran

Sergeant **Arthur Tyne Wright**, 80361, Armoured Car Section, Machine Gun Corps (Motors) died in Persia on the 8th October 1918. He was born on the 15th January 1898 in Ash Grove and resided at 77 Ransom Road. Arthur was employed as a machine tool fitter until enlisting in May 1918. The *'City of Coventry: Roll of the Fallen'* suggests he is buried in Kermanshah and the CWGC commemorates him on the Tehran War Cemetery.

The Tehran Memorial commemorates casualties of the Indian, United Kingdom and New Zealand Forces who lost their lives during the campaign in Iran (formerly known as Persia) and who have no known grave. The memorial comprises six free-standing memorial walls, three on each side of the central avenue leading to the Cross of Sacrifice. A central feature commemorates the names of 3,590 soldiers who died in Iran and in neighbouring lands during the Great War and who have no known grave.

Tehran Memorial

Gallipoli

The *'Roll of Honour'* was to increase further when His Majesty's forces landed on the shores of the Gallipoli Peninsula on the 25th April 1915. For 260 days the combined forces battled the Ottoman Empire (now Turkey) in the Gallipoli campaign for control of the peninsula and a strategic waterway known as the Dardanelles. By controlling the Dardanelles, the Allies hoped to threaten the Ottoman capital, Constantinople (now Istanbul) and knock the Turks out of the war.

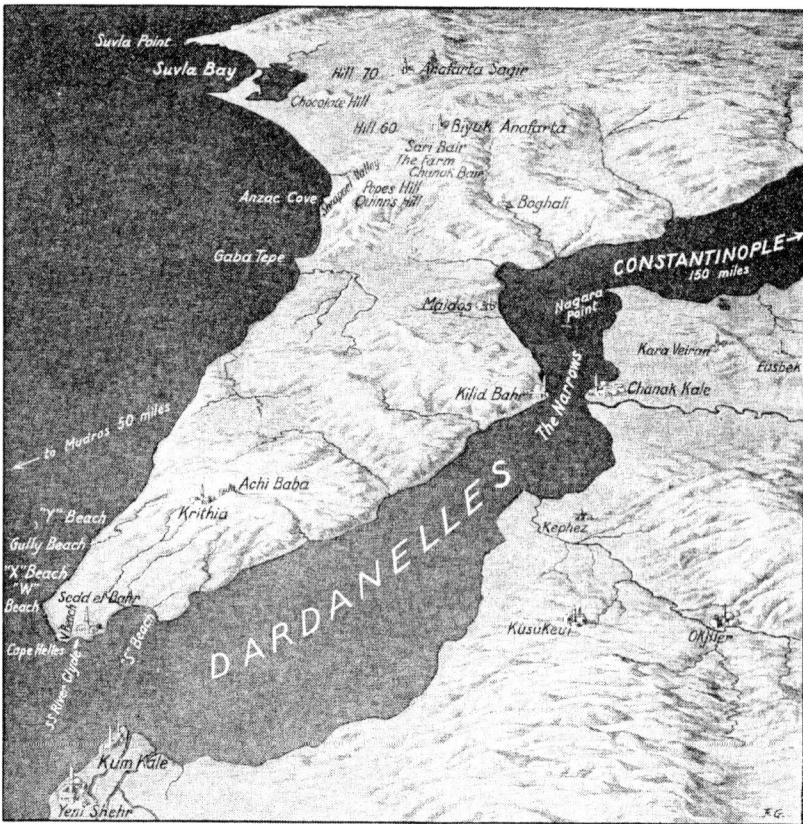

Map of the Dardanelles

This unsuccessful campaign was to prove rather costly and diverted much needed resources from the Western Front. When the order was received to withdraw, a number of ingenious methods were employed to give the illusion that the fighting forces were still there: guns were rigged to fire long after the owners had left; men ran along the trenches firing to give the impression of a bigger force and those going to the boats wore mufflers on their shoes. The withdrawal was planned with precision, so that every surviving man had been evacuated safely. The Gallipoli campaign was to account for the loss of four men commemorated in the War Memorial Park. Three of these are commemorated on the Helles Memorial to the missing, this memorial bears more than 21,000 names. Private Swingler is buried in Sulva bay.

Private **Ernest Jacob Higton** was born in Birmingham and employed at Siddeley Deasy Motors Ltd. He enlisted on the 5th September 1914 in Coventry with the Oxfordshire and Buckinghamshire Light Infantry and went with the 2nd Battalion to France and Flanders on the 26th January 1915. In July 1915, the Battalion were moved out to Lemnos to support ongoing activities in Gallipoli.

Theatre of War is not shown

The Battalions of the Oxfordshire and Buckinghamshire landed at Lemnos about 10.00am on July the 17th and were joined by the Hampshire Regiment who were at Lemnos for a well deserved rest from the fighting in Gallipoli. On landing the Hampshires found a warm welcome, a draft of approximately 300 men awaiting them, these men came mainly from other Regiments, notably the Oxfordshire and Buckinghamshire Light Infantry, but the officers with them came from the 3rd and 13th Battalions of the Hampshires. Private Higton was one of those promptly transferred to the 2nd Battalion, Hampshire Regiment.

This influx of men enabled the 2nd Hampshire to be reorganised with four platoons apiece, each platoon having an officer, commander and one adjutant. Other ranks now stood at 732 and officers at 24, giving a total strength of 756.

The 2nd Hampshires should have had a full fortnight at Lemnos, where the conditions were far from ideal, a dusty camp site: no canteen or means of supplementing the monotonous rations, except by purchase at exorbitant rates from the inhabitants, and few amenities, but they were away from the front and continuous shelling. An alarm of intended Turkish attack cut the division's rest short and on the 28th July the 2nd Hampshires were back at Cape Helles, being in brigade reserve at Gully Beach, mainly occupied in road making. Two officers and 110 men now joined and with 16 men returning from hospital the Battalion was stronger then it had been since landing.

After five days in reserve line the 88th brigade took over the right sub section of the divisional line, east of gully ravine, in readiness for another attempt on its old objectives, H12a, H12 and H13 on August the 6th. The 42nd Division were ready to exploit any success by attacking next day beyond the Krithia Nullah. The Turkish position had been considerably strengthened since the Allies' last attack, and the Hampshires had the nastiest piece of work, for their left had to tackle a formidable redoubt while their right and centre had nearly 300 yards of open ground to cross to reach objective H.13, a re-entrant point.

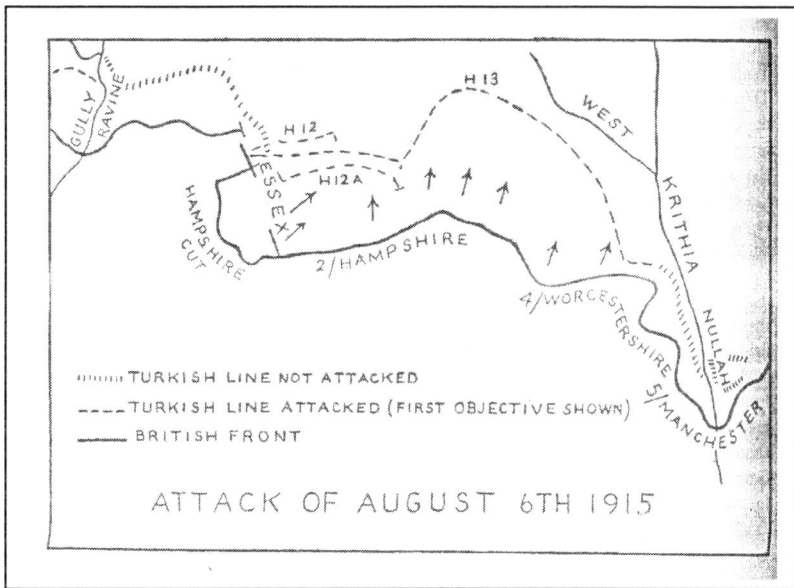

ATTACK OF AUGUST 6TH 1915

The assaulting troops were in position by 8.00am on August the 6th but had to wait for six hours before the bombardment started. The artillery support was utterly inadequate, falling short of the western front standard, the volume and vigour of the Turkish reply showed that they were unpleasantly ready for the attack and augured ill for its chances. After an hour's deliberate bombardment by a handful of heavy guns, the field guns took up the tale and for thirty minutes plastered the objective as vigorously as their scanty ammunition would allow; then at 3.50pm the infantry went forward with the utmost dash and gallantry, the Hampshires attacking in four waves. A low crest line fifty yards from the Hampshires front was crossed almost without loss but then machine guns opened up on all sides and mowed the attackers down wholesale before many of them had got any way across no man's land, some guns across the Krithia Nullah on the Battalion's right being particularly deadly. The guns could do nothing to subdue their fire and under it the attack soon withered away. The Hampshires suffered terribly and one of the officers Second Lieutenant C. Moor fell on the Turkish parapet which a few of the leading wave seemed to have reached.

The supports lost as heavily as the leaders but pressed forward with equal determination and some men entered the Turkish lines and established themselves in H12a, some apparently even reaching H13. Within a few minutes the attack had come to a standstill, the unhit survivors lying out amongst the dead and wounded, pinned to the ground by machine gun fire, unable to move till darkness let them and the more slightly wounded crawl back. It had been the worst day in the whole story of Cape Helles.

Inadequate artillery had led to a sacrifice of lives, nothing had been gained locally and even if the Turks had been distracted from the main attack at Suvla, its unavailing gallantry had left the 88th Brigade a wreck, the Hampshire lost 18 officers with 224 other ranks killed and missing; 2 officers and 210 men were wounded. This left the Battalion with 5 officers and 400 other ranks. During the night any wounded were brought in and the surviving Hampshires made their way back to Gully Beach where they were warmly congratulated by General de Lisle only to take over the line again on the 14th August from the 86th Brigade. Private Higton was originally reported as missing but later he was confirmed as one of those killed in the attack.

Pioneer **Herbert Joseph Payne,** 72nd Field Company, Royal Engineers was killed in action, aged 34 on the 8th August 1915. Five days after his death he was featured in '*The Coventry Graphic*' as one of a series of brothers who had responded nobly to the Call to Arms, the family at this point would not have been notified about his death.

Brothers with the Colours

The three brothers were the sons of Alfred and Ellen Elizabeth Payne of 4 Court, 2 House, Cox Street, Coventry. The pictures shows Private K. Payne (left) and Corporal A. Payne (middle) both served with the 2/7th Battalion, Royal Warwickshire Regiment and Herbert on the right. Herbert was born on the 3rd August 1882 at 72 West Orchard. He attended Bablake School and had already seen action serving in the South African War as a Trooper in the Imperial Yeomanry. He enlisted at the outbreak of war, prior to which he was occupied as an examiner residing at 16 Gas Street. Herbert served for exactly twelve months. Notification of his death was announced in *'The Coventry Graphic'*: *"News has been received that Driver Payne has been killed in action at the Dardanelles. Driver Payne was well known in Coventry having been prominently associated with Rugby football and he was formerly employed by the Daimler Co."*

The next casualty was **Private William Stagg**, 9th Battalion, Royal Warwickshire Regiment who died aged 22 on the 8th August 1915. He was the son of Mr. and Mrs. A. Stagg of 3 Court, 10 House, Castle Street, Coventry . William resided with his parents and was born on the 6th December 1892 in Well Street. He was previously employed as a hardener and enlisted at the outbreak of war.

The 9th Battalion Royal Warwickshire Regiment embarked at Lemnos for Anzac on the 3rd August 1915 about 4.30pm on board the troop transporters HMTB Renard, HMT's Redbreast and El Tiharah. 20 officers and 667 other ranks landed at Anzac at 1.00am the following day and moved into a location known as Canterbury Rest Gully. At 10.00pm on the 6th August, the Battalion moved on again for Aghyl Dere, reaching Walden Point at 4.00am on the 7th.

They remained there in Divisional reserve until about 10.00am when they moved to Brigade reserve and instructions were received to attack the enemy position at once. The Battalion proceeded to carry out these instructions without delay and advanced to a new position and relieved the Ghurkas. Night came before this relief could be accomplished and instructions were received to remain in the location known as Farm Gully. The effective strength was 16 officers and 608 other ranks.

At 2.00am on the 8th, the Battalion moved from Aghyl Dere Gully and advanced over Bauchops Hill. A Company and three platoons of B Company reached the Farm Plateau and the rest of the Battalion were instructed to relieve the Worcester Regiment, relief taking place at 5.00pm. Instructions were received to entrench on spur 3 at 8.00pm; D Company accordingly moved up over the crest of the ridge and dug itself in, connecting up with the Worcesters on the right. Eighty sappers assisted in this work. Casualties during the day were: killed 4 other ranks, wounded 2 officers 26 other ranks, sick 1 officer and 5 other ranks. Eleven days after leaving Lemnos the 9th Battalion of the Royal Warwicks had lost 16 officers and 360 other ranks as a result of sickness, wounds or killed in action.

Private **Frank Swingler,** 5th Battalion Dorsetshire Regiment died of wounds aged 20 on the 9th August 1915. The 5th Battalion, Dorsetshire Regiment were attached to the 11th Northern Division. On the 1st July 1915 the troops set sail from Liverpool, bound for Alexandria, and on to Mudros. Once all the troops were concentrated on the 28th July 1915, they set sail for Suvla Bay, Gallipoli landing there on 7th August 1915. Frank was mortally wounded in the initial landing and attack; those that survived dug in just above the beaches on which they had landed.

Frank was born on the 8th January 1894 at Coventry and resided at 35 Bramble Street with his parents John and Ellen Swingler. He was employed on the Admin Staff, Transport Department, Coventry Corporation and the *'Corporation: Roll of Honour'* notes he was one of the *"Earliest recruits of Kitchener's army"*. Frank enlisted in Nuneaton one month after the start of the war in September 1914 and is buried in Green Hill Cemetery, Suvla.

Green Hill Cemetery was made after the Armistice when isolated graves were brought in from the battlefields of August 1915 and from small burial grounds in the surrounding area. There are 2,971 service men of the First World War buried or commemorated in this cemetery. 2,472 of the burials are unidentified. Private Frank Swingler is one of the known graves.

Malta

Private **Wallace Towe,** 7th (Service) Battalion, Gloucestershire Regiment died of wounds received at Suvla Bay, Gallipoli, aged 21 on the 20th December 1915. He was the son of Wallace and Emma Towe, of 30 Mickleton Road, Earsldon, Coventry and was born on the 5th February 1894 at Daltons Cottages, Allesley Old Road. He resided at Yardley, Birmingham being employed as a tailor's cutter before the war and enlisted in September, 1914. He is buried in Pieta Military Cemetery, Malta.

There are 1,303 casualties of the First World War buried or commemorated at Pieta Military Cemetery. From the spring of 1915, the hospitals and convalescent depots established on the islands of Malta and Gozo dealt with over 135,000 sick and wounded, chiefly from the campaigns in Gallipoli and Salonika.

Pieta Military Cemetery

Palestine

Private **William Ivens Patchett,** 1st /1st Warwickshire Yeomanry, 1st South Midland Mounted Brigade, 2nd Mounted Division died of wounds aged 38 on the 14th November 1917, in Palestine.

William was born on the 4th July 1879 in Clifton, Rugby and married Ellen Robinson Colton on the 13th June 1904. They had two children Nellie born the 8th September 1905 (died 14th May 1997) and William Charles Herbert born 26th October 1910 (died 16th April 1982). William Ivens Patchett was described as a Printer of Clifton, Rugby on his marriage certificate but as a Compositor on his son's birth certificate where his residence was stated as 7 Manor Road, Rugby. William Ivens` father was Bethuel Patchett who was born on the 9th May 1853 and died sixteen years after his son in 1933.

In a letter written by William Ivens sent to his two children who were eleven and six years old at the time, he observed "the *Bedouin gathering corn and tending their animals*", a second sent to his wife Ellen from Egypt following a rough sea passage through the Bay of Biscay in the Saturnia included accounts of *"dodging submarines"*. *'The Manchester Guardian'* of Monday the 12th November 1917 gave an account of the action on the 8th November in Palestine in which William Ivens Patchett was mortally wounded: *"Details have now been received of an action of the Warwickshire Yeomanry. A General Officer Commanding reconnoitring near Huj saw a considerable body of the enemy with guns marching about 2,500 yards away in a north-*

easterly direction. He ordered the Yeomanry to charge the retiring enemy. The charge was at once carried out, in face of heavy gun and machine-gun and rifle fire, with a gallantry and dash worthy of the best traditions of British cavalry. Twelve guns were captured, the Austrian gunners being killed or wounded at the guns. Three machine guns and a hundred prisoners were also captured. This completely broke the hostile resistance and enabled us to push on to Huj."

Private Patchett, was shot in the attack. His Field Medical Card bears details of his transfer to 53rd Divisional Field Ambulance (Immobile) with a gun shot wound to the back. He suffered from tympanites and retention of urine. His wound was re-dressed at 9.15pm when he was catheterised. A.T. 500 units were injected and ¼ grammes of morphine. Despite this medical treatment Private Patchett died on the 14th November 1917. Second Lieutenant H. C. Alan Williams, C squadron, wrote to his widow Ellen on the 13th December apologising for the delay quoting *"he had experienced difficulty gaining her address"*. He stated, *"Your husband was a brave and gallant soldier and died taking part in one of the most brilliant charges of the war. It was instantaneous and he was buried within a few yards of the guns he so nobly assisted in capturing. Always so willing, reliable and thorough it was a real pleasure to command men like him and I shall miss him personally very much when I return to the Regiment"*.

William Ivens Patchett was buried in a local grave. His widow, was informed that his remains had been exhumed and re-buried in Beersheba Military Cemetery under guidance of the Imperial War Graves Commission. This cemetery was made immediately on the fall of the town, remaining in use until July 1918, by which time 139 burials had been made. It was greatly increased after the Armistice when burials were brought in from a number of scattered sites and small burial grounds. The cemetery now contains 1,241 burials of the First World War, 67 of them unidentified.

His widow Ellen, then resident at 6 Rowland Street, Rugby faced the task of supporting her two children but a large Patchett family lived in Rugby and rallied to bring comfort and practical assistance. Ellen lived as a widow for a further eighteen years and died in a Coventry hospital in 1935 having been cared for by her daughter in her final months of illness.

Mesopotamia

Turkey's entry into the war on the 29th October 1914 immediately prompted Britain to open a new front in the remote Ottoman province of Mesopotamia, now present-day Iraq.   To protect British oil interests (a vital necessity to numerous campaigns), British and Indian troops were mobilized and dispatched to the Persian Gulf. Encountering minimal Turkish resistance the forces made good ground and by 28th September were one hundred and twenty miles south of the capital, Baghdad.

At the Battle of Ctesiphon on the 22nd to the 26th November 1915 under the command of General Townshend, events took a turn for the worse and the Turks withstood a large attack. Half of the British force numbering some 8,500 were killed or wounded. Survivors fled, retreating to Kut-el-Amara, without sufficient resources including medical and transport facilities. After the epic retreat Kut-el-Amara was finally reached on the 3rd December 1915.

Turkish reinforcements saw to it that the town was besieged for one hundred and forty seven days, during which time the men endured horrendous conditions, including an epidemic of sickness, before finally surrendering on the 29th April 1916. Attempts were made to rescue the besieged town including air drops but they all failed and the British suffered another defeat by the Turks. The Mesopotamia campaign continued, Kut-el-Amara was recaptured on the 24th February 1917 and Baghdad on the 11th March.

Of the six men who died in Mesopotamia, four are either buried in Amara War Cemetery or Basra War Cemetery. The remaining two men, Private Frederick William Garner and Sergeant Leonard Dufner who have no known grave are commemorated on the Basra Memorial. Amara War Cemetery contains 4,621 burials of the First World War, more than 3,000 of which were brought into the cemetery after the Armistice. 925 of the graves are unidentified. A screen wall in the cemetery has the names of those buried in the cemetery engraved upon it.

The Basra War Cemetery contains 2,551 burials of the War, 74 of them unidentified and is an amalgamation of Makina Masul Old Cemetery, Makina Masul New Extension and other burial grounds whilst the Basra Memorial bears the names of more than 40,500 men who died in the operations in Mesopotamia from the Autumn of 1914 to the end of August 1921 and whose graves are not known.

Basra was occupied by the 6th (Poona) Division in November 1914, from which date the town became the base of the Mesopotamian Expeditionary Force and

Amara was occupied eight months later on the 3rd June 1915, immediately becoming a hospital centre.

The first casualty commemorated in the War Memorial Park to die in Mesopotamia was Sergeant (Battery Quartermaster) **Arthur Richard 'Tim' Voice,** D Battery, 66th Brigade, Royal Field Artillery who died of wounds received at Kut age 33 on the 13th March 1916. Arthur was the son of Walter and Emma Voice of Coventry and was born on the 26th October 1883 at Cardiff. Arthur was employed in the Council as a rate collector and enlisted in Rugby in October 1914. He is buried at Basra Cemetery and commemorated on the memorial to those who fell from the Finance department at the Council House. The *'Corporation: Roll of Honour'* notes *"Arthur Richard Voice came of a family well known and respected in the Hillfields district of Coventry. He joined the army in the early days of the war. His genial disposition and his deep sense of duty endeared him to all his friends by whom his untimely death is greatly mourned".*

Ten months later, Private **William Alfred Owen,** 9th Battalion, Royal Warwickshire Regiment was killed in action, aged 23 on the 25th January 1917. William was born on the 20th May 1894 at 9c. 5h. Chauntry Place and resided at 67 Northfield Road. He was the son of Mr. and Mrs. J. Owen of 107, Nicholls Street, Coventry and enlisted in 1914 being previously employed as a labourer.

The *'Battalion War Diary'* noted on the 25th January 1917, that the 9th Battalion were in position in Kala Haji Fahan Nullah and at 9.30am they were in immediate support of the assaulting Battalions. After an intensive artillery bombardment, the Worcestershire Regiment on the Battalion's right and the North Staffordshire Regiment on the left stormed and secured the enemy front and began consolidation. Meanwhile the 9th Battalion moved up and occupied a position known as Queen's trench and King's trench, ready to meet a counter attack; the latter trench had been vacated by the assaulting troops. About noon a strong Turkish counter attack, consisting mainly of bombers and supported by Minenwerfer was launched; the Battalion were ordered to advance and support the Worcesters and North Staffords who were being gradually overwhelmed.

Under leadership the Battalion recaptured the trench driving the enemy back to the second line. At 3.00pm the enemy commenced a second big counter attack working down communication trenches on the left supported by trench howitzer and artillery fire. The Turks' superiority in numbers gradually gained the ascendancy and forced the Warwicks to withdraw. The retirement was carried out in an orderly manner in quick time in spite and of heavy enemy rifle and artillery fire. In the evening the Battalion were drawn into reserve, a roll call showed casualties as 4 officers killed, 7 wounded, other ranks 177 killed wounded or missing. A Congratulatory telegram from the Corps commander was received which read " *Bravo the Warwicks"*.

Two days later on the 27th January, salvaging and burying parties were sent out and by the 28th the following was confirmed 4 officers killed, 1 died of wounds, 46 other ranks were killed or died of wounds with 118 wounded and 18 missing. Private Owen died on the 16th of January and is buried in Amara War Cemetery.

One of the men of the 9th Battalion

Private **Frederick William Garner,** 4th Battalion, South Wales Borderers was killed in action aged 31 on the 10th February 1917. He was married to Alice (nee Docker) of 44 Little Fields, Stoke Heath, Coventry and the son of Joseph Henry and Victoria Elizabeth of 57 White Friars Street, Coventry. Frederick was born on the 1st August 1887 in Vernon Street, Coventry and was employed as a cycle enameller until enlisting in May 1916. Frederick has no known grave and is commemorated on the Basra Memorial.

Three days later, **Corporal Arthur Albert Rubley,** 39th Battalion, Machine Gun Corps (Infantry) formerly Royal Warwickshire Regiment was killed in action five days short of his 23rd birthday. Arthur was born on 18th February 1894, in Spon Street and resided at 91 The Butts with his wife. He enlisted at the outbreak of war and prior to this was employed as a fitter at Siddeley Deasy.

In August 1915 whilst serving with the 9th Battalion Royal Warwickshire Regiment, Private Rubley was wounded in the Dardanelles. The official notification to his mother received in September 1915 and replicated in '*The Coventry Graphic*' stated that a bullet had passed through his leg. He recovered from this and was later transferred to the Machine Gun Corps, He died on the 13th February 1917. An officer wrote to his widow to the effect that her husband was killed instantly by a high explosive shell, "*his death is a great loss to the company and the deceased was most popular with both officers and men*". Private Rubley is commemorated in Amara War Cemetery and St. John's Church.

On March the 16th 1917, Private **Edward Arthur Kelly,** 9th Battalion Royal Warwickshire Regiment died of wounds. Edward was born on the 31st July 1895 at Foleshill, residing at 38 Princes Street, he was employed as a clerk prior to enlisting in February 1916. The '*Battalion War Diary*' for the 1st March states "*all ranks were warned that owing to present difficulties of supply part of today's rations should be reserved for later consumption*" at this time the Battalion were half way between Kut and Baghdad. The arrival of a ration ship on the 3rd March bought some relief but it was noted that it took "*150 men four hours to unload*". The 12th to the 16th of March saw three other ranks report as sick. Edward died on the 16th March and is buried in Amara War Cemetery.

The last of the men to die in Mesopotamia was Sergeant **Leonard Bennett Dufner,** 6th Light Armoured Motor Battery, Machine Gun Corps (Motors) who was killed in action, near Baku aged 21 on the 26th August 1918. He was born on the 2nd September 1897 in Clifton Terrace, Lower Ford Street and employed as an engineer until enlisted in March 1918. Leonard was the son of Herbert John and Elizabeth Dufner of 108 Sir Thomas Whites Road, Coventry and his plaque reads "*part of Locker Lampson Brigade, Armoured Cars, MGC*". Leonard died along with another man from Coventry, Sergeant Thomas Braithwaite Chadwick. He was born on the 10th April 1894 at Ulverston, resided at 13 Gun Lane, Stoke Heath and was employed as a turner and fitter prior to enlisting in March 1918 (probably with Leonard).

Mr. Oliver Locker Lampson was granted permission to equip and organise an Armoured Car-Squadron in 1914 and in doing so was granted the rank of Lieutenant Commander. Twenty one men who enlisted in Coventry, with Leonard's regiment died. Only four of these resided in Coventry, the remaining seventeen men had no obvious connection to Coventry. One of the four, Sergeant Arthur Tyne Wright also has a plaque in the War Memorial Park. Sergeant Dufner has no known grave and is remembered on the Basra Memorial.

Italy

Six of the men commemorated in the War Memorial Park died in Italy. Private Hollister Clare Franklin and Corporal Joseph Richards died in January 1918, Private Stonier in June 1918 with Privates Herbert Henry Griffin and George Peters dying in October 1918. The Armistice came into effect in Italy on the 4th November 1918, Private Herbert Henry Oswin died several weeks after this on the 22nd November 1918.

The Italians entered the war on the Allied side, declaring war on Austria, in May 1915. British forces were at the Italian front between November 1917 and November 1918. Rest camps and medical units were established at various locations in northern Italy behind the front, some of them remaining until 1919.

On 4 December 1917, the XIth and XIVth Corps relieved the Italians on the Montello sector of the Piave front, with the French on their left. The Montello sector acted as a hinge to the whole Italian line, joining that portion facing north from Mount Tomba to Lake Garda with the defensive line of the River Piave covering Venice, which was held by the Third Italian Army. The troops in this sector were not involved in any large operations, but they carried out continuous patrol work across the River Piave, as well as much successful counter battery work. In March 1918, the troops on the Montello sector were relieved. Three Divisions (7th, 48th and 23rd) took over the Asiago sector in the mountains north of Vicenza, and two Divisions (5th and 41st) were despatched to France. In October, the 7th and 23rd Divisions were withdrawn from the Asiago Plateau to take over the northern portion of the X1th Italian Corps front from Salletuol to Palazzon, on the River Piave. These Divisions took a prominent part in the Passage of the Piave (23 October-4 November 1918) during the final Battle of Vittorio-Veneto. Men who died in defending the Piave from December 1917, to March 1918, and those who fell on the west of the river during the Passage of the Piave, are buried in this cemetery.

This cemetery contains 417 burials of the First World War and three of these plots are taken by men commemorated in the War Memorial Park.

Private **Hollister Clare Franklin,** 2nd Battalion, Honourable Artillery Company died of wounds, aged 34 on the 22nd January 1918. He was not a native of Coventry but born in 1882 at Malmesbury, Wiltshire. His parents Mr. And Mrs. John Hollister Franklin were residents of Cricklade, Wiltshire. Hollister resided at 5, Stoney Road and worked as a cashier in a bank until enlisting in May, 1917.

Corporal Fitter **Joseph Richards,** 35th Battery, 22nd Brigade; Royal Field Artillery (Territorial Force and Howitzer Battery) was called up at the outbreak of war and had initially been in service in France where he was wounded. At some point after recovery he was transferred from France to Italy and was killed in action, aged 21 on the 26th January 1918. The son of Joseph and Hannah of Coventry, he was born in Coventry on the 26th November 1897 and resided at 7 Stockton Road. He was a fitter at the Ordnance works prior to the outbreak of war. After his death a letter was received from his Major by his parents stating " *I much regret to inform you of the death (in action) of your son Corporal Fitter J. Richards last evening (26th January 1918). He was killed instantaneously by shell fire and can have suffered no pain. He had recently been promoted and I regarded him as most promising and efficient at his work. I can only assure you of my most sincere sympathy with you in your loss"*. The name of Joseph Richards appears on the panels at Holy Trinity Church.

Private **William Stonier,** 55130, 23rd Battalion, Machine Gun Corps formerly 20256 Royal Warwickshire Regiment was killed in action aged 34 on the 23rd June 1918. He was the husband of Alice Stonier, of 152 Widdrington Road, Coventry and a native of Macclesfield. *'The Macclesfield Times'* of 1918 revealed William Stonier was killed by shell fire and previously lived at Cumberland Street, Macclesfield. William was a member of the Sunderland Street Methodist Chapel, he attended Mill Street School and left Macclesfield in 1911 to work at Courtaulds, Coventry.

He had previously served in the Boer war with the Cheshire Regiment and married Alice in June 1915 in Coventry. William's name appears on the Macclesfield Memorial and is on the memorial in St. Michael's Parish Church. William's brother, Frederick is also commemorated on these memorials and he was killed on the 26th March 1918 in the German offensive.

Private **George William Peters,** 33586, 1st/1st Battalion, Oxfordshire and Buckinghamshire Light Infantry died of wounds at Marseilles, Italy aged 23 on the 8th October 1918. He had received a gunshot wound to the abdomen on the 26th August 1918.

George was born on the 15th December 1895 at Walsgrave on Sowe, Coventry and lived with his parents Arthur and Ada Peters at 30 Primrose Hill Street, Coventry. He was employed as a ribbon dresser until enlisting in August 1914 being with the first draft of reinforcements. Initially he was 5451, 1st Battalion, Rifle Brigade and then transferred to the 7th Battalion. Following this he was transferred as 35560 Private 1st Battalion, Hants Regiment and finally to A Company, 1/1st Battalion, Oxfordshire and Buckinghamshire Light Infantry on the 10th July 1917 entering France and Flanders on the 12th July 1917.

In 1915 ' *The Coventry Graphic'*, ran the headline *'Coventry Rifleman Pierced By Shrapnel'*. This article covered a remarkable escape from death by Rifleman Peters. He was present at the Battle of Aisne and was amongst the British troops transferred to Northern France to extend the line. At Soisssons his shoulder strap was struck and pierced by a bullet missing his body. He kept the shoulder strap as a souvenir. In the desperate fighting near Armentieres in October 1914, Private Peters was in the trenches when the Germans repulsed. Whilst the fight was being waged, a shrapnel shell burst just above his head and he was struck by a missile. In describing the experience, he says *"The shell burst directly over the trench and almost immediately I seemed to shrivel up internally. I did not actually feel a blow; I just felt as if I was paralysed across the chest and had no use in my body. I stood still for a moment, then fell and remembered no more till I was being attended to in hospital."*

What had happened was that a piece of metal had entered his back on the right side, and passed right through his body till the left breast. The wound was very dangerous and he escaped death by the narrowest margin. He was taken to hospital at Boulogne where the metal was extracted. He remained in the hospital for two months before being removed to Netley. Notwithstanding his hazardous experience he was looking forward to returning to the firing line, being anxious to be in at the finish in Berlin. The white disc shows where the metal was extracted after piercing his chest from the right shoulder blade. Rifleman Peters is an old

Swan Lane school boy and formerly worked at Messrs Hamiltons, Much Park Street. He also had a brother serving at the Front with the Royal Engineers.

On the 6th December 1917, he received seven days Field Punishment No.1 for using obscene language to an NCO and was subsequently sent to Italy.

News of his death was covered by *'The Coventry Graphic'*: "*Mr and Mrs A. Peters, 30 Primrose Hill Street, Coventry have been informed of the death from wounds received in action in Italy of their son. Private George William Peters before joining the colours at the commencement of war he was employed at Hammertons, Much Park Street and went to France in August 1914, taking part in the retreat from Mons and being seriously wounded at Armentieres in November of that year. He returned to France in 1915 and was gassed at Ypres 1916. Peters returned to the front again in 1917*". His eldest brother Arthur was a Sergeant serving with the RFA and his younger brother Fred of the Dorsetshire Regiment was in the Royal Infirmary, Leicester suffering from shrapnel wounds. Private Peters is buried in Mazargues War Cemetery Extension, Marseilles.

Private **Herbert Henry Griffin**, 2nd Battalion, Royal Warwickshire Regiment was killed on the 21st October 1918. Herbert was the husband of Mrs A. M. Griffin, of 36 Meadway, Stoke Heath, Coventry and was born 10th September, 1891 at 35, Yardley Street, Coventry, residing at 1 North Street. Previously a tailor he enlisted in Coventry in April 1916.

A Family Photograph of Herbert Griffin

A postcard sent to his wife in 1916 revealed he was fighting on the Austrian front to the north of Venice. A note written on the reverse of a postcard reads *'Friday 1st*

December 1916. Dear All, just a line to let you know I am alright. I wrote a letter yesterday but you needn't worry if I don't write for a day or two as I may not have the chance you understand, and please tell Mother if you have the chance XXXX Love Bert'. The card had been censored by Sergeant Edwards.

The *'Battalion War Diary'* on this day did not record any casualties, but notes that they were in the line, with the headquarters at Fornice, East of Macerada. Half the Battalion (C and D companies) were on the left of the Sallateuil Road, the other half, A and B companies were occupying a Dyke in the rear of Sallateuil Road. The close proximity of the headquarters to the enemy is noted on the 22nd October as it was shelled with gas shells. Reference to an attack was made on the 23rd on Grave Di Papadopolli after crossing the Piave and the only note made on the 24th is weather fine. Private Griffin is buried in Giavera British Cemetery.

The final casualty in Italy commemorated in the War Memorial Park was Private **Herbert Henry Oswin,** 93rd Mechanical Transport Company, Army Service Corps who died aged 30 on the 22nd November 1918. A native of Coventry he was born on the 22nd September, 1888 and resided at 46 Stanley Road being employed as a motor body builder. He was the son of Herbert Henry and Annie Elizabeth Oswin and enlisted in October, 1914. Herbert is buried in Montecchio Precalcino Communal Cemetery Extension, one of 439 graves. Between April 1918 and February 1919 those who died from wounds or disease in the 9th , 24th and 39th Casualty Clearing Stations were buried at Montecchio or at Dueville. A resident of Earlsdon, Private Oswin's name appears on St. Barbara's Memorial.

East Africa

At the outbreak of the First World War Tanzania was the core of German East Africa. On the 8th August 1914, the first recorded British action of the war took place here, when HMS Astraea shelled the German wireless station and boarded and disabled two merchant ships - the Konig and the Feldmarschall. From the invasion of April 1915, a protracted and difficult campaign was fought against a relatively small but highly-skilled German force under the command of General von Lettow-Vorbeck. The Royal Navy systematically shelled Dar es Salaam from mid August 1916, and at 8.00am on the 4th September the Deputy Burgermeister was received aboard HMS Echo to accept the terms of surrender.

Troops, headed by the 129th Baluchis, then entered the City. On the 12th September 1916, Divisional General Head Quarters moved to Dar es Salaam, and later No 3 East African Stationary Hospital was stationed there. The town became the chief sea base for movement of supplies and for the evacuation of the sick and wounded.

In December 1916 General Smuts launched an offensive in German East Africa designed to prevent a merger of the two main German forces and to trap Lettow-Vorbeck, or at least to bring him to that elusive decisive engagement which would end the campaign. Van Deventer, operating south of Iringa, was slowed by mountains covered with dense bush and valleys the rains had filled with water. He was late and once again Lettow-Vorbeck slipped through his fingers, this time by crossing at Rufugi. As Lettow-Vorbeck once said *"There is always a way out, even of an apparently hopeless position, if the leader makes his mind up to face the risks"*.

Captain **Alan Caldicott,** 10th Battalion, the Loyal North Lancashire Regiment was killed in action in this engagement on the 7th December 1916 whilst attached to the 1st/2nd King's African Rifles. The Regimental History regrettably, does not note the circumstances of his death. Alan was born on the 19th March 1887 and resided at 4, Spencer Road, Coventry. Initially he was educated at Lindley Lodge near Nuneaton and then entered Bradfield College, Berkshire which he attended from September 1901 to July 1905. In 1907 he worked for the Imperial Tobacco Company, Nyasaland (now known as Malawi).

Prior to the war he was employed by W. D. and H. O. Wills Ltd, of Bristol where he had lived for two years residing at Sloanwick Road, Redland, Bristol. He was recommended for a commission by Walter Paul, a Justice of the Peace, in Bristol on the 25th August 1914. Alan joined the Public Schools Battalion and was posted as Private to the Middlesex Public Schools Battalion receiving a temporary Commission as a Second Lieutenant on the 29th September 1914.

In the Autumn of 1915 he was gazetted to the Loyal North Lancashire Regiment, served at the front, and was invalided home at Christmas 1915. He returned to the firing line in the summer and had been in action several times before being killed. His brother Captain R. Caldicott was in the Motor Transport Services and another brother Captain J. Caldicott was in the Royal Warwickshire Regiment. Alan is buried in Dar es Salaam War Cemetery; his brothers survived the war.

When the Germans finally surrendered on the 23rd November 1918, twelve days after the European armistice, their numbers had been reduced to 155 European and 1,168 African troops. Dar es Salaam was the capital of German East Africa. Dar es Salaam War Cemetery was created in 1968 when 660 First World War graves at Dar es Salaam (Ocean Road) Cemetery had to be moved to facilitate the construction of a new road. They were reburied in collective graves, each marked by a screen wall memorial. During the early 1970s, a further 1,000 graves were brought into this site from cemeteries all over Tanzania, where maintenance could no longer be assured. Dar es Salaam War Cemetery now contains 1,764 Commonwealth burials of the First World War, sixty of them unidentified.

Captain Caldicott is not only commemorated in The War Memorial Park but also on a war memorial at Clifton Rugby Football Club in Bristol along with forty four former players.

Greece

Two men from the War Memorial Park are commemorated in Greece. Sapper Royston Stephen Merrett is on the Doiran Memorial and Captain Frederick Julian Horner MC is buried in Sturma Military Cemetery.

Sapper **Royston Stephen Merrett**, Signal Service Training Centre (Worcester), Royal Engineers was originally reported as missing. In June 1917 it was confirmed to his mother that he had drowned at sea on the 5th May 1917 aged 28. He was born on the 30th September 1888 at Campden, Gloucestershire and was employed by Coventry Ordnance Works Ltd prior to enlisting in July 1915. His parents lived at 34 Sparkbrook Street, Coventry. The exact circumstances of his death are not known, his body was not recovered and he is commemorated on the Doiran Memorial, Greece. His plaque states he was in the Wireless Section.

From October 1915 to the end of November 1918, the British Salonika Force suffered some 2,800 deaths in action, 1,400 from wounds and 4,200 from sickness. The Doiran Memorial serves the dual purpose of Battle memorial of the British Salonika Force (for which a large sum of money was subscribed by the officers and men of that force), and as a place of commemoration for the men who died in Macedonia and whose graves are not known.

Captain **Frederick Julian Horner,** MC, was attached to the 2nd Battalion Cheshire Regiment from the Royal Warwickshire Regiment when he died of wounds age 22 on the 15th April 1918. He was the son of Frederick and Julia Horner, of Burnt Post, Coventry and born in 1896. He received his education at King Edward VI School in Birmingham and King Henry VIII School in Coventry. Prior to the outbreak of war he was employed by Coventry Corporation as an articled clerk. His name appears on the Corporation memorial to those who fell from the Town Clerk's Office and in his former school, King Henry VIII.

The '*Battalion War Diary*' on the 7th March 1918 notes that the Battalion were in the vicinity of Todorovo and that Lieutenant F. J. Horner rejoined the Battalion from hospital. A week later he was part of a Court of Inquiry with Major Valentine Brown and Lieutenant J. A. V. Babbington "*into the circumstances under which a Short Lee Enfield rifle and other Government property became damaged by fire and to express an opinion as to whom the charges should be debited*".

'*The Report of Operations*' for the 14th, 15th and 16th April 1918 provide a detailed account into the circumstances of how Second Lieutenant Horner was mortally wounded. On the 14th the head of the force crossed the Sturma at 8.15pm and halted South of Elisan where the forces were divided into parties for allotted tasks.

The advance party pushed forward to Kumli whilst the main body waited at Elisan for a status report that declared Kumli clear of the enemy, this being entered at 00.30am on the 15th April and the Barakli patrol left. Three hours later a defensive line had been established around Kumli and the artillery sent for, telephone contact was established with the Barakli patrol at 6.00am. In telephone conversations with the troops based at Kjupri at 8.10am, sniping and enemy artillery fire were reported which was getting heavier. Thirty minutes later the telephone conversation ceased and an observation post reported men returning.

Reports show at about 8.20am the enemy had appeared in a large number of about 500 men and despite the best efforts the patrol and the forward posts were overrun. After all the officers had either been killed or wounded and other ranks suffering about seventy casualties they were forced to withdraw. In contrast it was estimated the enemy suffered eighty casualties.

At 9.00am enemy sniping was received by the Barakli patrol and this increased at 10.20am and artillery was called for which started about 10.40am and lasted for twenty minutes. This patrol reported that the village of Barakli was empty on arrival but gradually rifle fire turned into artillery attacks. The posts were rushed by the enemy who forced the patrol to withdraw west of **Kumli** village; the support platoon was ordered to withdraw last but due to the strength of the enemy the whole of this platoon was taken. The casualties were stated as one officer and about fifty other ranks as wounded or missing. Lieutenant Frederick Julian Horner was listed on the *'Nominal Roll of Battle Casualties'* for the 2nd Battalion on the 15th April 1918 and is buried in **Struma Military Cemetery**. This cemetery contains 947 Commonwealth burials of the First World War, 51 of them unidentified.

News of his death was recorded in *'The Coventry Graphic'* : *"Mr. Frederick Horner secretary to the Coventry Education Committee has received intimation from the war office that his only son Lieutenant F. J. Horner Royal Warwickshire Regiment (attached 2nd Cheshire Regiment), died of wounds on 15th April, received on the Salonica front. Lieutenant Horner had been previously wounded, and his Colonel then wrote to his parents expressing his satisfaction with his gallantry, and mentioned his name in official dispatches. He was an articled pupil to Mr. George Sutton, Town Clerk. Every sympathy will be extended to his parents in their sad bereavement."*

In June 1918, Captain Horner was awarded the Military Cross whilst at the Salonica front, *"for consistent and conspicuous gallantry over an extended period"*. Captain Horner was one of the 69 employees who died from Coventry Corporation and his name is inscribed on a memorial in the Council House to those that fell from the Town Clerk's Department. In total the Cheshire regiment lost 378 officers during the war.

Captain Horner's Plaque awaiting restoration

The Western Front

1914

The first casualty on the western front and commemorated in the War Memorial Park was Private **Alfred Burrows,** 1st Battalion, Royal Warwickshire Regiment. He was killed in action age 35 at Meteren, Belgium on the 13th October 1914. Meteren had become occupied by the Germans at the beginning of the month. Alfred was born on the 19th December, 1879 and was the son of William and Alice Burrows of 11 Norfolk Street, although he resided at 23 Stanton Street. He was employed as a cycle finisher and was a reservist prior to the war.

On the 12th October at 6.30pm, the Battalion left their current location by bus for Caustre arriving at 2.00am when they went into billets. At 9.20am they received orders to move to Meteren and by 9.30am A and C companies formed an advanced guard under Major Poole with the Divisional Cyclist company and the cavalry in front. At 10.00am the Battalion reached Fletre, where the enemy were reported to be holding high ground along a ridge in front of Meteren. A and B companies were deployed. A on the left side and B on the right, they were to advance if possible to a cross roads. D company under Major Christie were sent up for support and behind C company. Noted in the *'Battalion War Diary'*, *"the enemy retired into and just outside Meteren occupying trenches and houses"*.

An hour later, the Regiment were ordered to push on and endeavour to drive the enemy out. At 1.00pm the outskirts of the village had been gained, but a further advance was held up and the companies were in great need of support. C and D companies tried to advance and in doing so took several trenches but suffered severely. At 1.30pm the Regiment were ordered to halt whilst the village was attacked from the North and South by the 10th and 12th Brigades; these attacks commenced at 2.00pm. By 3.00pm the Seaforth Highlanders attacked on the Battalion's left and through A company which withdrew at dusk to Planeboon – C and D companies under Captain Freeman and Major Christie were unable to withdrew till much later owing to heavy fire but about 8.00pm the King's Own Regiment came up and passed through them.

At 10.00pm C and D companies joined the Battalion at Planeboon, the Regiment becoming reserve to Brigade. Meteren was taken during the night and held until the German offensive of April 1918. It was very wet all day, the casualties were 42 killed and 85 wounded. The *'Battalion War Diary'* notes a perfect advance by companies concerned and *"dash & spirit shown by all concerned"*. In 1919 those buried in this area and neighbouring battlefields were bought into Meteren Cemetery. Private Burrows' exact grave location is not known but the

Commonwealth War Grave Commission state he is buried near Row III, Aisle F, Plot 712. F. His name appears on a stained glass panel in St. John's church.

Two days later, Private **Reginald Harold Hotton** was killed in action at Crux Barbe, Normandy on the 15th October 1914 aged 20, whilst serving with the 2nd Battalion, Lothian Regiment, Royal Scots. Reginald was born on the 20th May 1894 at Lancaster and resided at Coventry, being employed as a coach painter. He was well known in Coventry and lived with his parents Harold and Caroline Hotton of 173 Narrow Lane, Coventry. He is buried in Vieille Chapelle, New Military Cemetery, Lacoutre.

Private **Ernest Peter Prior,** 2nd Battalion Border Regiment was killed in action aged 26 on the 28th October 1914 at Kruiseik in Flanders. A soldier by profession his Regimental number, 9901, indicates that he enlisted as a regular soldier in November 1911. Ernest would have completed his basic training at Carlisle Castle, the Regimental depot of the Border Regiment. He was then posted to the 2nd Battalion, one of the Regiment's two regular Battalions. At this time the 2nd Battalion were based in the UK at Martinique Barracks, Bordon in Hampshire and in September 1912 moved to Manorbier Barracks at Pembroke dock in South Wales.

The Battalion were mobilised on 4th August and joined the 20th Brigade of the 7th Division. Ernest was serving in D Company when the Battalion embarked for France on 5th October 1914 sailing on SS Minneapolis. The Border Regiment were one of the first to arrive at Zeebrugge from where they went on by train to Bruges. On arrival the *'Battalion War Diary'* states *"the people were very good to our men but would take their cap and collar badges, a great nuisance as afterwards it was impossible to tell a man's unit"*.

On the nights of the 25th to the 26th October , the enemy had advanced considerably and had concentrated in large numbers in woods on the Battalion's front. The enemy launched an attack on the 28th October about 9.00am and succeeded in taking the front line trenches. They were eventually held up by the scouts and machine guns. The attack resulted in heavy casualties: Officers 4 killed, 5 wounded or missing, other ranks killed 25 ,wounded 65 and missing 174.

Ernest was the son of Peter and Rachel Prior of 7, Craven Street, Chapelfields, Coventry. He was born on the 25th January 1889 at Banbury and resided at 25, Allesley Old Road. He has no known grave and is commemorated on the Menin Gate Memorial. His name is recorded in the 'WW1 *Book of Remembrance*' in the Border Regiment's Chapel in Carlisle Cathedral.

Also commemorated on the Menin Gate is Private **Arthur Johnson**, 6th Dragoon Guards (Carabineers), who went missing and was subsequently believed killed, at the Battle of Ypres on the 1st November 1914, aged 38. Arthur was the husband of Kathleen Johnson of 21 Maycock Road, Foleshill and was born on the 2nd January 1877 to Rosa and Henry Johnson. Private Johnson was a reservist, employed as a watchmaker prior to the war and enlisted in Nuneaton.

Private **George John Stokes,** 11811, 1st Battalion, Worcestershire Regiment was killed in action at Neuve Chapelle on the 11th December 1914 aged 26. George was born on the 19th January 1888, at Coventry and was a professional soldier. He resided at 45, Swanswell Street with his parents, Sarah Ann and William Thomas. Private Stokes has no known grave and is commemorated on the Le Touret Memorial. His date of death is recorded inaccurately in the '*City of Coventry: Roll of the Fallen*' as the 11th January 1915.

In September 1914, the 1st Battalion set sail for England from Cairo having been based in Egypt for the previous two years. They arrived in Liverpool on the 16th October, having changed the destination from Southampton to Liverpool due to the risk of submarine attacks. On arrival the men were sent for training at Winchester and left Southampton on the 5th of November on board the transport ship Maidan. Issues with logistics meant the men did not leave for the front until the 9th November.

The Battalion formed part of the 8th Division and by a mixture of train journeys and marching the men were facing the trenches of Neuve Chappelle by the 14th November relieving the 1st Royal Scots. The position was far from ideal being very exposed and in some places only fifty yards from the enemy, an exchange of fire was constant. At dawn, on the following morning the enemy bombarded the Battalion's position killing six men and wounding twenty four. The men stayed in the line under conditions of rain and snow experiencing intermittent shell and rifle fire until the 19th November, when they were relieved by the 2nd Sherwood Foresters. The men then marched six miles to billets at La Gorgue, on the following morning one in four men had a reported case of frostbite to either their hands or feet and 150 men were sent back to base with cases of trench foot.

Until mid December 1914 the 1st Battalion were in trenches on the Bassée Road. During this period when out of line the men of the Battalion were in billets either at Estaires or in the hamlets of La Gorgue and Rouge Croix. Due to the extreme conditions and the proximity of the enemy the Battalion suffered many casualties during the period from the 19th November until mid December either from enemy fire or frostbite.

The last man to be commemorated in the War Memorial Park for 1914 is Private **Andrew Thomas Townend,** 147, 2nd Battalion, Royal Warwickshire Regiment. He was killed in action, aged 27 on the 19th December 1914. Andrew was the husband of Elizabeth Townend and resided at 1c. 5h. Paynes Lane, Coventry. He was born in 1886 at Ford Street. A reservist, he was employed by Humber Limited. Private Townend featured in two articles in 'The Coventry Graphic'. The first was an article about him and Bandsmen Sidney Carter from 96 Nicholls Street, Coventry both of whom had been injured in the retreat from Mons, and the second, to report his death.

The Royal Warwickshire Regiment left Harrow for Boulogne on August 22nd. On arrival in France they marched from Boulogne to Amiens where they caught their first glimpse of the Germans. Marching day and night they eventually worked their way to Mons. The men were supposed to have fifteen minutes sleep every three miles but this was forbidden and the men were very tired.

During the march a scouting party captured three German officers and their horses. At midnight the Germans came upon the Royal Warwickshire Regiment in full force quite unexpectedly and the Regiment were forced to fall back. Bandsman Carter describes the events *"We were on the march until 7.00am the next morning to get out off their way .Instead we fell straight into their trap and we met them in full force. There seemed to be about three million of them to 5,000 of us"*. He also described how at Cambrai they encountered some cavalry dressed in French uniform who beckoned them and waved to the British soldiers to go forward. This they did but when they were within two or three hundred yards they discovered to their surprise that the supposedly French soldiers were the enemy who immediately opened fire, at this point the men realised they were in a trap.

During this engagement, Private Townend was shot in his calf on the right leg and Bandsman Carter (left), who doubled up as a stretcher bearer came to his aid. Whilst carrying Private Townend, Private Carter saw and heard from another Coventry man Sergeant Harry Tompkins who said " *Sid it doesn't look like we will see Coventry again so long*". Shortly after this conversation, Bandsmen Carter was shot through his right leg which forced him to drop the stretcher. The order was given from the Commanding Officer " *For God's sake men, buck up; every man for himself*".

On hearing the order Private Townend and Bandsman Carter scrambled to the hospital ¾ mile away; on arrival they were treated in a church. It was not long before the Medical Officer came around and ordered those who could help themselves to get out as artillery was falling around the church. Bandsman Carter estimated 200 people were ultimately killed in the church. The wounded were taken to St. Quentin, coming under attack from enemy aeroplanes en route, but were soon ordered to move on again to Cambrai where they were moved to their final destination Le Havre.

Eight of the wounded from the Royal Warwickshire Regiment were treated at Netley hospital with an estimated 120 men from other Regiments also receiving treatment. All the men were sent home at the same time for fourteen days leave and told to report to the nearest hospital. The two comrades were amongst the first soldiers to arrive in Coventry from the scene of operations at Mons and returned to their respective homes. After their leave was completed, Private Townend and Bandsman Carter went back to the front.

On the 18th December the 2nd Battalion was based at Fleurbaix. An order was received to advance in three lines at 4.30pm to attack and take the German trenches which were in front of Le Malsnil. The attack was preceded by a heavy artillery bombardment to which the enemy hardly made any reply. The attack was started by B Company on the right led by Captain Haddon, advancing in two lines with D Company in the centre. C Company formed the third line with entrenching tools ready to dig in and hold a new position. Immediately the attack was started, the enemy opened a very heavy rifle and machine gun fire, the Battalion advanced under this with steadiness, but suffered very heavy casualties.

The 2nd Queen's Regiment sent in further companies but the attack still failed in its objective, although bodies of the advancing lines were observed a few yards from the German trenches. The remainder of the Battalion subsequently retired into the starting trenches. Shortly after daylight on the 19th December the enemy came out and started examining the British dead. Parties were sent out from the British lines and buried some of the officers and collected discs from some of the killed. The Germans refused to allow the British to remove the wounded who were being made prisoners. Two officers of the Queen's Regiment and several small parties of the Royal Warwickshire Regiment were fired upon when engaged in carrying our wounded into the enemy's lines. During this evacuation and also owing to Lieutenant Henry Raymond Syndercombe Bower, South Staffordshire Regiment being killed while helping to collect our wounded, the informal armistice was terminated.

Lieutenant Colonel Robert Henry Watkin Brewis was found killed about forty yards from the enemy's line and Captain Brownfield and four other Lieutenants were found together with thirty four men a few yards from a German machine gun. From evidence available it was apparent that Captain Reginald John Brownfield though previously wounded continued to lead the attack on the machine gun's position.

The following day the Battalion mustered in the trenches: 149 non-commissioned officers and men. The remainder of the 2nd Battalion, Royal Warwickshire Regiment had retired by order after the action into reserve at Cronballot. The total number of men reported as dead, injured or missing was 57 killed, 87 wounded and 219 missing. On the 20th December the Battalion received congratulations from the Officer Commanding the 7th Division for their gallant action on the 18th.

Private Townend was killed in the attack and his obituary in 'The Coventry Graphic' stated "The deceased will be regarded by all who knew him as a real hero, for he had not long returned to the firing line after being invalided home with severe wounds. Private Townend was well-known locally as a footballer, playing with St. Michael's, the Catholics and Longford teams. At the Humber works he will be long remembered for his genial good nature which earned him the appropriate nickname 'Happy'". Private Townend has no known grave; he is commemorated on the Ploegsteert Memorial and his plaque shows his nickname 'Happy'. Bandsmen Carter and Sergeant Harry Tompkins survived the war.

1915

The first casualty in 1915 commemorated in the War Memorial Park is Private **Charles Ponder DCM**, 2nd Battalion, Duke of Cornwall's Light Infantry who was killed in action, aged 26 on the 15th February 1915. Charles was the son of Thomas Martin Ponder and Mary Ann Ponder, of 171, Walsgrave Road, Coventry. A native of Coventry he was born on the 21st December, 1888, and was employed in the City as an iron polisher.

Charles enlisted at Warwick on the 20th April 1908 when he was 19 years old. At this point he weighed 130 lbs and was just under 5' 9" tall with his religion being specified as Church of England. Private Ponder originally joined A company of the 1st Battalion on the 18th September 1908. The 2nd Battalion were in Hong Kong at the outbreak of war and after their return they were equipped and landed in France on 21st December 1914. By February 1915 Charles had transferred from the 1st to the 2nd Battalion; at this point the 2nd Battalion were in trenches near St. Eloi, Ypres Salient. As this was a period of extremely cold weather the troops spent only two days in the line with one in support and two in reserve, additionally mud and water caused many problems and the enemy were active with rifle grenades, shell fire and sniping. During a period out of the line the Battalion were ordered forward to counter attack after the Germans had launched a strong assault on trenches occupied by the Leinsters.

The Battalion left their packs in a barn near Voormezeele, but it was extremely dark and the march forward became a nightmare as the grounds were heavily pitted with water filled shell holes and ditches. Shortly after midnight, a consultation took place between Lieutenant Colonel Tuson, 2nd Battalion, Duke of Cornwall's Light Infantry and the Officer Commanding 3rd Battalion, Kings Royal Rifles. This exchange resulted in verbal orders being given to draw up in two lines. The 2nd Battalion were to lead a counter attack on trenches 21 and 22, with the Kings Royal Rifles attacking trenches 19 and 20. After a short artillery barrage, the attack went forward at 4.00am with both Regiments capturing their objectives. Lieutenant Carkeet-James and 28 other ranks were wounded.

Private Ponder was awarded the DCM for conspicuous gallantry when he rushed forward at great risk under a heavy fire and dragged back to his trench Lieutenant Carkeet-James. In the continuing action, he was shot by a sniper and died instantly. He was originally recommended for the Victoria Cross but as he was killed later in the same day this was brought down to a DCM.

Private Ponder's citation appeared in *'The London Gazette'* on the 1st April 1915 and in the Regimental Magazine *'One and All'*. This was the first award to the Battalion after arriving in France and their first attack upon the enemy trenches. Charles has no known grave and is commemorated on the Menin gate and in St. Michael's Church.

Over two months later Private **Bert Rawlins,** 1st Battalion Royal Warwickshire Regiment was killed in action aged 34 on the 25th April 1915. Bert was the son of William Rawlins and the husband of Mrs. M. A. Rawlins (nee Beaumont) of 13, Lower Ford Street, Coventry. He was born on the 18th November 1881 in Far Gosford Street. On the 25th April 1915, the Battalion were at Ypres and left at midnight for Vielje where orders were received for an attack. At 4.30am the Brigade attacked a wood on the left of the line with the 7th Argyll and Sutherland Highlanders, whilst in support were the Seaforth Highlanders. The Royal Irish Fusiliers and Royal Dublin Fusiliers attacked to the Brigade's right at St. Julien.

Owing to the German trenches being insufficiently shelled, and supports unable to come up the line the brigade retired at about 7.00am to trenches near a farm and consolidated this position. The Battalion's casualties were very heavy: 17 officers with 500 other ranks, killed, wounded and missing. The *'Battalion War Diary'* notes in suggestions *"inadvisable to attack on enemy's position, unless properly prepared supported by artillery fire beforehand and thorough reconnaissance made beforehand".*

'The Coventry Graphic' in May 1915 included an appeal by Mrs Rawlins "as she was anxious for information respecting her husband, who has been posted as missing since April the 25th. Mrs Rawlings last heard from him on April 20th". Private Rawlins was one of a group of soldiers whose photograph taken in the trenches was reproduced on the front page of *'The Coventry Graphic'* on April the 16th.

His son Bertram was born on the 29th July 1914 and less then a week old when his father was called up to go out with the Expeditionary Force. Bertram can confirm that his sister paid for a copper beech tree and that his father served at one point as a batman to an officer. Bert has no known grave and is commemorated on the Menin Gate.

Gunner **Sydney Reginald Stebbing,** 3rd Battery, Machine Gun Corps (Motors) died of wounds received at Zonnebeke age 21 on the 4th May 1915. He was fourth son of Edwin Robert and Annabella Rebecca Stebbing, of 10, Craven Road, Rugby. Sydney was a member of a military family, his father served as Bandmaster in various Regiments for a total of fifty three years and his three brothers went through the Boer war without injury.

Sydney was born on the 3rd October, 1893 in Springfield Terrace. He lived in Coventry and was employed as a Machine Tool Maker at the Rudge Works where he had worked for over four years prior to enlisting. Gunner Stebbing joined Kitchener's army on 28th November, 1914 and left for the front with the Motor Machine Gun Service on April 24th 1915. He was immediately detailed for the firing line and was in the trenches on May 3rd at the reconstruction of the line at Ypres, when he was wounded by maxim fire and died the next day. He is buried in Hazebrouck Communal Cemetery.

Shortly before his death he wrote a letter to his colleagues :

Dear Sirs,
Received the box you so kindly sent, for which I must thank you very much indeed. I am sure the contents will be very useful, as Bisley is in such a state owing to the bad weather. I hope you will excuse me for not writing and letting you know before, as I have been laid up, but am better now. Again thank you very much for your generous gift.

Yours Sincerely
Gunner Stebbing

Also buried in Hazebrouck Communal Cemetery is Lance Corporal **John Musson** 2nd Battalion King's Own (Royal Lancaster Regiment) who was killed in action on the 5th May 1915. He was born in Ulverston, enlisted in Barrow-In-Furness and has no obvious connection with Coventry. His name does not appear in the *'Roll of the Fallen'*. Casualty clearing stations were posted at Hazebrouck, from October 1914 to September 1917, at first burials were made amongst the civilian graves but after the Armistice they were removed to a Commonwealth section . Lance Corporal Musson was one of six fatalities recorded with the 2nd Battalion on the 5th May 1915.

Private **John Adams,** 1st/7th Battalion Royal Warwickshire Regiment was killed in action near Messines on the 9th May 1915. He was the brother of Mr. F. Adams of 10, Thomas Street, Butts, Coventry and resided at the back of 3, Moat House. John was born on the 13th October 1891 in Coventry and prior to enlisting in September 1914 was employed in the city as a turret hand at the Siddeley Deasy works.

On the 6th May the Battalion were stationed at Steenbeck Trenches, Wulverghem. The 9th of May saw the Battalion take part in a demonstration against German lines according to special orders received and the *'Battalion War Diary'* notes *"A very fine day. Heavy shelling by enemy during day. Casualties three killed Corporal T. F. Johnson (from Rugby), Private E. Corbett (from Nuneaton) and Private Abbot. Twelve men being wounded"*. As the death of a Private Abbot could not be verified it would seem an error has occurred in the *'War Diary'* as Private Adams is buried at La Plus Douve Farm Cemetery, Ploegsteert next to his comrades Private Corbett and Corporal Johnson. The three men are buried in Row V, Plot C, Graves six to eight. La Plus Douve Cemetery was begun in April 1915 by the 48th (South Midland) Division.

'The Coventry Graphic' reported that Private Jack Adams was killed by shell fire and also injured by the same shell was Private J. Wormall of Coventry who was treated at Birmingham Hospital. He was subsequently one of the first Coventry Territorials to be treated at Coventry hospital.

Second Lieutenant **Edward Mason,** 3rd Battalion (attached 2nd Battalion), Northamptonshire Regiment was killed in action near Fromelles, Armentieres aged 36 on the 9th May 1915. He was an only son and born on the 24th June, 1878 at Coventry, to Jeremiah and Sarah Mason who later resided at 1 Ingoldsby Mansions, Avonmore Road, West Kensington, London. He was married to Jessie

Mason (professionally known as Jessie Grimson), and lived with her in Chelsea, London. His father maintained a business in Coventry running the firm Messrs Johnson and Mason.

Uniformed and Civilian Pictures of Second Lieutenant Mason

After being educated privately, he took up music as a profession, and became famous as a violoncello player and conductor. He received his musical training at the Royal College of Music, where during an exceptionally brilliant career as a student he won several exhibitions, became a favourite at the college concerts, and obtained his diploma as Associate Royal College of Music (ARCM). As a cellist he was principally known in London as a member of the Grimson String Quartet, of which his wife, Miss Jessie Grimson was the distinguished leader. He was also a Director and the principal cellist of the New Symphony Orchestra, which he conducted at its initial concert at the Queen's Hall in 1906. This was his first prominent appearance as a conductor, and his power of direction at once received the recognition of the public and the press and unsolicited tributes from some of the leading musicians of the day.

Edward Mason was on the musical staff at Eton College, a position he held for over seventeen years but was not an old Etonian himself. Whilst at Eton he was also a Principal Cellist at the Royal Albert Hall Orchestra. He frequently played as a soloist at Eton in Windsor and the neighbourhood also at chamber concerts in town as well as in the provinces. He was also a great favourite in his native town Coventry. It was however, as a quartet player that he excelled but he was also a good violinist and pianist. Edward was the founder and conductor of the Edward Mason Choir, and held a high place in the musical world of England. On at least one occasion he returned to Queen's Hall with the Edward Mason Choir

Even though he was married and in a prosperous position the call of patriotism came to him so strongly that he sacrificed everything in order to serve his country. He joined the army on the outbreak of war enlisting in the Public Schools Battalion of Kitchener's Army and subsequently received a commission as a Second

Lieutenant in the 3rd Battalion, Northamptonshire Regiment. At the time of his death he was attached to the 2nd Battalion.

On Sunday the 9th May 1915, Second Lieutenant Mason was killed leading his men in a charge on German trenches at Fromelles. His obituary appeared in *'The Eton College Chronicle'* on the 20th May 1915 and also in *'The Coventry Graphic'*. His late chief at Eton College, Dr C. H. Lloyd, said of him *"he was a fine fellow and one of the best musicians I ever knew"*, and as a special honour to his memory the Dead March in "Saul" was played in the college chapel by order of the Vice Provost and at the request of the senior boys. A fellow officer writing an account of his death said *"He was killed gallantly leading his men in the attack on the 9th May against the German trenches"*, and his Platoon Sergeant wrote that *"the detachment came under a devastating fire from German machine guns and he fell in a hail of bullets"*. Obituaries from unknown resources state *"Mr. Mason who was the first well-known London musician to fall in the war, was open hearted and generous to a fault. He hated pretence and cant, and, a lover of all healthy, open-air pursuits was the very antithesis to the conventional type of musician"*.

Although reports suggest Second Lieutenant Mason was buried near Fromelles, he has no known grave and is commemorated on the Ploegsteert Memorial.

By the end of the week Rifleman **Herbert Lawrenson,** 1st Battalion, Kings Royal Rifle Corps was killed in action, near Festubert age 34 on the 15th May 1915.

Herbert was a native of Coventry, born in the City on the 23rd March, 1882 in the Parish of St. Thomas to John and Emily Lawrenson. He resided with his wife, Annie Louise and one child at 27, Trafalgar Street. Rifleman Lawrenson was called up as a reservist and formerly employed at Rex Motor works and prior to this Williamson Motor works where he had worked as a motor mechanic.

On the 15th May 1915, Herbert was in the heat of the battle at Festubert. Heavy artillery bombardment continued on both sides and the assault on the enemy's trenches so often postponed was ordered for the end of the day. Preparations for the attack were made during the afternoon with the plan of attack as follows:

Assault to take place at 11.30pm, orders to seize and hold the first two lines of enemy trenches leading to the enemy's rear. If the assault is successful, fresh troops will be sent forward to push the attack further about daybreak. The Battalion's first objective was the front line of German trenches running parallel to the British lines.

The distance from the British front to the Germans was roughly 350 yards but considerably less in other places. The ground was flat ploughed with rough grass on it, parallel to the Battalion's line and about 20 yards in front of the line ran a ditch twelve feet wide full of water and again on the far side of the ditch a disused trench which presented no obstacle.

To prepare for the attack, two leading lines filed out quietly by two prepared openings in the parapet and lay down in front of a the ditch ready to assault when ordered. The left party crossed the ditch by bridges which had been prepared; the right party's opening was in front of the ditch where it entered the Battalion's lines. The Battalion left its billets at 9.00pm and everything went smoothly. Ordinary sniping (into the air) was carried on from our trenches to disarm suspicion, and our artillery which had been cutting the enemy's wire by deliberate fire for several days, fired an occasional shell throughout the evening. There was no moon and the night was pretty dark. Three signallers accompanied D Company taking with them a telephone instrument, two motor lamps and paying out wire as they went. They were ordered to light one motor lamp if they captured the German first line, two if they captured the second and were also told to signal back if other means failed with an electric torch, using Morse code.

For five minutes after 11.30pm when the advance began, quiet reigned. The Germans fired no lights and there was nothing more then the usual sniping. Then came a sudden burst of fire, mostly on the Battalion's left and the enemy began to send up lights in all directions. The advancing lines appeared to be quite close to the German trenches, advancing steadily, and as they gained them, the lights from that part failed to go up. Very heavy machine gun fire and rifle fire came from the left and it did not diminish much as time went on. A signal was received to say "secured enemy's second line", with heavy bombing the third line of German trenches was taken before daybreak. This position was consolidated and the making of a communication trench to our old lines was at once commenced. The Battalion losses on this day were 27 other ranks killed and 5 officers, with 192 wounded and 88 missing.

Annie Louise Lawrenson originally received information from the front that her husband was officially reported as one of those missing by his Commanding Officer. In a letter the Commanding Officer stated *"regret at being unable to trace Rifleman Lawrenson and he was very sorry to lose him"*. One of Herbert's chums also informed Mrs Lawrenson that *" there is not the slightest doubt he was killed on the night of the 15th May in a charge in which two German trenches were captured. He was killed between the first and the second trenches, for he spoke to his mate in the first trench and when they reached the second trench he was missing. He was quite fearless and did his duty like a Briton"*. Rifleman Lawrenson has no known grave and is commemorated on the Le Touret Memorial and in St. John's Church.

Mortally wounded in the fighting at Festubert was Private **Mark Henry Smith,** 2nd Battalion Royal Warwickshire Regiment who died age 35 on the 16th May 1915. He had completed almost sixteen years of service having previously served in the Boer War; he held the South African war medal with four clasps. Mark was the son of Thomas Smith and resided of 10 Stanway Road, Earlsdon, Coventry with his wife Mary Smith and daughter. Mark was born on the 29th July, 1879 in Coventry. A reservist he was called back to serve at the start of the war. A trained motor mechanic he was employed at the Rover Works as a turner.

Early in the morning on the 16th May A, B, C and D companies of the 2nd Battalion advanced on the line. C and D moved at 5.00am whilst A Company were in a communication trench. B company arrived further up the line at 7.30am. The *'Battalion War Diary'* notes " *All these companies advanced with great dash and quickness and arrived at desired objective"*. At 8.45am platoons of C and D companies received orders to get in touch with the Scots Guards on the left, protect the left flank and put the position of Rue La Quinque in a state of defence.

These orders were acted upon immediately and five minutes later the required platoons were en route. At 11.40am C Company were ordered to advance in support of the Royal Scots in their attack. Several hours later at 3.45pm, two platoons of D Company moved towards the farm on La Quinque Rue to put it in a state of defence, but found advanced British troops retiring. It was noted in the *'War Diary'* that the 2nd Battalion only retired from the line on receipt of orders from Captain Stockwell Commanding the Royal Welsh Fusiliers as the trenches were untenable owing to enfilade fire.

At dusk the Battalion was ordered to hold the first German trench and by 9.00pm the whole Battalion was reorganised and formed up in this position. On the morning of the 17th , the Battalion took up a position at Rue De Cailloux apart from one platoon of D Company which moved up to support the Royal Scots. This platoon stayed here until midnight, when it withdrew to first line British trench. During the night of the 17/18th the battlefield was cleaned and the dead buried. Throughout the 18th the Battalion remained in support of the Royal Scots and at

8.00pm the Battalion left the field and proceeded into billets at Vendin-les-Bethune. The casualties of the Battalion during the operations were as follows: officers killed 2, officers wounded 3, other ranks 24 killed,157 wounded and 21 missing. One of those killed in the various attacks on the German defences was Private Smith and he is buried in Bethune Town Cemetery.

Private J. Isaacs of the Regimental Police, in writing a letter to Private Smith's wife, stated" *Your husband was always such a good comrade and always so cheerful no matter what kind of task was before him. You and his little daughter were his constant thoughts and he never tired of talking of you both. I have been informed that his end was quite cheerful and he was just the same as cheerful as ever when he knew he was going before his Maker. He died a soldier's death. Our sincere regret is with you madam in this terrible blow that is happening to you"*.

The next two casualties also died in the Battle of Festubert, Private George Wagstaff and Sergeant Arthur Stagg who were with the 1st Battalion, Royal Welch Fusiliers.

Private **George Wagstaff,** 1st Battalion, Royal Welch Fusiliers was killed in action, near Festubert, aged 28 on the 16th May 1915. George was born in 1887, at Foleshill the son of Amos and Anna Wagstaff, of 150, Nicholls Street, Coventry. He resided with his wife, Jane Elizabeth (nee Gill) at 50 Well Street, Coventry. An engineer he was employed at Siddeley Deasy. He has no known grave and is commemorated on the Le Touret Memorial.

Sergeant **Arthur Stagg,** 1st Battalion Royal Welch Fusiliers was killed in action on the following day, the 17th of May. He was slightly younger than Private Wagstaffe and was born on the 12th March 1891 in Spon Street. A professional soldier he resided at 3c. 10h. Castle Street with his wife Mrs M. Stagg (nee Box) and his parents Mr. and Mrs. A. Stagg.

On the 15th May 1915, the 1st Battalion were engaged in operations against Aubers Ridge and Festubert by the 1st Army and the Canadians. At 8.30pm the 22nd Infantry Brigade moved from billets at Essars near Bethune to take up a line in the trenches. The Battalion formed up along a parapet resting on the Rue Cailloux on a frontage of 350 yards. The front parapet was held by the 2nd Battalion, Bedfordshire Regiment who maintained fire on the breaches made in the enemy's parapet by our artillery on the 14th and 15th. The 1st Battalion Royal Warwicks were in support trenches behind the Bedfordshire Regiment; the Battalion strength in the trenches at this point was 806 NCO's and men with 25 officers.

On the following day, the Battalion were ordered to assault the German trenches on a front of 200 yards, take the Germans 1st and 2nd line trenches moving on due East; from the 2nd line trenches the Battalion was to move South East and take up a line facing South East between the Rue Quinque and the Rue D'ouvert with its left on the road joining these two. The line allotted was formed by a big German high command communication trench- reported heavily bastioned and probably prepared for use as a fire trench. At 2.45am the intense bombardment commenced and ceased at 3.16am; the Battalion immediately assaulted, each company in two lines, company behind company in the order A, B, C and D. The parapet was mounted by scaling ladders – the wire had previously been cut and bridges thrown across a broad ditch which ran along the Battalion's front. The Battalion suffered very heavily from shell and machine gun fire both in crossing the parapet and the space between their parapet and the German front line.

Many fell severely wounded. The German first line however was quickly stormed, the German 2nd line was also carried and the line pushed on. A heavy machine gun and rifle fire then opened up from the left front. The Scots Guards lost direction to face the fire drawing a portion of the Battalion with them. The rear half of the Battalion suffered heavily in getting to the German trenches; A and B were rapidly advancing, C company directed towards La Quinque Rue – D company proceeded to reverse the German parapet to make the line captured tenable. Those heading towards La Quinque Rue were forced to halt by the fire from our own guns from which they suffered severely. Sergeant Stagg was one of the many casualties suffered on this day and he is buried in Bethune Town Cemetery.

The next casualty, one month later on the 23rd June 1915 was Private **William Simmons** who was serving with the 1/7th Battalion, Royal Warwickshire Regiment. William, also known as 'Bill', was the son of Walter and Emily Simmons of 29 Rudge Road, Coventry and engaged to be married. He enlisted in September 1914 at the age of 26, and prior to this worked at the Rotherams clock and watch manufacturer as a machinist. Whilst at Rotherams he proved himself as a champion shot in the works rifle club. He and another champion shot were egged on to enlist by their work-mates. On the way to the recruiting station William's colleague backed out but William stuck to his word " *I'd said I'll go so I'll go*".

Infantry and Civilian Photographs

On the 23rd June 1915, the Battalion were in trenches near Ploegsteert Wood and had just relieved the 1/8th Battalion, Royal Warwickshire Regiment. The *'Battalion War Diary'* states *"the weather was a thunderstorm followed by hot sun, the flies and mosquitoes very troublesome, one casualty Private Simmons shot by a sniper"*. News of his death was conveyed to his parents from Second Lieutenant Brian Ash (Platoon Officer) who wrote *"It is with deep regret that I have to tell you your son was killed in action last night. He was shot whilst doing sentry duty and his death was painless and instantaneous. I can assure you through his death I have lost one of my most trustworthy men."* The report of his death in *'The Coventry Graphic'* stated *"He was shot through the head whilst on sentry duty and died instantly"*.

These accounts were confirmed by the sentry on duty with William who visited his parents after the War and declared *"he had not suffered and had received a single shot to the head"*. Private Simmons was the only casualty recorded on this day by the 1/7th Battalion. One of a family of twelve, three other brothers also joined the colours one of them being injured in the leg.

William's mother, Emily Simmons attended the dedication of the cenotaph as a dignatory in October 1927. William was a member of the Queen's Road Church and is commemorated on a stained glass memorial in the church. He is buried in Rifle House Cemetery, Warneton, Belgium.

Corporal **John Jackson,** B Company, 2nd Battalion, Lancashire Fusiliers was killed in action at Ypres age 31 on the 29th June 1915. He was born on the 26th December, 1883 at Ratley, near Banbury and the son of Joshua and Sarah Jackson who also resided at Ratley. John was married to Florence Jackson; they had one child and resided at 68, Harnall Lane East, Coventry.

'The Coventry Graphic' reported *"he had been shot in the head whilst serving with the Lancashire fusiliers. The deceased soldier was well known in Coventry as a prominent member of the Demon Cycle and Motor club and the Oddfellows friendly society. Prior to the outbreak of war he was employed as an accumulator of work and joined the Lancashire Fusiliers as a reservist in August 1914. He was quickly promoted to Corporal; and at the time of his death was recommended for further promotion for holding a trench near Ypres when all other Non Commissioned Officers had been gassed".* Corporal Jackson is buried in Bard Cottage Cemetery, Boesinghe, Belgium.

Two soldiers commemorated in the War Memorial Park, Private John Henry Gutteridge and Corporal Alfred Ernest Ison were two of several soldiers killed with the 2nd Battalion, Oxfordshire and Buckinghamshire Light Infantry on the 27th August 1915 at Givenchy, France when members of the Battalion were attacked by bombs.

Private **John Henry Gutteridge** was born on Christmas day 1892 in Coventry and resided at 11 Henry Street. He worked as a coremaker for Messrs Johnson and Mason until enlisting in September 1914 . His employer Mason had lost his son, Edward in the war on the 9th May 1915 and was also losing his employees. Private Gutteridge had been in France for exactly four months.

Corporal **Alfred Ernest Ison** was the son of Joseph Albert and Isabella Ison of 54, Mount Street, Allesley Old Road, Coventry although he was born in Battersea on the 9th August 1895. Alfred enlisted in September 1914 and went to France on the 26th May 1915. An engineer with British Thompson Houston Co. his name appears on their memorial in the Royal Warwicks Club with those of twelve of his colleagues.

The news of his death was conveyed to his mother in a letter from Captain R. M. Owen (Commanding A Company) *"On Thursday night last we were in a very tight corner only a few yards from the Germans, who made an attempt to get into our trench by attacking us with bombs and we had to prevent them by using the same bombs. We succeeded in doing so but had six men killed one of whom was your son. He was killed instantly by a bomb and died a gallant death. I saw him only a few minutes before; he was then very cheerfully carrying out his duty. He was buried together with his comrade by a Chaplain and a neat tombstone marks the spot where he lies. May I offer you my deepest sympathy in your loss and please believe me. Yours Very Sincerely".*

Corporal Ison II.C.10 and Private Gutteridge II.G.8 died as a result of the bomb attack and are buried in Guards Cemetery, Windy Corner, Cuinchy.

Three men commemorated in the War Memorial Park died on the first day of the Battle of Loos, the 25th September 1915. Private Frederick Grant, C Company, 5th Battalion Oxfordshire and Buckinghamshire Light Infantry, Private Henry Bartlett, 1st Battalion, Northamptonshire Regiment and Second Lieutenant Theo Edward Newsome, 2nd Battalion, Royal Warwickshire Regiment.

Private **Frederick Grant** was the husband of Rose Hannah (nee Benny) and resided at 7 Court, 5 House, Much Park Street, Coventry. The couple had one child. Frederick was born at Quorndon, Leicestershire and was employed by Siddeley Deasy Motors Ltd. He had been in France just over a month arriving on the 19th August 1915. Private Grant's obituary appeared in *'The Coventry Graphic'* of October 1915 and he is commemorated on the Menin Gate.

Private **Henry Bartlett,** 1st Battalion, Northamptonshire Regiment was killed in action at Loos on the 25th September 1915. He was born on the 23rd August 1891 in Coventry but resided at Northampton. Prior to the war he was employed in the Turnery Department of the Rudge works as a fitter; his father Mr J. Bartlett was also employed at Rudge but in the aeroplanes Parts Department. Private Bartlett enlisted in December 1914 originally with the Royal Army Medical Corps but was attached to the 1st Battalion, Northamptonshire Regiment.

'The Coventry Graphic' dated May 7th 1915 detailed how Private Bartlett of 80 Paynes Lane, had helped uphold the traditions of his Regiment as he participated in the desperate fighting which checked the German rush on Paris and the German attempt to reach Calais. During a bayonet charge in the German trenches he was wounded in the arm. The subsequent trench warfare under awful conditions of rain and cold undermined his health with the result that he developed rheumatic fever and was invalided home. He recovered sufficiently to perform light duties and was sent back to the front. Private Bartlett has no known grave and is commemorated on the Loos Memorial.

Second Lieutenant **Theo Edward Newsome.,** 2nd Battalion, Royal Warwickshire Regiment was killed in action at Loos aged 21 on the 25th September 1915. A native of Coventry he was born on the 24th February, 1894 to Samuel Theo and Kate Newsome of Fairhill, Warwick Road, Coventry Theo was the eldest son and resided close to his parents in Oaklands, Belvedere Road. His father, formerly the head of a watchmaking factory, had become the Managing director of the Coventry Hippodrome.

Theo was educated at King Henry VIII prior to studying at Birmingham University. Upon leaving University he went to the Daimler company to whom he was articled and was in their employ when he enlisted on August 8th 1914. He was sent out to France with the first batch of Daimler cars and lorries, less than a week later on August the 14th.

In late September he wrote to one of his former teachers, stating he was enjoying the work and was hoping to transfer permanently to the motor cycle staff. Shortly after reaching the front he was attached to the motor transport of the army transport corps engaged as a dispatch rider to his colonel and later acted as a consulting engineer to the 4th division of transports. In December 1914 he was promoted to corporal. Theo transferred again to the Artists' Rifles and received his commission from the Brigadier General. In the summer of this year, he chose the 2nd Battalion Royal Warwickshire Regiment and took up a position with the Regiment on July the 26th.

Having celebrated his 21st birthday in February at the Front, he came home for a period of three to four days leave in August for the benefit of his health. This was his first leave since August 1914 and he promptly went back to the front on completion of his leave.

On the 25th September 1915 the Battalion's general headquarters were at Noyelles. The enemy's positions were bombarded and the advance commenced at 6.30am. The attacking force took the German front line trench, then the support trench and moved on to the Quarries as far as St. Elie. About sixty prisoners were captured and this position was reached at 9.30am. The occupation of the quarries was kept until midnight when the Battalion took up a retiring position in the support trench 400 yards west of the Quarries. This was due to the 9th Division on their left retiring.

During the day the Battalion lost 8 officers killed including Second lieutenant Newsome, with 10 officers wounded and 1 missing. Other ranks suffered 64 killed, with 171 wounded and 273 missing. The Battalion could only muster 1 officer and 140 men at the end of the day.

A telegraph received by the family stated he was killed between the 25th and 27th September. Additionally his Father received a letter from A. G. Pritchard the Commander of the 2nd Battalion stating *"I have only recently taken up command of the 2nd Battalion, and therefore do not know the Regiment well and never met your son. Those officers who knew him miss him very much. He was one of the right sort. It may be slight consolation to you to know that he was very popular and he died gallantly"*. News of his death was also announced in *'The Coventry Herald'* as follows: *"He fell in the Loos battle, his death will come as a blow for the many people in Coventry who knew him for he was a bright and intelligent young man and much esteemed. Whilst articled at Daimler he entered for the £200 scholarship offered by the firm and had the distinction of winning it. He was a member of Coventry and Warwickshire motor club and was a very keen rider attending regularly all the club events in peace time. The club has a roll of honour of 36 members , several have been wounded, but Lieutenant Newsome is the first to be lost".*

None of the men killed on the first day of the Battle of Loos and commemorated in the War Memorial Park have a known grave. Private Grant is commemorated on the Menin Gate. Private Jones, Private Bartlett and Second Lieutenant Newsome are commemorated on the Loos Memorial.

Lance Corporal George Percy Warner , B Company and Private Frederick Henry Mence, 1st/7th Battalion Royal Warwickshire Regiment were killed in action together at Foncquevillers on the 8th October 1915.

Lance Corporal **George Percy Warner** was the son of William Horne and Elizabeth Warner and resided with them at 145 Station Street East, Coventry. He was born on the 11th of November, 1893 at Halstead, Essex and was employed in the City as a printer prior to enlisting in November 1914. George was the brother of Eric and Stanley Warner who also have plaques in the War Memorial Park.

The Plaques of the Warner Family

Private Frederick Henry Mence was the son of Frederick Henry and Mary Elizabeth Mence and resided with them at 35 Priory Street, Coventry. He was born on the 27th June 1893 at Coventry and employed as an engineer prior to enlisting in August 1914. Early in May 1915 he was wounded at the front and removed to a base hospital. A label on a parcel sent out to him was marked *"Unable to trace"* and *"Hospital"*. Frederick recovered sufficiently to be able to write a letter in which he states *"'We had a very hard time last Sunday, having two killed and eleven wounded. I was one of the lucky ones being wounded in the head and right eye. I have been in four hospitals and am about to be moved again. There are many Coventry fellows here and it feels nice to see men from the Old spot"*.

On the 8th October, the 1/7th Battalion relieved the 1/8th Battalion, Royal Warwickshire Regiment in Foncquevillers trenches, the relief being completed at 3.15pm. Between 9.00pm and 9.30pm, the enemy fired nine 200lb Minenwerfer. *'The Battalion War Diary'* notes *"One pitched in front line trench killing four men and wounding an additional five. Killed along with Lance Corporal Warner and Private Mence were Privates George Alfred Wright and John Harold Birtwhistle. Wounded in the attack were Privates Clarke, Lewis, Brady, Osborne and Nichols. No other damage was reported"*.

Those killed are buried in Foncquevillers Military Cemetery. Private Mence is buried in Plot I, Row D, Grave 24 , Lance Corporal Warner is nearby in Grave 26, Private Wright Grave 23 and Private Birtwhistle Grave 22. In addition Private Mence's names appears on the Holy Trinity panels.

Lance Corporal **Isaac Norman Price,** 1st/6th Battalion, South Staffordshire Regiment was killed in action at Loos aged 19 on the 13th October 1915. Isaac's father was also called Isaac and his mother was Mary Price. The family lived at 43 Churchill Avenue, Coventry. Isaac was born on the 22nd of March 1896 at Worksop and resided in Coventry employed as an engineer although he enlisted in Wolverhampton in August 1914. He has no known grave and is commemorated on the Loos Memorial.

1916

Four days into 1916 saw the death of **Herbert Charles Collingbourne,** a Gunner with the 1st Warwick Battery, Royal Horse Artillery (RHA), who had responsibility for the light mobile guns. Gunner Collingbourne was in the Coventry section of the Warwickshire RHA, during their first fourteen months of action in France they had been immune from casualties, but this excellent and fortunate record had to be sacrificed as the result of a bombardment when several Coventry men were injured by the bursting of a high explosive shell. The battery was the first territorial regiment to go to France arriving there on November 1st 1914, they claimed they had been more in action than any other battery and were complemented on their splendid work by General French. The incident occurred when the man sought safety in an old cellar protected by sandbags, one of the enemy shells forced its way through the structure and according to local papers *"played havoc amongst the men"*.

An account of the disastrous bombardment was given in a letter from Gunner Croydon who in writing home says :-" *We all went down a cellar for safety because they were shelling us. And as soon as we got down there one of the 5.9 shells came in and burst. The result was bricks and bits of shrapnel were flying all over the place. About six of us got hurt, Fletcher, Short, Collingbourne, Barklett and myself. I believe Chattaway was hit but I don't know, (Spot) Phillips was not there at all so was not hurt thank God. I was the only one able to stand so got out and went for help. I believe I am on my way for England but don't know. I must look funny. I was hit in the face and you can only see one eye and enough of my mouth to but a fag in. The nurses are very good to me and the Doctor is a Leamington man (Dr. Gibbons Ward, Medical Officer of health for Leamington is one of the best). I am on a barge on the canal on the way to the coast. Chattaway it is believed is seriously hurt".*

The Chattaway referred to was Herbert Walter, the son of Architect of the City who had attended King Henry VIII, later reports advised he was seriously injured, but a successful operation was performed and he was visited in hospital in France by his father. Other reports suggested Gunner Richard Hunt Croydon also a former King Henry VIII pupil and son of Mr. Richard Croydon was brought back to Colchester Hospital. The other men who were injured and well known locally were Collingbourne, Short, Traherne (probably Herbert Leslie a former King Henry's pupil from Chapelfields) and Reginald Fletcher.

Herbert also known as 'Bert' was treated at the hospital centre in St. Omer. The extent of his wounds ultimately led to his death and he was buried in Longuenesse (St. Omer) Cemetery. The General headquarters of the British Expeditionary Force (BEF) were based at St. Omer until March 1916. Herbert was one of five children, the son of David Charles and Sarah Jane Collingbourne, of 52, Nicholas Street, Coventry. He was born on the 9th May 1892 in Colchester Street, Coventry and resided at 41 King Richard Street.

A territorial Herbert chose to enlist in Leamington in 1914, swapping his uniform from that of a telegraphist and sorter at the Post Office to that of the RHA. His brother George also served with the RHA as a Sergeant and survived the war. Herbert had been home on a short leave in August 1915. His family paid for his plaque, his name also appears on the Post Office Memorial and the Bablake School Memorial.

Private **George Edward Everest,** C Company, 1st Battalion, Bedfordshire Regiment died aged 28 on the 23rd January 1916. He was born in Woolwich and resided at 21 Stanley Street, Foleshill with his parents William and Susannah Everest and enlisted in St. Albans. At the start of January 1916, the Battalion were in billets at Bray Sur Somme. The following day they relieved the Norfolks in a subsector and throughout the coming weeks they were engaged in mining fatigues, cutting the enemy's wire and reconnaissance. The Battalion returned to their billets on January the 22nd. On the following day, C Company were sent on mining fatigue and whilst carrying out this task, Private Everest lost his life. He was the only casualty on this day and is buried in Citadel New Military Cemetery, Fricourt.

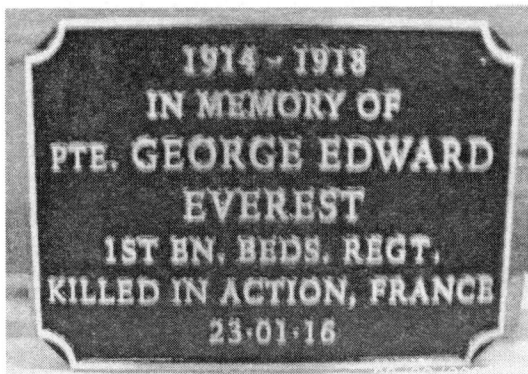

1914 - 1918
IN MEMORY OF
PTE. GEORGE EDWARD
EVEREST
1ST BN. BEDS. REGT.
KILLED IN ACTION, FRANCE
23·01·16

Lance Sergeant **Henry Smith Craven,** 6th Battalion, The Buffs (East Kent Regiment) was killed in action at Givenchy aged 24 on the 6th March 1916. Henry was born on the 22nd February, 1892 in St. Peter's Parish and lived with his parents at 27 Spencer Street, Coventry. He started his education at St. Peter's Elementary School before attending Bablake School. Whilst at Bablake he excelled in batting and also played football gaining praise as a splendid tackler. He secured a boy clerkship in the civil service and by working part time for a Scottish newspaper, paid for his younger sister to go to Barrs Hill School until she was old enough to secure a scholarship.

He conceived a great desire to be at the opening of the panama canal and managed to get there by working his way as a purser on the Orduna, the opening was delayed and on the return journey war was declared. Harry was responsible for announcing this in four languages as the ship zigzagged across the Atlantic to avoid the German submarines. On his return he was eager to enlist and did so at Canterbury in October 1914. Whilst a Corporal he was wounded and returned home.

He returned to France, by this time he had become engaged to Miss Carrie Morgan, and was promoted to Lance Sergeant. The *'Historical Records'* for the 6th Battalion show they were involved in securing a large crater near Hohenzollern Redoubt. Henry has no known grave and is commemorated on the Loos Memorial and on the Bablake School Memorial.

The following two men, Gunner Jenkins and Private Cooke are not only commemorated in the War Memorial Park but also on a stained glass memorial in Queens Road Church. As the men died so close together a combined memorial service was held in one of the early morning classes held at the church.

Gunner **George Reginald Jenkins,** 4th Battery, Royal Field Artillery died at Hebuterne, aged 20 on the 14th March 1916. *'The Coventry Graphic'* reported he was accidentally killed and his plaque states that he died of wounds. George was the son of Alfred and Sarah Ann Jenkins, of 141 Hearsall Lane, Chapelfields, he was born on the 15th May at Coventry. Employed as a sign writer at Messrs Hamilton, sign writers of Coventry, he resided at 46 Craven Street and enlisted in August, 1914. George is buried in Beauval Communal Cemetery and was probably treated at the 4th Casualty Clearing Station.

Private **William Frederick Cooke,** A Company, 1st/7th Battalion, Royal Warwickshire Regiment was mortally wounded at Foncquevillers aged 21 on the 17th March 1916. William was born in October 1894, at St. Stevens, Hounslow to Thomas William and Eleanor Eliza Cooke and resided with them at 13 Lord Street, Chapelfields. He was an Engineering Apprentice to Coventry Chain Company, enlisted in August 1914 and was well known in local sporting circles. He was at one point the secretary of the works cricket club and in the winter months he was a player for the Queen's Road Football club.

The *'Battalion War Diary'* shows that on the 17th March 1916 the Battalion were subject to intermittent shelling. A bomb landed near A Company slightly wounding four men and mortally wounding Private Cooke. He was the only Battalion fatality on this day and is buried in Foncquevillers Military Cemetery. His comrade and chum wrote a letter to the family and explained the way in which William had died *"We were in the trenches just after midnight and the men of the machine gun section of which I was in charge were talking together. We were in the best of spirits when without warning a rifle grenade came from the German lines and burst amongst us. Five of the boys including William were struck with fragments of the grenade. Private Cooke died an hour after his arrival at the ambulance station and did not once complain. He was laid to rest in the cemetery here today and the funeral was attended by the Colonel, Lieutenant Jagger (officer commanding the machine gun section) and a great many friends".*

William's father was a Sergeant Major and rendered service with the local Battalion of the 7th Royal Warwickshire Regiment. The family received many letters of condolence upon the death of William. Another brother also died in service for his country. Locally William is commemorated on the Coventry Chain Memorial and on the stained glass panels in Queen's Road Church.

Private **Ernest Lumbert**, 27th Battalion Canadian Infantry (Manitoba Regiment) was initially reported as missing, and then confirmed as being killed at St. Eloi, Belgium aged 33 on the 4th April 1916. Ernest was born on the 15th November 1882, at Birmingham and was the son of Clara Lumbert, of The Hawthorns, Harefield Road, Stoke, Coventry.

Ernest emigrated to Winnipeg, Canada at the age of nineteen and held a position in the post office. Prior to emigrating he resided at Claremont, Northumberland Road and worked in the City as a postal clerk and was also actively engaged in local athletics. Ernest was considered fit for joining the Canadian Infantry on the 26th October 1914 and had previously experienced army life as a volunteer with the 2nd Warwicks. His *'Attestation Papers'* note he was 5' 8" tall, had a 40" chest, brown hair, cited his religion as Church of England and was a bachelor.

On the 3rd of April 1916, two platoons of C Company along with B and D companies left their billets at 5.00pm to relieve the 1st Gordons and the King's Own regiment to take over captured trenches in front of St. Eloi. During the night of the 4th the trenches were subjected to a terrific artillery bombardment which resulted in 13 other ranks being killed and 46 men wounded. Private Lumbert has no known grave and is commemorated on the Menin Gate.

Private **Joseph Peddie**, 1st Battalion, North Staffordshire Regiment was killed in action aged 42 on the 30th April 1916. He was married to Mary Peddie and lived at 67, High Street, Bucknall, Stoke on Trent. He was also born in Stoke on Trent. Joseph was employed at the Siddeley Deasy works, resided in Coventry and enlisted in Nuneaton. Joseph is buried in Dranoutre Military Cemetery, Belgium. This cemetery was used by fighting units and field ambulances until March 1918, many of the burials being carried out by the 72nd Brigade (24th Division) in April-June 1916.

Private **Charles Edward Mann**, 2nd Battalion, Royal Warwickshire Regiment died of wounds aged 23 on the 24th May 1916 and is buried in Corbie Communal Cemetery Extension. Charles was born in Harbury to John and Laura Mann, of 1 Ufton, Southam, Warwickshire and enlisted in Warwick. The *'Battalion War Diary'* shows that on the 24th May 1916, *"A company proceeded to trenches and relieved C company in the front line; one other rank was wounded"*.

Pioneer **Sidney Arthur Abel,** Corps of Royal Engineers (formerly G/11742, Middlesex Regiment, 1st Battalion Special Brigade) was killed in action by being gassed on the Somme on the 26th June 1916 aged 20. Whilst attached to the Royal Engineers he was badly gassed owing to a shell bursting a pipe through which asphyxiating gas was being discharged. His death took place only a few hours afterwards. On receipt of his injuries he was probably treated at a field ambulance but they were unable to save him and he is buried in Louvencourt Military Cemetery. A touching reference was made to this sad event by the Reverend J. E. Thomas of Warwick Road Church at a service in July 1916. Sidney was born on the

8th February 1896 at Brighton to Sidney and Mary Eliza Abel, and resided with them at 92 Widdrington Road, Coventry. His brother Frederick Cecil Abel also died in the war on the 20th June 1917 and also has a plaque in the War Memorial Park. Prior to the war, Sidney was employed in the City as a brass finisher until enlisting in December 1915 at Harlesden, Middlesex.

The Battle of the Somme started on the 1st July 1916, thirteen divisions launched an offensive on a line from North of Gommecourt to Maricourt. Prior to the start of the battle, an intense artillery bombardment pounded the German lines for seven days with the intention of eliminating any likely resistance. When zero hour came on the 1st July at 7.30am, the men went over the top and worked at a steady pace towards the enemy positions. In spite of the shelling many of the German positions were unscathed and were able to open fire with machine guns on the advancing masses which were met with this unexpectedly fierce resistance. Ground that was gained initially was lost over the coming days. In the first few days of the Somme the British Army lost over 52,000 troops. The Commonwealth War Graves Commission attributes 18,721 deaths on this day.

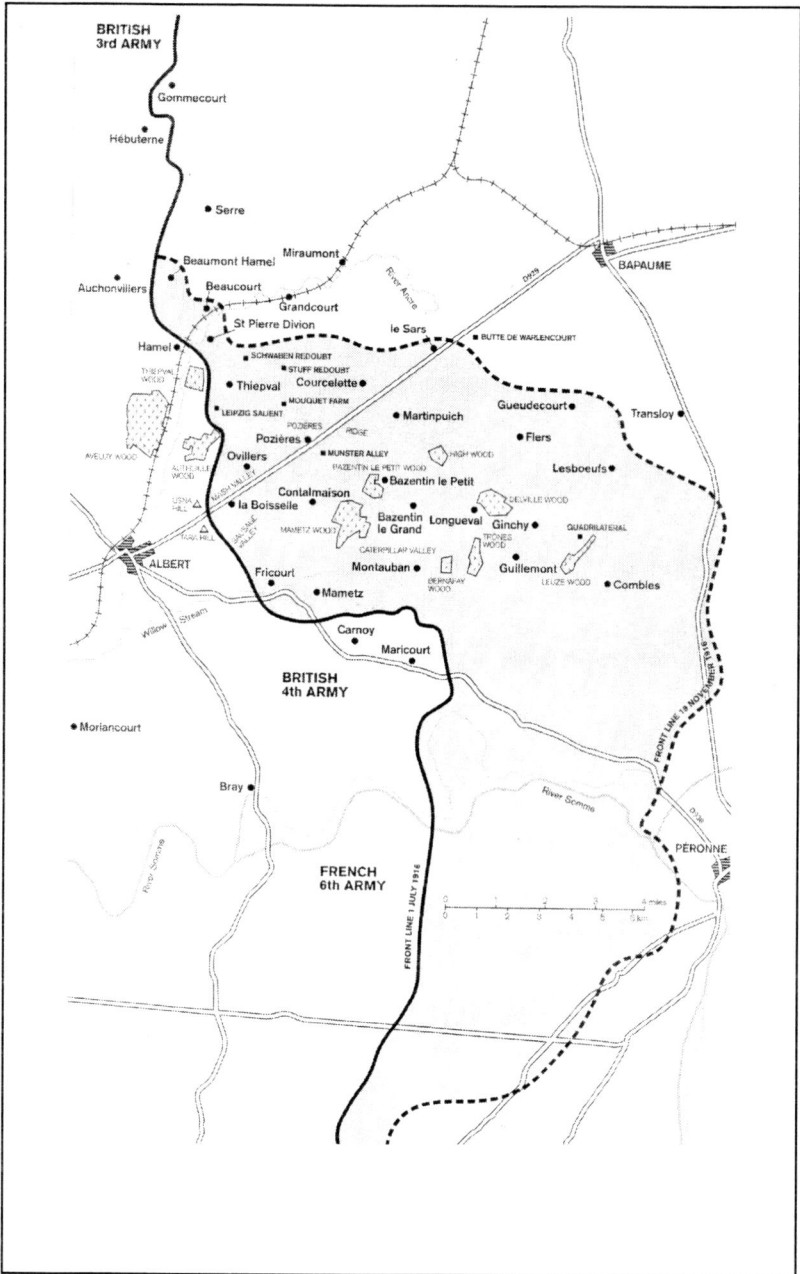

Map of the Somme

Private **Eric Keppell Purnell,** 1st/6th Battalion Royal Warwickshire Regiment was reported as missing and subsequently presumed killed on the 1st July 1916. Eric was born on the 6th January, 1887 at Kenilworth to E. J. and A. Purnell of Coventry. He was educated at King Henry VIII and became a tailor's manager, resided at 20 Sir Thomas White's Road prior to enlisting in October 1915.

The 'Battalion War Diary' states "*the Battalion left their assembly trenches at 7.40am, 10 minutes after the 1st/8th Battalion Royal Warwickshire Regiment who had left at the zero hour of 7.30am. About eighty men were killed before crossing the British lines. On reaching the German Lines the Battalion mingled with the 1/8th Royal Warwickshire Regiment and worked up as far as the third line. The first and second wave Battalions on the right had advanced no further than this and the 31st Division on the left had units which reached Serre. The enemy's opposition was a well distributed barrage and severe cross machine gun fire.*

The 12th Infantry Brigade followed but were unable to advance further than the line held by the 11th Infantry Brigade. The one officer unhit, Second Lieutenant J. G. Cooper returned with a message to Brigade Headquarters between 11.00am and 12.00am.The line which was being consolidated was severely pressed on the flanks and the Battalion were forced to withdraw; the few remaining men were sent back to our lines about 7.00pm. All that could be collected were taken back to Mailly at Midnight. The estimated casualties were 120 killed with a further 316 missing or wounded". Private Purnell is commemorated on the Thiepval Memorial and the King Henry VIII School Memorial.

Gunner **Frederick Stanley Shepperd,** 4th South Midland Howitzer Brigade, Royal Field Artillery was killed in action on the second day of the Battle of the Somme, age 21. He was the son of Mrs E. M. Shepperd, and lived with his mother at 67, Broomfield Road, Coventry. Frederick was born on the 31st December, 1894, at 52 Winchester Street and employed as an engineer until enlisting in late 1914. He is commemorated on the Thiepval Memorial but his family received notification that he was buried in Carnoy Military Cemetery. This cemetery contains 850 graves, thirty are unidentified, seventeen soldiers are known to be amongst them.

Sapper **Percy John (Jack) Francis,** 90th Field Company, Royal Engineers was killed in action at Montauban age 31 on the 3rd July 1916. He was killed with two comrades whilst working on the defences of a village which had been recently stormed and taken. His parents were landlords at the Fox and Vixen, Gosford Street. Percy was born on the 7th August, 1886 at 46 Howard Street and resided in Wolverhampton where he was employed as a fitter with Sunbeam. Prior to this he served an apprenticeship at Daimler and was a Freeman of the City. He enlisted in October, 1914 and is buried in Quarry Cemetery, Montauban. This cemetery was begun in July 1916 at an advanced dressing station.

Sergeant **William Toms** was killed on the 3rd July aged 24. Sergeant Toms was married to Mrs. M. A. Toms and resided with his wife at 190, Spon Street, Coventry. Born in Coventry on 14th February 1892 he was employed in the city as an elementary school teacher, before enlisting in September 1914 at Oxford. This probably influenced his decision and he joined the 2/4th Battalion Oxfordshire and Buckinghamshire Light Infantry. The first part of his education was spent at St. Michael's Elementary School; he then spent four years at Bablake before going to Culham Training College.

He is buried at Laventie Military Cemetery, La Gorgue. After the armistice a number of graves were removed from other burial grounds and re-interred in this cemetery. Billets were placed at Laventie as it was approximately two miles from the front line, this area was however subject to shelling as it came within range of the German field guns. William's name is on the Bablake Memorial and on a plaque in the Council House to those who fell from the Education Department.

Sergeant **Arthur Day,** 1st Battalion Worcestershire Regiment went missing, assumed killed age 34 between the 6th of July 1916 and the 10th of July 1916. He was the son of John and Annie Day, of Belbroughton, Stourbridge and husband of Mary Day of 67 Kingston Road, Coventry. Arthur was born on the 6th October, 1881 at Belbroughton. A reservist, he was employed as a storekeeper at Siddeley Deasy.

The 1st Battalion were attached to 23rd Division during this time and he probably fell with them during the assaults on Contalmaison. This is directly North West of Mametz Wood, which was in front of the German second line on the 1st July 1916 and was an objective of 34th Division that day. The assaults failed with large losses and during the next few days more efforts were made.

Over the period Sergeant Day went missing the Battalion attacked North East from Shelter Wood and to the left of Pearl Alley (the South West to North East side of the four-sided Quadrangle trench system) and in to Contalmaison, receiving heavy casualties from machine gun fire before reaching the village. The Battalion were engaged in fierce hand-to-hand combat in the cellars and houses, making it to the area of the church where they tried to dig in. The Germans appeared to have shelled their own line and the attackers indiscriminately at this time and the 1st Battalion had to withdraw as they were out of bombs and low on ammunition. The 1st Battalion had been fighting alongside the 2nd Battalion, East Lancashire Regiment and to this point both battalions had lost 800 officers and other ranks. The final effort by the 1st Battalion was on the 8th September when they again were unable to gain ground. Sergeant Day has no known grave and is commemorated on the Thiepval Memorial, many men were buried where they fell and subsequent attacks and shelling destroyed the graves or lost the markers.

Also commemorated on the Thiepval Memorial is Private **Frank Ellis Hattersley**, 8th Battalion, South Lancashire Regiment who was killed in action at the Battle of the Somme aged 27 on the 15th July 1916. Frank was the adopted son of W. H. and Polly Hattersley and resided with them at 253, Swan Lane, Coventry. He was born on the 25th February 1889 in Sheffield and employed in Coventry as a mechanic before enlisting in Birmingham in May 1915.

The 8th Battalion embarked for France in September 1915 and on arrival they were concentrated in the Armentieres area. As winter set in they carried out tours of duty with no outstanding incidents to report. At the beginning of January 1916, the Battalion were in the line near Creslus Farm and moved to billets in Ploegsteert Wood by the 6th January. In February they moved to rest billets at Courtecroix carrying out company training. In March the Battalion, along with the rest of the 25th Division, moved further south to Marquay in corps reserve and remained there until April 28th when they moved to take over a section of the line due east of Neuville St. Vaast. Here the Battalion were subjected to various forms of German activity, shelling and grenades until the 5th May when they were relieved by the 2nd Battalion and moved back to their billets.

The Battalion moved to prepare for the Battle of the Somme and by the 1st July the Battalion were at Hedauville having marched in short stages; these movements

149

were mostly by night to hide the concentration of troops. During the first week of the battle the Battalion did not go into battle but were in reserve with the 75th Brigade near Aveluy wood. On the afternoon of the 7th July the Battalion moved forward in readiness for an attack of the enemy's defence south of Ovillers and north of La Boisselle.

At 11.30pm the position was reached and at 4.00am the following morning an advance was made practically without opposition. During the day further advances were made and the Battalion were on the outskirts of Ovillers having made contact with the Royal Sussex on the left and 11th Lancashire Fusiliers on the right.

On the 9th of July local attacks were made to capture centres of resistance that were holding up the advance and the Battalion was subjected to shelling as the Germans ranged on the position. The following day the Battalion retired until the night of the 12th and 13th July when two companies were called in to support the capture of Ovillers. On the 14th and 15th of July the Battalion stood by, to advance and establish touch with the advancing troops on the right. This did not happen due to the resistance of the enemy. The Battalion held on to its position in the ruins of Ovillers despite counter attacks by the crack Prussian Guard Fusiliers. Private Hattersley is not only commemorated on the Thiepval Memorial but is also commemorated in the *'Regimental Book Of Remembrance'* for the South Lancashire Regiment which records 5,428 names.

Sergeant **Thomas Yates** MM, 11th Battalion, Royal Warwickshire Regiment died on the 9th July 1916. He was born in Holborn, Middlesex, and was employed by Siddeley Deasy Motors Ltd, Coventry and enlisted near his home in Warley, Middlesex. Thomas has no known grave and is commemorated on the Thiepval Memorial, news of his Military Medal appeared in the London Gazette on the 8th August 1916 and was probably awarded at the beginning of 1916.

The *'Battalion War Diary'* shows that on the 8th July, they were near Albert. At 2.30pm on the 9th, the *'Diary'* states *"a patrol of B company, reconnoitered the ground leading to Contalmaison Wood and found three abandoned 77mm guns and also made three prisoners in the battery dugout. Half a platoon was left to hold the battery position. Many useful maps were also found , one marking the defences of Ovillers on the Battalion's left, still held by the enemy. During the afternoon the Battalion's position was heavily shelled. The detachment guiding the guns being partially surrounded was withdrawn. Heavy shell fire (chiefly 150mm) on the Battalion's position continued throughout the night. The Battalions casualties during the day were four officers wounded, other ranks ten killed and eighty six wounded mostly from shell fire".*

Private **Leonard Joseph Worrall,** 8th Battalion, South Staffordshire Regiment enlisted in September 1914 and was killed in the Battle of the Somme on the 10th July 1916. He was born on the 26th August 1896 in Coventry and resided in Birmingham. Prior to the outbreak of war he worked in the GEC Witton Works as an Electrical engineer in the switchgear Department where he had been for a period of about six months prior to his enlistment. 252 men from the GEC lost their lives during the war and the *'GEC Roll of Honour'* states *"He was killed in action in the advance on the 1st July 1916".* His death is officially recorded as the 10th July 1916.

The 14th of July 1916 was to account for the loss of six men with the 1st/7th Battalion, Royal Warwickshire Regiment who are commemorated in the War Memorial Park. Second Lieutenant Henry Acton Bullock, Private Lawrence Cecil Cox, Private Percy Elliman, Private Albert Jeffs, Private Edward Ernest Waring and Private James William Wilcox.

The *'Battalion War Diary'* notes; *"the 13th of July was a fine and warm day and the Battalion were based at Bouzincourt. At 1.30pm the Battalion moved by motor lorries to just outside Bouzincourt. From there, they moved in fighting order to Albert where they lay down in a field until midnight, having had orders that the Battalion would attack North East of La Boisselle at 7.30am.*

On the 14th July the Battalion moved into position in trenches and were heavily shelled going into La Boisselle. At 7.30am after artillery preparation A and B Companies proceeded to assault and reached their objective. Many casualties resulted chiefly from machine guns the following officers being killed: Lieutenant Bullock and the following attached officers of the 3rd Dorset Regiment, Second Lieutenant Jones, Second Lieutenant Baker and Second Lieutenant Forman. The Battalion held the trench for seven hours but they had to evacuate it on account of the enemy's extremely heavy enfilade fire both shell and machine guns. Lieutenant Colonel Knox who lead the attack and who had shown the greatest bravery throughout was wounded later. Major Hanson then took command of the Battalion. The casualties were estimated at 150 of whom 68 were reported killed".

Second Lieutenant **Henry Acton Linton Bullock,** BA, was born on the 6th January, 1885 at Coventry and resided in Coundon Road with his parents, Frederick and Lousie. He was initially educated at King Henry VIII School from 1895 to 1903 and won a scholarship to attend St. John's College, Oxford. Whilst at Oxford, he was a member of the college debating society and gained a 2nd Class degree in Natural Science, Chemistry in 1906. Four years later, he passed the final examinations of the law society and like his father, a partner with Messrs Goate and Bullock ,became a well-known solicitor. He enlisted in May 1915 and his obituary appeared in local papers and in College publications. He has no known grave and is commemorated on the Thiepval Memorial and St. John's Church; the 'City *of Coventry: Roll of The Fallen'* hints he was buried near Pozières.

Second Lieutenant Henry Acton Linton Bullock on the right

His youngest brother, Second Lieutenant Rowland William Bullock (pictured left) was also a former King Henry VIII pupil and head of the school at the time of leaving. Rowland was articled to Mr. Dadley, chartered accountant and enlisted seven months before his brother, in October 1914, with the Army Service corps Motor Transport (ASCMT) He accepted a commission to the 2nd/7th Royal Warwickshire Regiment. A few months later. Whilst with this Regiment he was wounded and survived the war.

Private **Lawrence Cecil Cox,** B Company was killed in action age 25. He was the eldest son of Richard and Lavinia Cox, of 4, Inchley's Buildings, King William Street, Coventry. Lawrence was born on the 6th May, 1891, at Nuneaton and had six siblings the youngest being Mary Ethel Cox who was born on the 18th January 1907. Lawrence was married on the 26th December 1914 and lived with his wife Gertrude Muriel Cox (nee Arnold), in Pridmore Road. Lawrence enlisted in October 1915 and prior to this was a manager at Foleshill Co-Operative store.

Private Cox has no known grave and is commemorated on the Thievpal Memorial although it is suggested he is buried at Ovillers Cemetery. His plaque was paid for by his mother, Lavinia. He is pictured below with his wife.

Private Cox pictured with his wife

Private **Percy Elliman** was born on the 28th January, 1888 in Stoke, Coventry and resided at 31 Moor Street, Earsldon. He enlisted in September 1914 and was employed as a chain finisher at Coventry Chain Company. A member of Well Street Congregational Church he left a widow and one child. He was pictured in '*The Coventry Graphic*' of November 17th 1916 with his brothers, Corporal Horace J. Elliman (middle), 13th Battalion, Royal Warwickshire Regiment and Private Matthew Elliman (right)2/7th Durham Light Infantry.

The Elliman Brothers

It was stated in this article that Percy had died in the "big push" and that his parents also had nine nephews serving in the army, a tenth had been killed. Private Elliman is commemorated on the Thiepval Memorial and more locally on the Coventry Chain Memorial and in St. Barbara's Church.

Private **James William Wilcox,** was the brother of Mrs S. J. Baynes, of Senyab, Binley Road, Coventry. He was born on the 17th February, 1890, in Old Tower Yard, Cook Street and resided at 27, Mount Street. He enlisted at the outbreak of war and prior to this was employed as a wood machinist. Like his comrades he is commemorated on the Thiepval Memorial and on the memorial to the men from Coventry Chain.

Private **Albert Jeffs** was killed in action age 22. The son of Harry Jeffs and Hannah Jeffs (formerly Booton) of 77 Newcombe Road, Coventry he was born on the 21st February, 1894 in St. John's Parish. Albert resided close to his parents at 6 Broomfield Terrace, Spon End and probably knew Private Percy Elliman as both men worked at Coventry Chain although Albert was a chain examiner. Albert enlisted in September 1914, and spent fifteen months in the trenches before going home on leave in June 1916. Albert returned to the front at the end of June and died a few weeks later, the 'Coventry Graphic' stating he died in the "*Great offensive*". Private Jeffs is commemorated on the Thievpal Memorial and on the Coventry Chain memorial.

Also commemorated on the Thiepval Memorial is Private **Ernest Edward Waring**, B Company who died age 28 on the 14th July 1916. He was the son of Joseph Waring of 22, Lamb Street, Coventry and the husband of Ada Waring, of 24, Moat Street, The Butts, Coventry and worked at Siddeley Deasy. Private Waring was featured in *'The Coventry Graphic'* of the 7th May 1915, under a headline of *'Coventry Territorial's Remarkable Escape, Saved by Tobacco Box'*.

The Cigarette Box that saved Private Waring

From the front, Ernest had sent to *'The Coventry Graphic'* a parcel containing a tobacco box, a German bullet and an exciting account of how the tobacco box saved him from being fatally wounded by the bullet. Private Waring said "*I was struck by the bullet on the morning of April 16th and there is little doubt that the box of tobacco saved my life. It happened about 7.00am, we had some trouble with a German sniper ever since daylight, and a very good shot he was. He had hit the top of the sandbags about six times and each time he sent a shower of dirt right into our breakfast. Everyone of his shots hit about the same place. After a time he slackened a little, so I, being the duty sentry at the time, got the periscope to look over the parapet and see if I could locate his position.*

I could not see him, but he must have seen the top of the periscope, for just as I was going to get down to the bottom of the trench a shot came right through the parapet and struck me over the right breast. It hit a tobacco box I was carrying in my pocket, then struck downwards through my two shirts and just caught my ribs. I was bowled clean over. I thought at the time that the bullet had entered my body, as it could not be found. I had to wait all day and until dark before being able to go out and see the doctor; but when he had examined the wound he assured me it was only a scratch. I was able to walk back to our billets (a large barn) and next morning I found the bullet in my sock, where it had fallen during the night"

The photograph included in 'The Coventry Graphic' shows how the bullet ripped up the side of the box. By a fortunate chance the missile struck the box exactly on the narrow strip where the lid overlaps and forms a double layer of metal. The bullet hitting this sideways partly tore it away, but in doing so expended its force. Had the bullet hit the side of the box at right angles it would probably have passed right through and made a severe wound. The tobacco box with the side ripped open by the bullet which is seen beside it is shown on the previous page, the force of the impact split the end of the bullet.

A memento from the war is kept by his relatives in the form of a letter from his mother which was posted to him and subsequently returned to his mother with the words 'killed in action'.

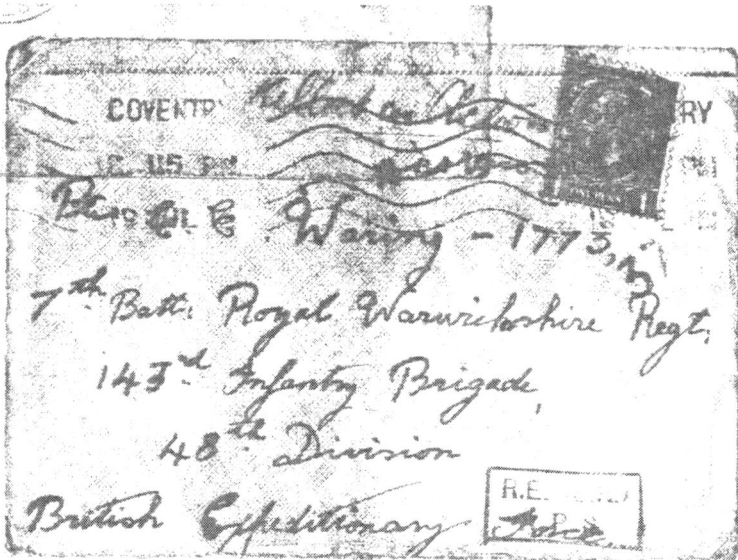

A letter addressed to Private Waring

Private E Waring – 1773
7th Battalion, Royal Warwickshire Regiment
143rd Infantry Brigade,
48th Division,
British Expeditionary Force.

Coventry B.115 PM.
Field Post mark 1st Aug 1916
Warwick post mark 6-Sept-1916
22 Lamb Street,
Coventry.
Dear Ted,
We were all very pleased to get your letter and to know that you have so far escaped any serious injury. I too pray that God in his mercy will bring you and Cyril both home safe and sound. We have not heard from Cyril for more than a fortnight or so. It was cheering to read that you had seen him and that he was well. As you suppose we have read the advances the boys are making.

We think with you it must be the beginning of the end. May it be soon.

I have not seen Ada lately and should like her to come and see me. We could at least try to cheer one another again even if we failed. You know Ted, we do try to be brave but after all we are only women and though we are proud to think you are doing your duty, our hearts ache when we think of the terrible risk your lives are exposed to.

We get news of a few casualties in the papers every night, of local men, and the pity is we shall get more, but still, as you say Ted, we must not get the wind up but wait patiently and hope for the best.

Now with the best wishes from all,

I am your loving mother

Sergeant **John Reddington**, 1st/7th Battalion, Royal Warwickshire Regiment died of wounds on the 18th July 1916. He was born on the 15th February, 1893 in Vauxhall Terrace, East Street and employed at the Rudge Works as an enameller prior to enlisting in August 1914. He spent seven years in the Territorials and after enlisting was appointed as an instructor of recruits. During a five day period of short leave in March 1915 he was married to Miss H. Parkes at Gosford Street Church, Coventry on March 13th and resided with his wife at 12, Hartlepool Road.

The picture on the left appeared in *'The Rudge Record'* and shows John with his wife. *'The Coventry Herald'* from April 1915 featured Mr and Mrs Reddington who had five sons (three of them married), serving in the Army. A picture was published of the five brothers all of them being at work in Coventry factories when war broke out.

Arthur in the centre is the only reservist amongst them; he was aged 26 and called as a reservist in the Coldstream Guards. Arthur came safely through the retreat from Mons and continued to be in hard fighting. By September 1915 he had escaped any injury and formerly served four years in India. He worked for Singer Ltd before going to the front. Top left is Alfred aged 18 who enlisted in the Worcesters in August giving up his job at O' Briens. Bottom left is William the eldest son who joined the 4th South Midland Howitzer Brigade early on, leaving his work at the Sparkbrook.

The Reddington Family

158

Top right is Corporal Jack (22) who had been a Territorial in the Warwicks for some years and left Coventry after the mobilisation. He crossed over to France in March 1915 with the Royal Warwickshire Regiment. Prior to the outbreak of war Jack was employed at Rudge Whitworth. At the bottom right is Herbert, 20, who originally joined the Royal Warwickshire Regiment but was later transferred to the 19th Cycling Corps. Herbert worked at the Humber works prior to enlisting in August 1914. The article also stated Mrs Reddington had a brother and brother in law in the army who were *"keeping fit and well"*.

On the 15th July 1916 at 12.30am a party was assembled for the purpose of capturing or putting out of action a machine gun which was situated South West of Pozières in a small wood on the right of the Albert- Pozières road. The *'Battalion War Diary'* notes *"this party was unable to reach this machine gun emplacement owing to the enemy bombing the party so heavily as to drive them back. The party reported the enemy holding the wood in force. Another party of D company under Second Lieutenant Vincent left our trenches about 1.30am to ascertain whether the enemy's trench opposite was still being held. They returned about 3.00am and reported the trenches were manned. Neither party had many casualties"*.

During the afternoon the Battalion received orders to attack and take the enemy's position on the opposing ridge. At 3.30pm, two platoons of C Company under Lieutenant E. W. Fowler proceeded in two parties to attack. They had scarcely left our trenches when a heavy fire from hostile machine guns was opened on them. The fire was so terrific that only the first leading men were able to leave the trench and these were promptly mown down. Lieutenant E. W. Fowler was killed. The Battalion came out of the line late at night and proceeded to bivouacs in a field near Albert.

On the 16th to the 19th July the Battalion remained in the trenches until relieved in the evening by 1/4th Royal Berkshire Regiment and proceeded to bivouacs at Bouzincourt. During the attack on the machine gun position on the 15th July, Sergeant Reddington was shot down and despite being severely wounded managed to get back to his own lines. *'The Coventry Graphic'* records *"every possible attention was given to him, and he succumbed to his injuries on the 18th July 1916. John also had four brothers who served with the colours. News of his death has come as a great shock to his widow, who lives at 37 Bramble Street, Coventry"*. Sergeant Reddington is buried in Heilly Station Cemetery, Mericourt-L'Abbe.

Private **Alfred John Clarke**, 2/7th Battalion, Royal Warwickshire Regiment was originally posted as missing and then believed killed at the Battle of the Somme on the 19th July 1916. John was born on the 2nd December 1880 in Tile Hill Lane, resided at 18, Junction Street and enlisted in December 1915. He was employed by

Armstrong Siddeley Deasy Motors Ltd and was the husband of Edith Bessie Clarke. Private Clarke is commemorated on the Loos Memorial.

On the 15th July 1916, the 2/7th Battalion were in trenches at Fauquissart. C and D companies were in the front line with A and B companies in reserve. In the morning a smoke attack was ordered for 8.30pm. The *'Battalion War Diary'* states *"some of the Battalion's men were gassed by the Royal Engineers in the afternoon when they turned on the gas taps by mistake"*. The smoke attack occurred as requested at 8.30pm, Second Lieutenant Crombie took out a patrol to see the effect, and found about twenty Germans sitting on their parapet. He promptly bombed them and estimated sixteen were killed. During the smoke attack, machine gun fire was very heavy around the Battalion Headquarters.

On the following day preparations were made for an imminent attack. On the 17th July it was so misty the batteries had been unable to register and the time of the intended attack had not been declared by 11.00am. Orders were received to send two companies to rest, D Company remained in the line with A in reserve. Preparations for the attack were still taking place on the 18th : A company took over from D Company to give them a rest. A company cut the wire opposite two sally posts during the night.

On the 19th of July, B and C companies moved in from Rue Bailleul and Major Welsh took up his position in the front line near the advanced signal station. It was stipulated that only 21 officers were allowed to join the attack which had a zero hour of 6.00pm. The first objective was the enemy's front and support trenches and the second to gain touch with the 2nd/6th Royal Warwickshire Regiment on the left by bombing along the front and support trenches.

At 5.30pm D and C companies got out through two sally posts without being seen and got in front of a low ditch which ran in front of the Battalion's parapet. At 5.50pm the attacking companies were in four waves 50 yards apart with company bombers behind the first wave and Lewis gunners behind the second. The Battalion bombers were behind the third and a section of the 182nd machine gun company behind the fourth. The companies started to move slowly towards the enemy trenches, at the same time B, the support company, moved out ready to advance.

Just after zero hour, the artillery lifted and the leading companies rushed the Germans from about 50 yards. The waves of men went over in perfect order and the final rush from about 40 yards was carried out with great dash. It was impossible to hold the line as the enemy appeared to be in greater strength than anticipated and had more men than the Battalion.

At 8.17pm orders were received to withdraw slowly and by 9.25pm all me who had started the attack had withdrawn and the wounded either came in or were brought in. The losses were 13 officers with 370 other ranks missing or killed. The effective strength was 28 officers and 656 men, though it was noted a number of bodies were still being recovered from no man's land. A report by Lieutenant Crombie timed at 9.45pm stated *"The Germans manned their front line and those who went over first are no more"*.

Second Lieutenant **Alan Percy Charles Loveitt,** 7th Battalion Royal Warwickshire Regiment was killed in action, near Pozières, France age 20 on the 25th July 1916. He was the only son of Mr. and Mrs. Percy George Loveitt (auctioneer and estate agent) of Anlaby, Davenport Road, Coventry. Alan was born on the 26th September 1895, at Kingston-upon-Thames. He was educated at Rugby School, which he entered in 1910 and left in 1914. Alan furthered his education and became an undergraduate at St. John's College, Oxford University.

He entered St. John's College in October 1914 and remained in residence for the academic year, leaving the college at the end of Trinity term in June 1915. Alan's name remained on the College books until his death so he clearly intended to return. Alan enlisted in August 1915 and was commissioned to the Royal Warwickshire Regiment joining them from the Oxford University Training Corps and went to the front in January 1916. The *'Battalion War Diary'* shows he joined the 1/7th Battalion on the 11th March 1916.

On the 25th July 1916 the Battalion were at Bouzincourt. At 2.00am owing to a bombing attack on the Battalion's left the Germans put up a very heavy barrage on the Battalion's trenches which prevented the company from coming up in time to make a planned attack on a known strong point before daylight. This scheme was then abandoned. Second Lieutenant Loveitt was killed by rifle fire whilst reconnoitring the ground in front preparatory to the attack; additional losses would occur throughout the day.

At 9.00am after a short bombardment of a strong post by the Stokes mortars, the Battalion endeavoured to bomb up the trench but owing to the Germans' heavy bombing the Battalion were unable to get past their barricade. About 1.00pm another attack was organised: two stokes guns were ordered to fire on the point for five minutes, bombing parties were to approach as near as possible under cover of the stokes gunfire and were then to rush the trench. Unfortunately for some reason (it is thought owing to the gun sinking in the soft ground) the stokes bombs all fell short and killed about 7 of the Battalion's men and wounded about 10. Naturally this disorganised the bombing parties and all the men were very shaken. At about 8.00pm the Battalion received orders from the Brigade to attack the strong point and take it at all costs. Casualties for this day amounted to approximately 18 killed, 27 wounded and 2 missing.

Second Lieutenant Loveitt has no known grave and is commemorated on the Thiepval Memorial, 'The *Coventry Graphic'* in August 1916 stated *'he fell during the great advance'*. The deceased's father, Mr. P. G. Loveitt, was well-known in the City: for twenty years he was connected with the 2nd Battalion Royal Warwickshire Regiment in which he took the keenest interest, retiring with the rank of Captain.

On the 26th July, Private **Thomas Hogan,** 1st/7th Battalion Royal Warwickshire Regiment was killed in action at Albert age 19. He was born on the 2nd October 1896 to William and Lizzie Hogan of 8, Mill Street, Coventry and resided with them at this address. Thomas was employed in the city as a machinist and enlisted in August 1915. The name T. Hogan appears on the Triumph and Gloria Works Memorial and its likely this is where he worked as a machinist.

At 1.30am on the 26th July 1916, three platoons of D Company with Captain Hoskins and Lieutenant Abbott attacked over the open ground. The other platoon of D Company under Lieutenant Caley bombed along the trench, at the same time a platoon of C Company under Lieutenant Murray bombed along the trench to meet the other parties. All parties arrived at the strong point simultaneously and drove the enemy out capturing about a dozen prisoners, some of whom were wounded. The bombing parties then proceeded up the trench where they got in touch with the Anzacs. The party then pushed on where they drove out a large number of the enemy into the open causing considerable casualties with rifles and bombs and capturing four more prisoners. Two German officers were killed in this trench.

The Germans were then rallied under an officer and prepared for a counter attack. The Battalion's party then withdrew as they had passed their objective. Later a strong point was made and a bombing party proceeded down a trench running due west of that point until held up by machine gun fire, and made a bomb stop. The Battalion were relieved about 2.00pm by the 1/8th Royal Warwicks and went to La Boisselle. Private Hogan died in this attack and he is officially commemorated on the Thiepval Memorial; the *'City of Coventry: Roll of the Fallen'* suggests he is buried at Tulloch Dump, near Pozières.

One of the those who fell in the Battle of the Somme

Also commemorated on the Thiepval Memorial and killed on the 27th July 1916 are Privates Kenneth Barry and Raymond Francis Harrow. With the Battle of the Somme continuing Private **Kenneth Barry**, 23rd Battalion, Royal Fusiliers was killed in action at Deville Wood, on the 27th July 1916 aged 20. He was the son of Oliver Barry (photographer of Process Block books) and Amy Barry of 83 Grafton Street, Coventry. He attended St. Peter's Elementary School and went on to Bablake from 1907 to 1911.

Kenneth continued his education at Manchester University as a student of textiles, he also previously worked as a clerk in a textile works. Kenneth enlisted in February 1916 in Manchester. Following the successful raids of the 14th July the right side of the new British Line was threatened by Deville Wood and uncaptured parts of Longueval village, for attacks to continue these areas needed to be captured. The task originally fell to the South African Brigade starting on the 15th July. After initial gains the Germans counter attacked forcing a withdrawal. Fighting for the wood continued until the 3rd September 1916. A renewed attack was made by the 2nd Division on the 27th July in which Private Barry lost his life. He is commemorated on the Thiepval Memorial and on the Bablake School Memorial; an appeal was made in *'The Coventry Herald'* by his family for any information.

Private **Raymond Francis Harrow** originally enlisted with the Oxfordshire and Buckinghamshire Light Infantry and transferred to the 95th Company, Machine Gun Corps (Infantry). He was born on the 23rd July, 1899 at 4 Berry Street, Coventry and resided with his parents, Robert and Mary Harrow. Raymond was an engineer's apprentice and enlisted in Nuneaton in August 1915 when he was 16 years old. He died shortly after his 17th birthday in the Battle of the Somme.

Sergeant **Oliver Bates,** A Company, 1st/7th Battalion Royal Warwickshire Regiment died of wounds aged 25 on 6th August 1916. He was born on the 26th July, 1891 in St. Michael's Parish to Oliver and Clara Bates and resided at 63 Beaconsfield Road, Stoke, Coventry. Oliver enlisted in September 1914 and was previously employed as a printer.

In April 1915, No 6 Base Supply Depot was started at Calais to help relieve the pressure on Boulogne and to provide a base nearer to the front than Le Havre or Rouen. The 30th, 35th and 38th General Hospitals, No 9 British Red Cross Hospital and No 10 Canadian Stationary Hospital were also stationed in the town. Sergeant Bates would have received treatment at one of these hospitals prior to his death and he is buried in Calais Southern Cemetery, France. This cemetery contains 721 First World War burials. Sergeant Bate's name appears on the memorial in St. Michael's Church.

Private **Thomas Speight Pearson,** 1st/10th Battalion, The King's (Liverpool) Regiment was killed in action in France age 24 on the 9th August 1916. He was the son of Alice and Arthur Pearson, of 68, Fishergate, Preston. Thomas was born in 1892 at Preston, enlisted in Liverpool on the 2nd October 1915. Curiously he gave two addresses,55 Park Road, Coventry and 128 Adelphi Street, Preston. He was employed in Coventry as a traveller. He is commemorated on the Thiepval Memorial.

Private **Charles Clifford Webster,** 14th Battalion, Gloucestershire Regiment died of wounds received in the Battle of the Somme age 20 on the 24th August 1916. He was born on the 8th September, 1895 at Halifax and resided at 6, Rayleigh Road, Coventry. Before enlisting in November 1915 he was employed as a clerk. Charles was the son of Mr. and Mrs. Frederick Webster, who also resided in Coventry. He is buried in Warloy-Baillon Communal Cemetery Extension and commemorated in St. Michael's Church, Coventry. By July 1st 1916, field ambulances had come to Warloy-Baillon in readiness for the attack on the German front line eight kilometres away. The fighting from July to November 1916 on the northern part of the Somme front accounts for the majority of the burials in the extension.

Lieutenant **Geoffrey George Edwin Cash,** 6th Battalion (attached 8th Battalion), The Loyal North Lancashire Regiment was killed in action, near Thievpal, France age 21 on the 27th August 1916. He was born on the 1st January 1885 in Coventry to Sidney and Elsie Cash, of Moat House, Keresley, Coventry. He was an undergraduate at Marlborough College and Magdalen College, Oxford. He entered Magdalen College as an exhibitor in October 1913 and never completed his degree prior to enlisting in August 1914 at the outbreak of war. During his stay at the front he wrote several letters back to the president of Magdalen College, Sir Herbert Warren. Lieutenant Cash is buried at A.I.F Burial Ground, Flers one of 4,000 soldiers whose burials were moved into this cemetery from the battlefields and surrounding areas. He is also commemorated on the Great War tablets near Magdalen's Chapel.

Lieutenant Cash: Pictured on the back row, third from left

Gunner **Alfred George Middleton,** D Battery 240th (South Midland) Brigade, Royal Field Artillery was killed in action near Aveluy, France age 23 on the 27th August 1916. He was born in 1893 at Collycroft, Bedworth and resided at 572 Foleshill Road. Alfred was the third son of Edward (a gas works engine wright) and Rebecca Middleton, of 78 Richmond Street, Stoke, Coventry. He attended Bablake School where he *"gave promise of a very bright future"*. An engineer by profession he enlisted in October 1914 and had been in France about 18 months. He was home on leave at Easter 1915 with his younger brother, Rupert who was a Corporal in the same battery; they both returned looking extremely well. Gunner Middleton prior to enlistment was employed at the Triumph works, was 23 years of age and single. Major Fowler, in writing to the deceased's parents, mentions that *"Alfred was one of the best gunners in the battery and a popular favourite with the officers and men"*. The Chaplain, Reverend Cyril A. Brown, writes *"There is not a man in the battery who does not feel his loss"*.

The story passed down through generations of the family is that he was killed as a result of a shell going off prematurely. He is buried at Aveluy Communal Cemetery, commemorated on the Bablake School Memorial and on the memorial to the sixty seven employees of the Triumph and Gloria Works who gave their lives for liberty in the Great War.

Private **Montague Johnson,** 16th Battalion Royal Warwickshire Regiment was killed in action at the Battle of the Somme age 21 on the 1st September 1916. Montague enlisted in Birmingham during November 1915 and joined the 7th Battalion of the Royal Warwickshire Regiment in January 1916. He was born on the 17th March 1895 in Coventry and resided at 14 Northumberland Road with his parents Herbert Arnold and Fanny Sophia Johnson. At the age of fourteen, he took his degree as a violinist and prior to enlisting worked in the City as a clerk and Professor of violin; he was an associate of the Victoria College of music and was a well known violinist at Public entertainment in the City. His officer writing to his home states *"he was killed instantaneously by a shell on September 1st 1916, whilst under heavy bombardment"*. Private Johnson has no known grave and is commemorated on the Thiepval Memorial and on a stained glass panel in St. John's Church.

Lance Corporal **Walter Bodin,** 1st/7th Battalion, Royal Warwickshire Regiment died of wounds in France on the 4th September 1916; his wounds were received in action on August 19th. Walter was born on the 1st December, 1894, at Dudley and resided at 28 George Street, Coventry. His parents lived at 129, Stoney Stanton Road, Coventry. Prior to enlisting in October 1914 he was employed as an apprentice in a printing works to Messrs, Caldicott and Feltham. Walter is buried in Etaples

Military Cemetery, France and his headstone reads *'Until the day breaks and the shadows flee away'*.

Private **Alexander Ross MacDonald,** 31st Battalion Canadian Infantry (Alberta Regiment) was killed in action at Courcelette age 32 on the 15th September 1916.
He was born in Glasgow on the 13th December 1885 and then moved to Coventry with his parents John and Isabella MacDonald, living at 19 Butts, Coventry. Before emigrating he was employed as an engineer and went on to reside at Lidstone, Canada changing his occupation to that of a farmer. His *'Attestation papers'* show he was certified as fit to enlist on the 15th September 1915. Alexander listed his father as his next of kin and his religion as Presbyterian. He had a dark complexion, blue eyes and dark hair and was 5' 9" tall.

Private MacDonald was killed exactly one year after enlisting. His Battalion were based near Pozières and the attack centred around Courcelette. On the 17th September the casualties for the 15th September were listed in an appendix of *'The Battalion War Diary'*. Private MacDonald's name appears with those of 67 of his comrades; he has no known grave and is commemorated on the Vimy Memorial.

Lieutenant **William Reginald Fitzthomas Wyley,** Royal Field Artillery was killed in action at Ovillers, age 24 on the 19th September 1916. He was born on the 23rd January, 1892 and the only son of William Fitzthomas and Clara Margaret Wyley of Charterhouse, Coventry.

Initially he was educated at Rugby School attending from 1906 to 1910 and on leaving Rugby school he entered Balliol College, Oxford University. He was at Balliol from 1910-1914 and studied Chemistry under Harold Brewer Hartley and David Henry Nagel. The college have no record of his final exam results or of his having taken up his degree. William coxed for the College Torpid, which was head of the river in 1911, played for the College Rugby XV and he was a member of the Oxford University Dramatic Society (OUDS). He also took part in several of the plays, being acting manager for the performance of the 'Acharnians' in 1914.

He was commissioned in November 1913 and enlisted at the outbreak of war. In October 1914 he was pictured in *'The Coventry Graphic'* with members of the Warwickshire Howitzer (the 4th South Midland) Brigade riding past the King. The officer leading in the photograph is Colonel West followed by Trumpeter Shelley, Lieutenant Wyley, Major Fowler, Sergeant Major Coulad and Sergeant Major Cadden.

Riding Past the King

William's obituary at Balliol College states he was *"Small in stature, with quick bright eyes and a merry smile. His keenness and friendliness and his readiness to help in anything, quickly won the affection of his contemporaries. Intellectual work never came very easily to him, but he progressed conscientiously and developed considerably while at Oxford. He threw himself into life at the College, and his cheery presence was a help to many team and crew. He played a plucky game at half-back for the college XV.(1911-1914), and coxed the Torpid that was head of the river in 1911 and the eight in 1911 and 1912.*

Like his father he was a keen territorial and held a commission in the Howitzer Brigade, RFA since November 1913. He was mobilised at the outbreak of war and went to France in March 1915. He served on the Brigade staff until April 1916, when he was appointed adjutant to the 240th Brigade, RFA. He was killed in action by a shell on September 19th, 1916, at Ovillers in the Battle of the Somme and was buried at Aveluy. A soldier by nature, he quickly became a first-rate officer, and the qualities that had endeared him to his Oxford friends speedily won for him the affection of his new comrades".

Colonel Lord Wynford, Commanding the 240th Brigade wrote of him *"whilst he had been my adjutant I had learnt to like the boy immensely and his work, especially lately, had been really excellent.... You may possibly know already what a great favourite he was not only in the brigade, but, I may almost say, right through the artillery of the division, thoroughly high-hearted, always kindly and good humoured and ready to infect others with his cheeriness on all occasions, no matter what the circumstances."*

His father had been Mayor of Coventry twice from 1911 to 1913 and purchased and presented to the City the ancient Cook Street gate in 1913 and was made an Honorary freeman of the City in 1924. Colonel Wyley writing in *'The Coventry Standard'* in 1937 stated *"The year 1916 was to me a very sad year owing to my retirement, my illness and the loss of my only son, who was killed in September at Ovillers near Albert. Among my lost officers were the only sons of two personal friends Lieutenant Bullock and Lieutenant Loveitt both charming and brave boys"*.

During the second World War, on the night of the 14th November 1940 more tragedy was to strike the Wyley family. The Provost of Coventry Cathedral and those on fire watching duty realising the fate that was about to befall the Cathedral managed to save furniture and the colours of the 7th Battalion Royal Warwickshire Regiment by dragging them from the sanctuary into the vestries, however they were forced to watch pitifully as a memorial screen to Sir William Wyley's only son was licked by flames, the Provost remarked how *"thankful we were that Sir William had not to bear the sight before he died!"*. The family's residence of the Charterhouse off the London Road was passed by Sir William's request to the City of Coventry in 1940. Lieutenant Wyley is buried in Aveluy Communal Cemetery Extension.

Private **William Herbert Cooke,** 1st/20th Battalion London Regiment formerly 4829 East Kent Regiment was killed in action on the 1st October 1916. William was born on the 4th February, 1886 at 42 Bond Street and resided there prior to his death. He enlisted in Coventry and was employed by Coventry Corporation as a meter repairer. He has no known grave and is commemorated on the Thiepval Memorial and the memorial in St. John's Church.

Rifleman **Hugh Conrad Pails,** 1/12th Battalion, London Regiment (The Rangers), formerly of the Queen's Westminster Rifles, was killed in action, aged 19 between Le Sars and Lesboeufs on the 7th October 1916. He was born the 16th of April 1897, at 7, Starley Road and resided there with his parents Hugh William (a warehouseman) and Clara Emma Pails. A pupil at St. John's Elementary School, he attended Bablake from 1909 to 1912. Hugh was a designer in a textile factory after leaving and enlisted in April 1916. He is also commemorated on the Thiepval Memorial and the Bablake War Memorial.

Private **Stanley Thomas Warner,** B Company, 11th Battalion, Royal Sussex Regiment was killed in action on the Somme age 28 on the 21st October 1916. He was born on the 6th March, 1888, at Halstead, Essex and resided at 145, Station Street East with his parents William Horne and Elizabeth Warner. A decorator he enlisted in Bedford in January 1916.

On the 21st October, the 11th Battalion were heavily engaged in the attack by the 39th Division on the Schwaben redoubt. The attack was successful, most of the redoubt being captured, including the feature called Stuff trench, the objective for the 116th Brigade. The losses for the Battalion were substantial, being 77 officers and men killed in action or died of wounds on that day. Stanley is buried in Regina Trench Cemetery, Grandcourt, and also commemorated on the Luton War Memorial. His brothers also died during the war and have plaques in the War Memorial Park.

Private **Mark Welch Rollason,** 1st Battalion, Royal Warwickshire Regiment was originally posted as missing then official notification received that he was killed in action at the Battle of the Somme on the 23rd October 1916. Mark was born on the 29th February, 1876, at West Bromwich and resided at 25, Swan Lane, Coventry employed as a labourer in the Daimler Foundry. Mark was married to Jane Lilley and had five children; he was one of the oldest men to be commemorated in the War Memorial Park and enlisted in Coventry in January 1915.

On the 23rd October 1916 at 10.30am the Battalion received a message to say zero hour was put forward to 2.30pm. At this time the barrage commenced and the attack launched. The *'Battalion War Diary'* states *"a wounded man came in and reported he was hit in No Man's land and that the companies were going ahead well"*, a note was also made that the barrage fire was very good and dense.

At 3.50pm a message was received by Battalion HQ from a forward post stating prisoners were coming in from a position known as Gun Pits. At 4.40pm the Company Sergeant Major of C Company returned wounded but could not state the time he left the line; his company was then about 400 yards north east of strong points at Hazy Trench. Less then three hours after the attack began it was held up by machine gun fire on all sides, resulting in heavy casualties. A message was sent back by the forward troops requesting reinforcements to bring up small arms ammunition and bombs as they were too weak to resist a possible counter attack. The final message received by Battalion HQ by a runner from A company was received at 5.30pm and timed at 4.30pm which stated that a mixed party of 50 Royal Warwicks and Royal Dublin Fusiliers were close up to Hazy Trench and digging in. The action on this day resulted in the death of 2 officers who died of wounds, 6 officers wounded and 150 other ranks killed, wounded and missing.

After he was posted as missing his friends made many inquiries concerning his fate. In August 1917, nearly a year after being posted as missing information was received by his family that he had met his death in the Battle of the Somme. Private Rollason was forty years of age and he left a widow and five children. His brother George, well-known as a footballer with Clifton View FC, was killed on the 9th September 1915 with the South Staffordshire Regiment.

Private Rollason has no known grave and is commemorated on the Thiepval Memorial, His family also have a headstone in London Road Cemetery with the words *"Private M. W. Rollason killed in action Battle of the Somme"*. This reveals his mother in law was Ann Bristow, his wife Jane Lilley died age 53 on the 20th July 1933 and one of his daughters Anne Elizabeth was also buried in the same plot.

Private **Leonard Faulks**, 1st/7th Battalion, Royal Warwickshire Regiment was killed in action towards the end of the Battle of the Somme on the 11th November 1916. He is commemorated on the Thievpal Memorial. Leonard was born on the 26th December 1896 at Foleshill and resided at 4, Crabmill Lane. He was employed by Siddeley Deasy as a driller and was a member of Well Street Congregational Church. The *'Battalion War Diary'* from the 10th November 1916 shows the Battalion relieved the 4th Royal Berkshire in the front line right of Le Sars. On the 11th of November A and B companies were in the front line with C and D in support. The day was fairly quiet except for shelling on D company which resulted in 1 killed and 16 wounded; Private Faulks was probably this fatality.

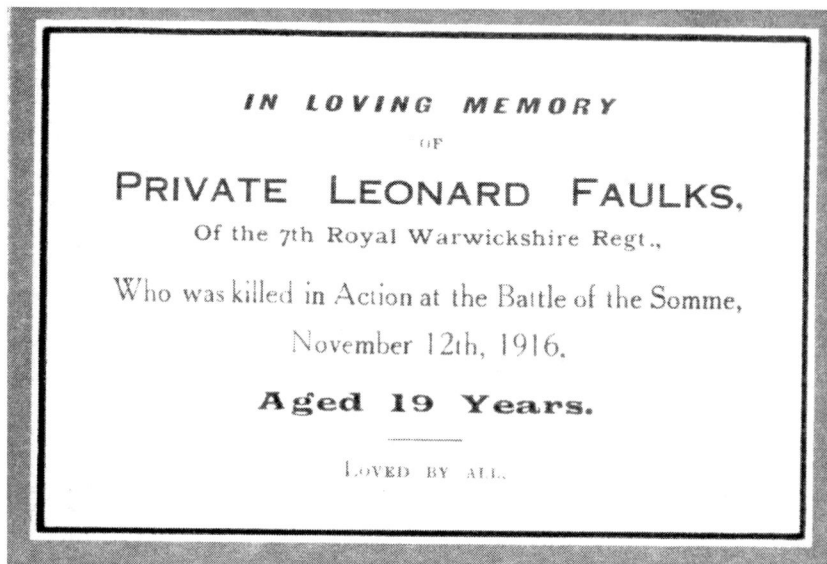

IN LOVING MEMORY

OF

PRIVATE LEONARD FAULKS,

Of the 7th Royal Warwickshire Regt.,

Who was killed in Action at the Battle of the Somme,

November 12th, 1916.

Aged 19 Years.

LOVED BY ALL.

A Memorial Card for Private Faulks

Private **Herbert George Wright**,1st/7th Battalion, Royal Warwickshire Regiment died of wounds age 38 on the 15th November 1916. He was the son of George and Rebecca Wright, and husband of Lilly Wright (nee Blood). He was born on the 27th December, 1877 at Stoke and resided at 2 Leigh Buildings, Stoney Stanton Road, Coventry. Herbert enlisted in September 1915 and was employed as a gardener prior to the outbreak of war. He is buried in Contalmaison Chateau Cemetery and could have been injured in the shelling that took the life of Private Faulks. Herbert is commemorated near his former home on the St. Michael's Memorial

Captain **Francis Noel Graham,** 11th Battalion Royal Warwickshire Regiment died of wounds at Beaumont Hamel age 31 on the 16th November 1916. He was the son of James and Sophia Graham and married to Alice Graham. He was born on the 31st December 1885 in Whitley and also resided in Whitley. As a scholar he was educated at Rugby School from 1899 to 1902 being in Donkin house. A Wine Merchant he enlisted in October, 1914 receiving his commission in February 1915.

Coventry men in the 11ᵗʰ Warwicks. Captain Graham in the centre

On the 14ᵗʰ November the Battalion were at a location known as White City; they moved forward to attack Frankfort trench passing over Munich trench. The attack was held up by hostile machine gun and rifle fire from Munich trench, which forced the Battalion to retire to Minden trench where it established its Headquarters. A further attack was launched at 9.00am on the following day with the 11ᵗʰ Battalion supporting but the objective was found to be very strongly defended which held up the attack and forced the Battalion to reorganise under the cover of darkness. On the 16ᵗʰ November the Battalion held on in Wagon Road but experienced a heavy hostile barrage during the afternoon. Captain Graham is buried in Contay British Cemetery, Contay.

Private **Charles Thomas Worrall,** 1ˢᵗ/6ᵗʰ Battalion, Royal Warwickshire Regiment was killed in action age 25 on the 29th November 1916. Charles was born on 4ᵗʰ May, 1891 at 9c. 4h., Chauntry Place and resided at 39, Cook Street. His father was also called Charles and his mother was Ellen Worrall. He enlisted in April 1916 and worked previously as a barman.

On the 29ᵗʰ November the Battalion were in trenches near Le Sars, the casualties reported were other ranks 1 killed and 8 wounded. The *'Battalion War Diary'* does not state any particular action on this day and his death was probably due to shelling. Private Worrall is commemorated on the Thiepval Memorial, one of the seventeen names commemorated on the Chauntry Place Roll of Honour now kept in the Royal Warwicks Club and also at Holy Trinity Church.

1917

Private **William Edwards,** 10th Battalion, Worcestershire Regiment died of wounds near Peronne age 27 on the 5th March 1917. William was the son of Edmund and Mary Ann Edwards and was born on the 3rd August 1887 at 36 Wellington Street. He was employed as a driller and miller, residing at 17 Highfield Road prior to enlisting in late 1914. William is buried at Hem-Monacu near Peronne. Some records state William was in the 1st Battalion and others the 10th Battalion, it is known that both of these Battalions were in the same region at the time of his death and William could have been transferred between the two.

Private **Thomas Edmund Griffin,** 16th Battalion Royal Warwickshire Regiment died of wounds in France age 24 on the 14th March 1917. Thomas was married to Mabel Winifred Griffin and they resided at 15 Stoke Row. He was born on the 8th December 1893 in Coventry and was employed as a hairdresser prior to enlisting in November 1916. The *'Battalion War Diary'* states the Battalion *"were in the location of Annequin and completed a relief at 2.40pm. In the middle of the relief the enemy opened fire on the front line with a trench mortar, killing one other rank and wounding three of whom one died later. Sergeant W. E. Fisher A company showed great gallantry in rescuing the wounded and helping to dig out those who were buried although under trench mortar fire all the time"*. Private Griffin is buried in Cambrin Military Cemetery.

Private **George Bell,** 1st/6th Battalion Royal Warwickshire Regiment was killed in action age 32 on 1st April 1917. He was the husband of Harriet E. Bell and resided at 49, Raglan Street, Coventry. He was employed as a packer at the Triumph works and was born on the 2nd November 1885 in Little Park Street. His parents resided at St. John's Street, Coventry.

On the 1st April 1917 the Battalion were based at Caulcourt and took part in an attack by the 143rd and 144th Infantry Brigade on Epehy and Pozières. The Battalion was supported by the 1/5th Royal Warwickshire Regiment. From the 1/6th B, C and D companies were lead, with A company in reserve. The attack commenced at dawn with the whole objective secured at 6.40am. Casualties were recorded as other ranks 9 killed, 2 died of wounds and 25 wounded. Private Bell is buried at Epehy Wood Farm Cemetery, Epehy. The village of Epehy was captured at the beginning of April 1917. It was lost on 22 March 1918 after a spirited defence and retaken in the Battle of Epehy on the 18th September 1918. Private Bell is buried in Plot I and the graves in Plot I were made by the 12th Division after the capture of the village.

Also buried from the Royal Warwickshire Regiment who died on the same day and commemorated in the *'City of Coventry; Roll of the Fallen'* are Lance Corporal A. Atkins, Private Ernest Frederick and Private Jesse Herbert. Other casualties included Second Lieutenant John Wallis Bisseker, Private Joseph William Harwood, Private Joyner E. H. Henley, Private Ramsay D. Smith, and Private Arthur Toplis.

Private **John Clews,** 9th Battalion King's Own Yorkshire Light Infantry formerly with the Royal Horse Artillery and Royal Field Artillery was killed in action near Arras age 30 on the 9th April 1917. John was the husband of Hannah Clews of 199 Heath End, Chilvers Coton, Nuneaton. The son of John and Ann Clews, of Chapel End, Atherstone he was born on the 30th June 1887, at Stockingford and previously resided in Lewis Road, Foleshill. He was employed as an insurance agent, enlisted in October 1916; he had served for eight months. He is buried in Cojeul British Cemetery, St. Martin-Sur-Cojeul near Arras.

For some days before going into operations on the 9th April, the Battalion had been practising for their attack on the Hindenburg Line. On the 7th, close reconnaissance of the effect of the British artillery on the Hindenburg Line was made by CSM J. W. Gill and Corporal A. Hammond who had crept in daylight 1,500 yards to bring back valuable information. For this action CSM Gill was awarded the DCM and Corporal Hammond the MM.

The assault on the 9th was made in the afternoon, with the objectives of position in the Hindenburg Line about the Henin-Heninel road. The artillery attack had failed to cut the wire sufficiently. Some of the companies managed to get through the gaps and capture the first objective. The second objective was found to be impenetrable; heavy losses were incurred in trying to cut gaps and efforts made to cut the wire with stokes mortars also failed. The men of the first and second wave had lost their leaders and took cover in shell holes. At about 6.00pm they withdrew to the first objective south of Heninel.

After dark the wounded were collected from around the second objective as this position was to be bombed the following day. The remaining men of the 9th Battalion were relieved by the 10th Battalion and the Durham Light Infantry. This forward position was technically in enemy territory and a bombers block was manned to prevent penetration of the front line trenches. In holding this block on the 10th April, Private H. Waller of the 10th Battalion was awarded the VC posthumously.

Twelve officers and 550 other ranks had taken part in the assault, 3 officers were killed and 26 other ranks, wounded were 99 and missing 49.

Sergeant **Albert Ernest Mann,** 10th Battalion Canadian Infantry (Alberta Regiment) was killed in action at Vimy Ridge aged 25 on the 9th April 1917. He was the husband of Irene Frances Annie Mann and prior to emigration had previously lived at St. Dunstan's School, Stoke Green, Coventry. He was born on the 17th March 1892 at Matlock and resided at Calgary, Canada where he worked as an engineer. He is commemorated on the Vimy Memorial and unofficial notification suggests he is buried at Vimy.

On enlisting the '*Attestation Papers*' show Albert was employed in Coventry as a machinist and had previously served four years with the 7th Royal Warwickshire Territorial's. He was 6' 1" tall with fair complexion, brown eyes, black hair; his religion was stated as Church of England and he had a noticeable scar across the top of his nose. He was considered fit for duty on the 25th January 1915 and died just over 2 years later.

The '*Battalion War Diary*' shows the attack was to capture and consolidate the area known as Pimple and to establish a line of continuous resistance. The assault was launched at 5.30am. One of the objectives was the taking of Hill 145 and the assault was not successful in this objective. At 9.30pm a conference took place to call for reinforcements to complete the taking of the hill. The total number of casualties was not recorded. Despite emigrating his family saw to it that his name is written on the memorial in St. Michael's Church, Stoke.

Private **Henry Herbert Riley,** 1st Battalion, Royal Warwickshire Regiment was posted as missing and then believed killed age 24 on the 11th April 1917. He was born on the 31st October, 1893, at London and lived with his parents John and Elizabeth Riley at 71, Huntingdon Road, Coventry. Henry enlisted in February 1916 in Leamington and was employed as a coach painter in the tramways department at Coventry Corporation.

He had been in France for eleven months and has no known grave. He is commemorated on the Arras Memorial, the Memorial in the council house to the Car Shed Workmen in the Tramway department and in St. Barbara's Church. His obituary appeared in '*The Coventry Graphic*' on the 15th June 1917.

On the 11th April 1917 the Battalion were based in a dugout south of Athies. At 2.30am a conference was held at Brigade Headquarters and orders issued that the 10th Brigade would attack at noon. At 8.30am the Battalion moved off west of Fampoux and arrived at the assembly position at a sunken road on the East Edge of Fampoux just before noon. A and C companies were to attack on a frontage of

500 yards per company and B Company followed in the rear as carriers. The attack commenced at noon, when the 1st Royal Inniskilling Fusiliers and 2nd Seaforth Highlanders started going forward. At 12.10pm the 1st Battalion attacked in support. The *'Battalion War Diary'* records *'"the enemy shelled the Battalion's assembly positions heavily before starting and they suffered many casualties. The enemy's machine gun fire held up the Battalion's attack almost from the start and the Brigade consolidated a line about 400 yards in front of the assembly position. Both Brigades on our right and left were held up also by machine gun fire. The enemy put up a heavy barrage on assembly positions and the vicinity. The Battalion dug in and held a line. The enemy was fairly quiet all night. Very cold and snow"*.

Lance Sergeant **Herbert William Harper**, 15th Battalion, Royal Warwickshire Regiment was killed in action age 24 on the 21st April 1917. Herbert was born on the 5th July 1893, at 28 Foleshill Road; his parents lived at 49, Queens Road, Coventry. Herbert resided at 211 Sovereign Road, Coventry with his wife Lizzie and was employed as a decorator prior to the outbreak of war.

On the 20th April 1917 the Battalion moved to support the 16th Royal Warwickshire Regiment on the East Side of Vimy Ridge near Givenchy-En-Gohelle and relieved the 1st Bedford Regiment. This relief was complete about 11.00pm and a note appears in the *'Battalion War Diary'* that the weather was good. The following day the Battalion were in support trenches. The situation was reported as normal but no visible movement was permissible owing to enemy observation. The Battalion moved up to the front line to relieve the 16th Battalion Royal Warwickshire Regiment. The relief of the companies in the front lines proved difficult owing to the nature of positions held. One of the reasons cited was the detached posts were some distance in front of the line of resistance and separated in some cases by several hundred yards. Communications by wire also needed to be established and maintained to the left front Company. The relief was completed at 1.45am, with the Battalion suffering three other ranks killed and four other ranks wounded. Lance Sergeant Harper is buried in La Chaudiere Military Cemetery, Vimy.

Private **Arthur Checkley**, 11th Battalion, Royal Warwickshire Regiment was killed in action near Arras on the 23rd April 1917. He was born on the 6th June, 1884, at 63, Edgwick Road and also resided at this address. He was employed as a bricklayer prior to enlisting in December 1914.

On the 22nd April 1917 the Battalion marched off at midnight to their position of assembly in Laurel trench; by 3.30am on the 23rd April the Battalion were at this position. At 4.45am orders were received to move to Hurrum- Hussar trench and a note made in the *'Battalion War Diary'* that *'"Heavy shelling over the whole area of the area covered by these operations continued throughout the day"*. Later in the afternoon at 3.50pm orders were received for an attack on Greenland Hill. At 6.00pm after thirty minutes artillery preparation (twenty five minutes shrapnel and five minutes High Explosive) the Battalion moved forward 100 yards east of the Gavrelle–Roeux Road. The Battalion were unable to advance any further owing to heavy machine gun fire from the chemical works on the Battalion's right and also owing to the fact that the Division on the right was held up, the Battalion consolidated the line.

This was the second action of the Battle of Arras and lasted from the 23rd to 29th April 1917. During this the Battalion had 2 officers killed, 8 wounded and 1 missing. Amongst the other ranks 37 were killed or died of wounds with 192 wounded and 59 missing. The initial Battle of Arras lasted from the 9th to the 13th of April and the Battalion reported 25 killed or died of wounds, 142 wounded and 8 men were missing. Private Checkley has no known grave and is commemorated on the Arras Memorial

Private **Edward Walter Newbold**, 10th Battalion, Royal Fusiliers was killed in action age 26 on the 28th April 1917. He was the husband of Elsie Newbold, of 72 Humber Avenue, Coventry and the son of Francis and Eliza Newbold. His father died prior to his enlisting and his widowed mother lived with Edward and his wife. Edward was born on the 10th July, 1890 in Coventry and prior to enlisting in March 1916 he was employed as an auctioneer's clerk to Messrs Eaves and Bird, Bishop Street. The *'Battalion War Diary'* shows that on the nights of the 25th to the 27th April 1917, enemy snipers were very active, the consolidation of Cuba Trench continued and the Battalion's position was shelled with shrapnel and high explosives. On the 28th April at 3.25am the Battalion frontage was extended on the left and the Battalion were ordered to support of the 13th Battalion, Royal Fusiliers.

Zero Hour was 4.25am and the attack commenced in line with the artillery programme, the objective being marked on the maps as a brown line. The reply to the artillery barrage was immediate and particularly heavy on Cuba Trench. Patrols were sent out to understand the locations of the other Battalions involved. At 10.00am the enemy started shelling the Battalion's position and this continued for about an hour. At 2.00pm another patrol was sent out to get in touch with the 63rd Brigade, the men retuned at 5.30pm having avoided enemy snipers. Neither patrol found any trace of the 63rd Brigade. At 6.00pm the shelling of Cuba Trench commenced again and this also lasted for about an hour.

During the night a party of 80 men assisted the Royal Engineers in supporting and constructing a strong position in front of Cuba Trench. The total men killed in operations from the 22nd to the 29th April 1917 was 4 officers and 42 other ranks. The wounded totalled 198 and 22 men were missing. .

Private Newbold's Grave

Private Newbold is buried in Chili Trench Cemetery. Pictured above are his original wooden cross and his mother with his headstone prior to the Second World War. Unfortunately his grave along with eighty five others was destroyed by shell fire during the Second World War and his name now appears on a special memorial to men known to be buried in the cemetery. Fortunately the panels in Holy Trinity Church survived the air raids of World War 2 as these also commemorate Private Newbold.

Rifleman **George Odey,** 13th Battalion, Kings Royal Rifle Corps died of wounds on the 28th April 1917. He was born in Burton-upon-Trent the son of Mrs Maria Odey of 15 Edward Street, Milverton, Leamington Spa. George was employed by Siddeley Deasy Motors Ltd.

The total casualties during operations from the 9th to the 12th resulted in the Battalion having an effective battle strength of 20 officers and 400 other ranks. In operations for these three days, 13 officers were killed or wounded, 26 other ranks were killed, 162 wounded and 24 were posted as missing.

Between April 19th to the 30th the Battalion passed through some very trying days, experienced severe fighting and gained the single distinction of being the only Battalion in the division to reach and hold its final objective. The *'War Diary'* notes that just after 5.35am on the 23rd when the barrage ceased the Battalion suffered heavy losses, due to tremendous shelling and machine gun fire, despite this they pushed on and took prisoners who were put to work digging in. The night was a busy one with hostile patrols. The enemy put down a heavy barrage and was seen massing aggressively on the Battalion's front but a return barrage broke this up. The Germans then put down a terrific bombardment of high explosive and gas shells and brought up strong forces. Rifleman Odey is buried in Duisans British Cemetery, Etrun and most of the graves in this cemetery relate to the Battle of Arras and the trench warfare that followed, as the site was selected due to its proximity to the 8th Casualty Clearing Station.

Lance Corporal **Joseph Sharratt,** 2nd Battalion Royal Warwickshire Regiment was originally reported as missing and then as killed in action at Bullecourt age 30 on the 4th May 1917. *The Coventry Graphic'* included an appeal from his brother William who *"would be grateful of any news"*. The article also stated Joseph had been wounded at Ypres and went back to the front nineteen months before his death. Joseph was born in Coventry in 1886, lived at 81 East Street, Coventry and enlisted at the outbreak of war. He was previously employed as a fitter.

At 6.45pm on the 3rd May 1917 the Battalion received orders for an attack on Bullicourt. The following day the Battalion left a railway cutting and moved under the cover of an embankment to the attack position, reaching this position at 3.45am. A conference was held and it was stated that communication would be sustained by three methods;
1) by runners,
2) by signalling (a visual and a receiving station to be established)
3) by pigeon.

The exact circumstances of the attack are not detailed in the *'Battalion War Diary'*, however concern was expressed for its success. The signalling lamp had been broken by shell fire and one pair of the pigeons died of shell shock. At 6.00am The Corporal in charge of Battalion runners was sent forward to try and discover the positions and strength of companies, also if possible to obtain written messages from remaining officers. Owing to heavy fire and bad visibility the men who survived the attack had started to withdraw and began to report at Battalion Headquarters at 8.30am. At 10.00am the Sergeant in charge of scouts and two men were sent to try and locate posts, find men, Lewis Guns etc and identify each position held by the companies.

At 12.30am Lieutenant W. C. Fowler (Battalion Intelligence Officer) was sent forward and corroborated the statements brought back by runners and scouts. Any exact positions and strengths of posts were difficult to obtain, but at 9.00am there were 20 men, 3 Lewis guns and 2 officers holding a line and on the railway embankment 40 men under NCO's. Both these parties were digging in. There were also scattered posts of men in shell holes unable to move owing to fire, it was not possible to ascertain exact numbers. Also 60 men had been collected and reformed behind a railway embankment.

The strength of the Battalion going in to action was 20 officers 609 other ranks, after action strength 8 officers, 362 other ranks. Sentries were posted to direct any stragglers. The *'Battalion War Diary'* offers several explanations as to the cause of the attack being a failure. The concentration of troops had probably been observed by the enemy as he put down a heavy barrage which had to be passed through and the Battalion's plans had been suddenly altered. The positions held by the enemy were protected heavily by machine guns and the second belt of wire had remained uncut on the front being attacked by the Battalion. The village was also honeycombed with dugouts and underground passages which allowed the enemy to get behind the Battalion's men and they also outranged the troops with a bomb attack. The difficulty of obtaining information was very great owing to the open nature of the ground and due to the large number of machine guns, snipers and extremely heavy shelling fifty percent of the men became casualties. Finally reference was made to the smoke and dust caused by shelling making it difficult to see any distance.

At 5.30pm it was agreed to push forward strong patrols in Bullecourt; about 200 men were collected and the attack recommenced at 11.00pm. The enemy held fire until the troops reached the second belt of wire, which was still uncut and then opened strong rifle and machine gun fire which caused heavy casualties. Lance Corporal Sharratt has no known grave and is commemorated on the Arras Memorial.

Sergeant **George Frederick Randall** (MM and Bar), 56th Battery, 34th Brigade, Royal Field Artillery was killed in action near Arras age 28 on the 5th or 6th May 1917. George was the son of John William and Mary Ann Randall and lived with his parents at 23 Stratford Street, Coventry. He was born, at Woodford, Northants on the 16th January 1899 and trained as a mechanic. He had spent about nine years in the army. His brother James William Randall also commemorated in the War Memorial Park had previously been killed on board HMS Arabis. *'The Coventry Graphic'* in June 1917 reported that Sergeant Randall had been killed by a shell.

Notification of his Military Medal appeared in *'The London Gazette'* in October 1916 and his second award in February 1917 probably for an award in late 1916. During the Great War approximately 5796 MM's and Bars were awarded. Sergeant Randall is commemorated on the Arras Memorial and the memorial to the men who fell from the Triumph and Gloria works.

Private **John Butler,** 8th Battalion, Royal Berkshire Regiment was killed in action in Belgium aged 24 on the 24th June 1917. He was born on the 21st September, 1892 in Gilbert Place, Brook Street and resided in Albert Street. His father William Butler, resided at 53 Coronation Road, Coventry. John was a machinist and enlisted in Rugby in August 1914 along with several of his colleagues from Messrs Singer Co. Ltd. On the 14th July 1916 *'The Coventry Graphic'* reported Private Butler had seen much severe fighting and although badly wounded rejoined his Regiment.

There are no *'Battalion War Diaries'* for the 24th June 1917, the *'War Diary'* from the 23rd June shows the Battalion were in trenches near Nieuport Les Bains early in the day and at 10.00pm they moved to trenches across Yser Canal and relieved the 16th Northumberland Fusiliers. It was noted *"the line consisted of shallow trenches in sand dunes and the enemy commanded the line from large dunes, these having the observation of practically the whole of our system of trenches. The enemy artillery was active during the day but quiet at night where the enemy then relied on machine gun fire. On relief the shelling increased 80% as soon as we took over the line and there was no sniping though the enemy had every opportunity of doing so ".*

The *'War Diary'* continues on the 25th June *"a heavy bombardment started at 4.30am and lasting till 8.30am on the Battalions' front and support trenches. The enemy took no further action, the communication trenches were badly damaged but no casualties. It was obvious the enemy know the location of headquarters etc. A lack of any good maps of area proves hampering".* Private Butler is commemorated on the Nieuport Memorial This memorial bears the names of 548 officers and men of United Kingdom forces who died during the First World War in operations on the Belgian coast, and whose graves are not known.

The next two men are both John King, unfortunately it is not confirmed which one is commemorated on the panels in Holy Trinity Church.

Private **John King,** 10th Battalion, South Wales Borderers formerly M/286518 Royal Army Service Corps was killed in action in Belgium age 37 on the 30th June 1917. John was born in 1880 at Coventry and was the son of John and Elizabeth King. John was married to Elizabeth King and they resided at the back of 11 Burges, Coventry. The only fatality for the 10th Battalion on the 30th June, he is buried in Bard Cottage Cemetery, Boesinghe. For much of the war, this village directly faced the German line across the Yser canal. Bard Cottage was a house set back from the line, close to a bridge called Bard's Causeway, and the cemetery was made nearby in a sheltered position under a high bank.

Private **John King,** C Company, 10th Battalion, Worcestershire Regiment was killed in action in France age 32 on the 7th July 1917. John was the son of James and Caroline King of 7 Chauntry Place, Coventry and was born on the 20th April 1885 in Birmingham. John was employed as a fruiterer prior to his enlisting in September 1916. At the point of his death the Battalion were in operations to the east of Oostaverne in the Southern Part of the Ypres Salient.

His three brothers also served. Samuel was with the Royal Berkshires, Private Charles King 14th Battalion Royal Warwickshire Regiment had previously been wounded and finally Private James King, Devonshire Regiment who was also at the front. Private John King's body was not recovered and he is commemorated on the Menin Gate and is also one of seventeen names on the Chauntry Place memorial now kept in the Royal Warwicks Club.

Gunner **William Richard Northall,** 681623, "B" Battery, 286th Brigade, Royal Field Artillery died of his wounds age 21 on the 7th July 1917. William was the son of William and Fanny Northall of Manchester and husband of Violet Northall. William was born at Newton Heath, Lancashire and resided with his wife at 30, St. George's Road, Coventry. He enlisted in Wolverhampton and is buried in Estaires Communal Cemetery Extension and commemorated on the roll of honour in St. Thomas's Church.

Gunner **George Nixon Punshon,** D Battery, 47th Brigade, Royal Field Artillery died of wounds on the 22nd July 1917. George was born on the 6th October, 1892 at London and resided in Coventry. He was employed as a cycle liner until enlisting in Coventry in September 1914 and lived with his parents at 59 Gilbert Street. George was one of five sons and shortly before his death the patriotic family appeared in *'The Coventry Graphic'.*

Pictured left to right is George, Sergeant T. E. Punshon, Private R. L. Punshon, Private E. Punshon and Private Alfred Punhson.   At the time the picture was published George was in France, Sergeant T. E. Punshon was in the King's Royal Rifles. He had been wounded twice and had then become a recruiting officer working in Sheerness. Private R. L. Punshon 1/7th Royal Warwickshire Regiment was suffering from the effects of shell stock. Private E. Punshon 2/7th Royal Warwickshire Regiment who had been awarded the Military Medal for gallant conduct in recovering, in the face of heavy enemy fire, a Lewis gun which had been put out of action. He was formerly employed by the Empire Meat Co. Ball Hill, Stoke. He received his decoration at the First Southern General Hospital, Birmingham and also the French Croix de Guerre. Finally Private Alfred Punshon who was with Queen's Own Hussars.

Gunner Punshon is buried in Lijssenthoek Military Cemetery. During the First World War, the village of Lijssenthoek was situated on the main communication line between the Allied military bases in the rear and the Ypres battlefields. Close to the Front, but out of the extreme range of most German field artillery, it became a natural place to establish casualty clearing stations.

Driver **Edward Ernest Mason**, 277th Brigade, Ammunition Column, Royal Field Artillery died of wounds age 18 on the 23rd July 1917 , although he actually served under the name of Edward Flinn. Edward was the son of Frederick William and Esther Mason of 70, Stanley Road, Earlsdon, Coventry. He was born on the 2nd January 1899 at Budbrook and employed as an apprentice at a machine tools company. Edward enlisted in July 1915 when he was sixteen, which is probably why he enlisted under the name of Flinn. Driver Mason is buried in Brandhoek Military Cemetery, Vlamertinghe.

Private **Thomas William Molloy**, 10th Battalion Royal Warwickshire Regiment was killed in action at Hazebrouck on the 24th July 1917 aged 27. He was born on the 6th December 1888 in New Buildings and resided in Spon End. Thomas was employed as an enameller/ liner at Messrs Calcotts and enlisted in Coventry in July 1916. Exactly one year after enlisting Private Molloy died of gunshot wounds in the head and eye, received in action in France. *'The Coventry Graphic'* from August 10th 1917, states *"He was well known in local athletic circles and played in St. Michaels and the catholic football teams. He was married and leaves a widow and one child "*.

The *'Battalion War Diary'* shows on this day that two other ranks were killed and three other ranks wounded in the trenches. As the Battalion was not involved in an offensive it is likely that Private Molloy and his comrades were shot by snipers. Private Molloy is buried in Hazebrouck Communal Cemetery, exactly one year after his death his wife placed a notice in memoriam in *'The Coventry Graphic'* as follows: *"Molloy T. W. Private T. Molloy 10th Royal Warwickshire Regiment died of wounds in France. Sadly missed by his wife (Nell)"*. Unusually his plaque reads *'fell at the Battle of Ypres'*.

Gunner **William John Evetts**, 48th Trench Mortar Battery, Royal Field Artillery was killed in action at Ypres aged 21 on the 27th July 1917; he had been reported wounded and missing. William was the son of John and Mary Evetts of 6, Brookville Terrace, London Road, Coventry and was born on the 12th April 1896 in Coventry. Gunner Evetts resided at 6, Brookville Terrace and had been employed as an engineer with the Maudslay Motor Co. since he left school. He enlisted in October 1914 and joined the Howitzers. William was killed less then three years later and is buried in La Brique Military Cemetery No.2, St Jean-les-Ypres.

His father received a letter from his Lieutenant Harris that stated *"It is with much regret that I have to inform you that your son is now reported as killed. After the affair took place no trace of your son could be found and it was therefore assumed that he had gone to the nearest dressing station wounded. We were notified however yesterday by another unit that they had found your son's body and had buried him. The loss to the battery is great but to you of course much greater. He was a good soldier, spoken of most highly by his officers and NCO's and that very day had been doing splendid work with his guns on the front line. It must be a consolation to you, as it is to us, that he died doing his duty and thereby setting an example to those of us who are left".*

Sapper **William Joseph Barnett,** 234th Field Company, Royal Engineers died age 22. He was reported as missing then presumed killed at Ypres on the 31st July 1917. His parents Ellen and Joseph were notified he was missing and an appeal was made by them in local newspapers as *'they would be grateful of any news'.* William was born on the 27th April 1895, at 40 King William Street and also resided at this address. Employed as a bricklayer, his body was not recovered and he is commemorated on the Menin Gate. His photograph is still on display in his relatives home and has always had a poppy behind it. In William's case the family paid for the plaque although his relatives *"could not imagine how the family found the money to pay for the plaque".*

Sergeant **Samuel Arthur Smith,** D Battery, 62nd Brigade, Royal Field Artillery was killed in action in France age 25 on the 2nd August 1917. He was the only son of Arthur and Rosa Smith, of 22 Clarendon Street, Earlsdon, Coventry and was born on the 10th September 1892, at Gainsborough, Lincolnshire. Sergeant Smith resided with his parents and enlisted in Coventry in August 1914, prior to this he worked as a machine tool maker. He died on the 2nd August 1917 and is buried in Tilloy British Cemetery, Tilloy-les-Mofflaines. The plaque for Sergeant Smith could not be found but reference was made to a plaque for Sergeant S. Smith. Two men fit this category in the *'Roll of the Fallen'* and both have been included, the other being Sergeant Sidney Harry Smith.

Gunner **Arthur Baxter,** 154th Heavy Battery, Royal Garrison Artillery formerly 17705 Royal Warwickshire Regiment died age 19 on the 15th August 1917 as a result of being gassed. He was the son of Mrs Emma Baxter, of 12 Waterloo Street, Hillfields, Coventry and was born on the 12th June, 1898 at 57 King William Street.

Arthur enlisted in Coventry on the 29th March 1916, but prior to enlisting he worked as a turner in the tool room at the Triumph works. He transferred in December 1916 to the Royal Garrison Artillery and had been in France since May the 29th 1917. Arthur is buried in the extension at Outtersteene Communal Cemetery, Bailleul. After the Armistice, graves were brought into the cemetery extension from the battlefields surrounding Outtersteene and from certain small cemeteries.

Gunner **Arthur Ernest Sparkes,** D Battery, 241st Brigade, Royal Field Artillery was killed in action at Ypres on the 18th August 1917. He was born on the 17th September 1896 and died a month before his 21st birthday. Arthur was born and resided at Much Park Street. Before enlisting at the outbreak of war he was employed as a turner. Gunner Sparks is buried in Vlamertinghe New Military Cemetery, Belgium.

Acting/Bombardier **Henry Walter Parnell,** A Battery 103rd Brigade, Royal Field Artillery was born on the 23rd December 1892 at Coventry. He resided at York where he worked as a Minstrel Musician at York Minster. Henry was killed in action at Ypres on the 20th August 1917. He is commemorated on the Choristers Memorial, this memorial can be found in the South Transept of York Minster and is dedicated to the losses of the Minster Choir through the First and Second World Wars. The monument is a Calvary with the arms of St. Peter and an Inscription. The figure was designed by William Foxley Norris, Dean 1917-25, and made by Lawrence A. Turner, sculptor and wood carver of Holborn, London. It was erected in 1922 and dedicated by Gordon Lang, Archbishop of York 1909 to 1929.

The memorial is inscribed *"The Calvary above was placed in grateful memory of those boys of the Minster Choir who gave their lives for their King and country in the war 1914 - 1918. remember them O God for good and bring them unto glory through the sufferings and death of our salvation"*. Henry Walter Parnell is one of thirteen names on the memorial. Acting Bombardier Parnell has no known grave and is commemorated on the Tyne Cot Memorial and in Coventry in St. John's Church.

Private **Harry Edward Kimberley,** 2nd/4th Battalion, Oxfordshire and Buckinghamshire Light Infantry was killed in action aged 24 on the 22nd August 1917. He was born on the 8th April 1893, in Gilbert Street and resided with his wife, Florence Lily at 53 Well Street. In civil life he was employed as a fitter with Singer & Co. prior to enlisting in September 1914. Harry went to France with the 6th Battalion Oxfordshire and Buckinghamshire Light Infantry and was transferred to the 2/4th Battalion on the 7th August 1915. Just over two years later he was killed and left a wife and one child. In writing to the family an officer stated *"that the deceased was one of the best men under him, and had he lived he would have been decorated for gallantry"*. Harry has no known grave and is commemorated on the Tyne Cot Memorial.

Gunner **Horace Preedy,** 48th Division Ammunition Column, Royal Field Artillery attached 48th Trench Mortar Battery died of wounds aged 23 on the 25th August 1917. Horace was the youngest son of Thomas and Elizabeth Preedy, of 17 Jenner Street, Coventry and was also born there on the 16th November, 1893. He was employed at the concrete works in Foleshill Road and enlisted at the outbreak of war. Formerly a Gunner in the Howitzer Battery, he had for two years served in the  divisional ammunition column and was transferred to a Trench Mortar Battery shortly before his death. Horace had only one leave after the outbreak of war, and was due home in September 1917. He is buried in Duhallow A.D.S Cemetery, Ypres.

Second Lieutenant **William Arthur Imber** served with the 7th Battalion, Royal Warwickshire Regiment and lost his life on the 27th August 1917 aged 23.

Born 6th July 1894 at Coventry, he was the son of William (a police superintendent) and Hannah Imber, of 'Astbury', 43 Spencer Avenue, Earlsdon, Coventry. An attendee at Spon Street Elementary School he also attended Bablake School. On leaving he was employed as a clerk to a Medical Officer of Health and then a banker's clerk at Barclays Bank. He joined the Army in December 1914 and was for a time attached to the University and Public School Corps. He was commissioned on the 16th June 1915.

Just over a year later, on the 26th June 1916 at 10.15am whilst serving with the 1/7th Battalion Royal Warwickshire Regiment Second Lieutenant Imber was slightly wounded. The enemy had put a barrage on the Battalion trenches causing considerable damage. 2 other ranks were killed, 12 were wounded. On the 27th August 1917, Second Lieutenant Imber was killed in action near St. Julien, Belgium.

The *'Battalion war diaries'* show that the 1/7th Battalion started an attack at 2.00pm. D Company captured Springfield and handed it over to the 8th Battalion Worcester Regiment who relieved them. The details of A Company and a portion of B Company were relieved from the line on the 27th by the 8th Battalion Royal Warwickshire Regiment and went by train to Poperinghe. Unusually Second Lieutenant Imber is not named in the diary and the casualty numbers are not recorded. Second Lieutenant Imber is commemorated on the Tyne Cot Memorial and at Bablake School.

Private **Cuthbert William Walker,** 2nd/7th Battalion Royal Warwickshire Regiment was killed in action, near St. Julien on the 30th August 1917. Cuthbert was born on the 5th February, 1898, in Lincolnshire and resided at Wisteria Cottage, Stivichall Common. His previous occupation was as a miller and he enlisted in February 1917. On the 30th August 1917 the *'Battalion War Diary'* notes *"this was a quiet night and the Battalion had moved left in the support sector to relieve the 2/6th Gloucesters in the reserve line and then forward to relieve the 2/4th Gloucesters in the front line. The companies left a canal bank at 4.30pm, arrived at the left support at 7.30pm moved off from the left support at 8.55pm. The relief was complete at 11.15pm, during this the Battalion were heavily shelled resulting in one man killed and three wounded".*

Private Walker has no known grave and is commemorated on the Tyne Cot Memorial. He is also commemorated on a brass plaque in St. Jame's Church, Stivichall along with four other members of the community.

Private **Leonard Leslie Bicknell,** 2nd/7th Battalion, Royal Warwickshire Regiment died of wounds in hospital on the 2nd September 1917. His fatal wounds were sustained on the 19th August 1917, on his first visit to the trenches near Poperinghe. Leonard was born on the 27th January 1898 at 32 Moor Street, Earlsdon but resided at 16 Hollis Road with his parents. He was formerly an apprentice in the grocery trade and is buried in Lijssenthoek Military Cemetery.

Captain **Percy Malin Pridmore MC** 2/6th Royal Warwickshire Regiment was killed in action near Ypres aged 31 on the 2nd September 1917. Percy was the only son of Alexander Percy (Elastic Web Manufacturer) and Florence Louise Pridmore and husband of Constance Margaret (nee Mitchell). Percy was born on 7th January 1886 at the Hollies, Foleshill Road, Coventry. He then resided in an area known as Burnt Post. He enlisted in August 1914 and prior to this was involved in the manufacture of small wares presumably for his Father who ran Pridmore & Co. in Park Street.

The award of the Military Cross was covered in *'The Coventry Graphic'* on June 9th 1916 under the headline *'The Mayor's Nephew Honoured'* and in *'The London Gazette'* dated 3rd June 1916.The MC was awarded for gallant conduct whilst in charge of the 48th Trench Mortar Battery, 48th Division. The article also noted *"Percy was the first local officer to secure the military cross which is a great honour not only to himself but to his Regiment. Just after his award he was wounded, and did not return to France until April 1917, during this spell on October the 18th 1916 he was married at Allesley Church to Miss Constance Kerby, daughter of Mr and Mrs Fred Kerby, Allesley".* He was also the brother of the Mayoress Miss Doris Pridmore. Percy joined the 1/6th Royal Warwickshire Regiment in September 1914 went to France and joining his Battalion on the 23rd March 1915. After serving in the trenches he was put in command of a trench mortar battery, he left his Battalion on the 1st August as a result of being wounded and went to St. Omer 'sick'. He embarked for England on the 7th August 1916 and was prescribed as suffering from Pyrexia, it was estimated he would be unfit for service for at least four weeks.

On August the 30th the Battalion moved into right support in dugouts along Oxford Road. The *'Battalion War Diary'* for the 2nd September 1917 states *"that commencing at about 8.30pm the relief of the 2/5th Royal Warwickshire Regiment in the right sub-sector of the front line was carried out. The relief was completed by 12.15am. The dispositions were A Company in Pommern Castle and in shell holes to the east of it, C Company in trenches and shell holes on North and North West of Hill 35, D Company holding Somme and Don't Trench with 1 platoon at Bank Farm and finally B Company in support having one platoon at Plum Farm and the remaining two platoons round Jasper and Uhlan Farms. Captain Pridmore, was killed by a shell as he was leading A company in. The other casualties were two other ranks killed, one wounded and two missing".*

Captain Pridmore is not only commemorated in the War Memorial Park but also on his family headstone in St. Michael's Church, Stoke. This indicates he was the Grandson of George Alexander and Sophie and reads *"P. M. Pridmore who was killed age 31 interred at Vlamertinghe. He died the noblest death a man can die, fighting for God and Right and liberty, and such a credit is immortality".* His family also presented three clocks to the City (one in Broadgate, the second in the Council House and third in Warwick Road), they also donated altar rails to Coventry Cathedral in memory of their son. The air raids of World War 2 left only the clock in the Council House remaining and the plaque reads *"This clock together with the clocks in Broadgate and Warwick Road was presented to The City of Coventry in Memory of Captain Percy Malin Pridmore MC, 6th Battalion, The Royal Warwickshire Regiment who was killed in action near Ypres on the 2nd September 1917 – While gallantly serving his country in The Great War".*

Clock in Broadgate next to Tram

His Commanding Officer wrote to the family *"He was mortally wounded by a shell the night we went in and died about an hour later without becoming conscious. We all miss him greatly. He was one of my best Company commanders and one on whom I could absolutely trust to do what he was asked to do. He is buried with many other British soldiers in a cemetery near here".* A former 2/6th Battalion, Regimental Sergeant Major A. H. Bradbury wrote to the local press and provided more details *" After the action his body was recovered and carried to Wieltje, thence by ambulance to Query Camp, immediately in rear of Goldfish Chateau behind Ypres. The following day I was given orders to bury his body in Artillery Cemetery in the Brandhoek area, 200 yards east of Vlamertinghe. He was given full military honours and a Christian burial denied to so many thousands of Infantry".* Captain Pridmore is buried in Vlamertinghe New Military Cemetery, Belgium.

Captain Pridmore's effects were valued at just over £1,668 and in probate at Birmingham in November went to his widow and Father.

Lieutenant Pridmore sitting on duckboards wearing a wristwatch.

Photograph taken by Captain Simms (RAMC) in trenches at Petit Douve Farm, Messines, April 1915

193

Vincent Arthur Bloxham enlisted in August 1914 and became Gunner, 840327, D Battery 240th Brigade, Royal Field Artillery (South Midland Howitzers). A pupil at Earlsdon Elementary he went on to Bablake and attended for three years from the 2nd September 1907 to the 21st July 1910.

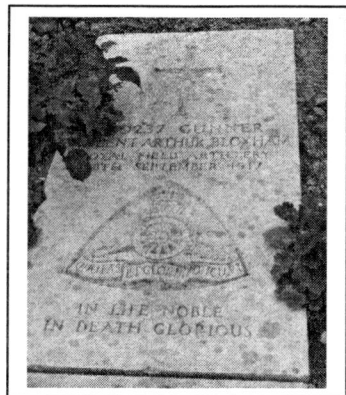

Vincent was born and raised in Earlsdon, Coventry moving from Moor Street where he was born in 1896 to 38, Earlsdon Street and then finally; 8 Stanway Road. He was the son of George and Alice Bloxham. Like his father he was employed as clerk and store assistant at a cycle works. He enlisted in August 1914 and died of wounds in Boulogne on the 18th September 1917 aged 21. He is buried in Wimereux Communal Cemetery and was pictured in *'The Coventry Graphic'* along with other members of his battery. Vincent is commemorated on the Bablake Memorial.

With The Battery
In the group are V. A. Bloxham, H. Round, E. Ward, C. Arnold and J. Burton

Wimereux was the headquarters of the Queen Mary's Army Auxiliary Corps during the First World War. From October 1914 onwards, Boulogne and Wimereux formed an important hospital centre and until June 1918, the medical units at Wimereux used the communal cemetery for burials. Buried among them is Lieutenant Colonel John McCrae, author of the poem *"In Flanders Fields"*. The headstone in this cemetery lay flat due to the sandy nature of the soil and Gunner Bloxham's reads *"In life noble in death glorious"*.

Corporal **John Blythe** (also known as Jack), 24th Division Ammunition Column, Royal Field Artillery died of injuries received in a railway accident at Calais on the 25th September 1917. He was the son of Mr. and Mrs J. Blythe of 5 Berry Street, Coventry and resided with his parents at this address. He was born on the 3rd January 1892 in Coventry and employed as a painter and decorator prior to enlisting in January 1915. John was one of the first burials at Les Baraques Military Cemetery, Sangatte as the Calais Southern Cemetery had reached capacity.

Private **Lawrence Jackson,** 14th Battalion, London Regiment (London Scottish) formerly 203559 5th Battalion Royal Warwickshire Regiment was killed in action age 27 on the 25th September 1917. He was the son of Edward and Ann Jackson and lived with his wife, Phoebe (nee Allen) at 67 Butts, Coventry. A native of Coventry he was born on the 19th December 1890 and employed as a clerk prior to enlisting in March 1917. He is buried in Anneux British Cemetery. The name L. Jackson appears on the memorial to the men who fell from Iliffe & Sons and it seems probable this is where he worked as a clerk.

One of the First Plaques

Gunner **Charles Alfred James,** 275th Siege Battery, Royal Garrison Artillery was killed in action at Ypres on the 29th September 1917. He was the son of Samuel and Hannah James and born on the 8th March 1888. Charles was married to Lily James and they resided at 18 Caludon Road, Stoke, Coventry. Charles was employed as an insurance agent and swapped his profession enlisting in August 1916. He was killed just over a year after enlisting and is buried in The Huts Cemetery, Dickebusch, Belgium. He had been at the front since March 1917 and left not only his widow but also a child.

Private 34032 **Henry Buckland,** 1st Battalion, Duke of Cornwall's Light Infantry, (formerly 20179 Royal Warwickshire Regiment), was killed in action on the 2nd October 1917 aged 42. He was born on the 16th July 1875 at 35 Norfolk Street. He was the son of William Buckland and lived with him at 23 Chester Street, Coventry and attended Bablake School in 1899. Together with other members of his family he was employed as a gold watch case maker.

Private Buckland is buried in Meteren Military Cemetery, France this cemetery contains 768 burials and was made in 1919 by the French authorities who brought in graves from the local battlefields and neighbouring cemeteries. His name appears on a plaque in Bablake School and he is also commemorated on a stained glass panel in St. John's Church.

Private **Arthur Edwin Berry,** 16579, 1st Battalion, Royal Warwickshire Regiment was killed in action at Passchendaele on the 4th October 1917. Arthur was born on the 28th April 1894 at 7 George Street and resided with his parents George and Mary Berry at 22 Perkins Street. He was employed as a clerk and enlisted in February 1916.

On the 3rd of October the Battalion were in a location known as Iron Cross in the vicinity of Langemarck/ Broombeek. At 8.15pm the Battalion moved up to Canal Bank End and then along a trench board track to Iron Cross where Battalion Head Quarters and the companies were assembled prior to the attack. The 1st Battalion were ready to move under orders from Battalion Headquarters should the 3/10th Middlesex Regiment become involved in the forward fighting. The dress was stated in the *'Battalion War Diary'* as *"Each man will carry 120 Small Arms Ammunition in pouches and 2 bandoliers (except rifle grenadiers and Lewis gunners, who will carry 50 rounds each in pouches, rifle grenadiers will carry 6 rifle grenades each). Every man (except Lewis Gunners) will carry two No.5 Mills Hand Bombs. Each man will carry one pick or one shovel in the proportion of four shovels to one pick respectively.*

Rations: Two Days rations and the iron ration will be carried by each man. In addition every fourth man may carry one tin of jam. Watches synchronised".

Zero hour for the attack was 6.00am on the 4th October. The 1st Battalion were in support and the Household Battalion in reserve at Soult camp. At 1.15pm orders were received from the 10th Infantry Brigade that the Battalion would be required to reinforce the 2nd Seaforth Highlanders. The companies marched off at 1.30pm by platoons at two minute intervals via Au Bon Gite and Langemarck in order A,B and C and arrived at Eagle Trench about 3.30pm. The Battalion came under the enemy's barrage just west and east of Langemarck and suffered a few casualties. The situation explained by the Officer Commanding 2nd Seaforth Highlanders was that his left flank was unsupported. A and B companies were sent forward to reinforce and get in touch with 2nd Seaforth Highlanders and C company to keep in close support.

The leading companies came in contact with the enemy before reaching Nineteen Metre Hill and were held up by machine gun and rifle fire from the left flank. Two strong patrols were sent forward and two pill boxes captured. The line advanced and took up position on the reverse slope of Nineteen Metre Hill. Patrols were again sent forward with the object of getting in touch with the troops on the left and right; connections were established on the right but none on the left. On the 5th of October, patrols were sent out again to find the advanced troops but were unable to advance more then 200 yards due to machine gun fire. The Battalion were relieved on the night of the 6th /7th, with the companies being very tired and fatigued. Notes were made in the *'War Diary'* that *"The whole Battalion performed gallantly under the most trying conditions"* these complimentary messages were received from General Officer Commanding Division and the Brigade commander. Private Berry was killed in action on the 4th October; he has no known grave and is commemorated on the Tyne Cot Memorial.

Second Lieutenant **Raymond Russell Cheshire,** 1/8th Battalion Royal Warwickshire Regiment was killed in action near St. Julien, Flanders age 19 on the 4th October 1917. He was one of two sons of William Woodward Cheshire (retired schoolmaster) and Emma Mary Cheshire, their other son was Harold Theodore. At the time of Raymond's death the family lived at 1 Grosvenor Villas, Grosvenor Road but later moved to Rayleigh, 96 Earlsdon Avenue, Coventry. A native of Handsworth he was born on the 6th April 1898 and worked as an auctioneer's articled pupil until enlisted in 1916 with the Birmingham Officer Training Corps.

On the 2nd and 3rd of October the Battalion were in a location known as Cheddar Villa. The following day the Battalion moved forward to an assembly position in support of the 143rd Brigade. At Zero hour, 6.00 am, B company moved forward to a position east of Vontirpitz Farm and a note made in the *'War Diary'* that Battalion Head Quarters and all Companies were under heavy shelling during the time they occupied this position. At 1.00pm C Company moved to the neighbourhood of Hubner Farm and together with A company with Captain Arnell commanding were placed under the Officer Commanding 1/6th Royal Warwickshire Regiment. During the afternoon these two companies attacked Burns house and Vacker Farm but were held up by heavy machine gun fire. At 2.00pm D Company moved to the Hubner Farm area.

At 3.30pm the Battalion received orders to collect as many men as possible from the 1/6th, 1/7th and 1/8th Battalions, Royal Warwickshire Regiments and push forward under a barrage commencing at 5.00pm. The objective was the taking of Burns, Vackers, Oxford and Berks Houses. The barrage commenced beyond Burns and Vickers farm both of which were strongly held by the enemy, so the men came under heavy fire and were unable to advance further than their present front line. A heavy rainstorm during the attack and darkness setting in made further operations impossible. The 5th Battalion relieved the 1/6th Battalion, Royal Warwickshire Regiment at dusk and any of the 1/5th Gloucesters who were in this area. The 6th Battalion reorganised and found a number of men still missing whilst the 8th Battalion moved by bus to Siege camp. During the operations, Second Lieutenants C. V. Samuel, Cheshire and Bastin were killed. The casualties in other ranks were 140 men. Second Lieutenant Cheshire has no known grave and is remembered on the Tyne Cot Memorial.

Private **Frank Harvey,** 201737, 1/5th Battalion, Royal Warwickshire Regiment was killed in action at Passchendaele age 30 on the 4th October 1917. He was the son of Mrs. Sarah Harvey of Yew Tree Cottage, Whichford, Shipston-on-Stour and was born on the 21st January 1887. He resided at 127 Aldbourne Road and enlisted in Coventry in April 1916; prior to this he was employed as a baker and confectioner.

The *'Battalion War Diary'* notes they were in action at Poelcappelle from the 1st to the 7th October 1917. At dusk on the 1st October officers went over their forming up ground and put in marking posts and they all returned before dawn. On the following day, the signalling officer and intelligence officer lay down directing tapes and on the 3rd October, officers and NCOs spent all day in the trenches taking compass bearings etc. From the 1st to 3rd October the objectives were observed as much as possible from observation points and any landmarks noted.

On the 4th October 1917, twenty minutes before zero hour the enemy opened a heavy fire along the Battalion's forming line. A company were the right company, B company on the left front, C company right support and finally D company left support. The attack commenced and from A company, No. 1 platoon quickly reached their objective with only a few casualties and consolidated their flanks. No. 2 platoon passed through No. 1 platoon and had some severe fighting around Winzig; they took twenty prisoners and consolidated their position. No. 3 and No.4 platoons came through No. 1 and No. 2 platoons but were pushed over to the left by the New Zealanders who were also involved in the attack but had lost direction.

Despite this No. 3 platoon got to the high ground and consolidated with the 1/6th Royal Warwickshire Regiment on the left and New Zealanders on the right who only had about ten men remaining. No. 4 platoon received casualties from machine gun fire on the left but reached their objective and dug in. About zero plus fifty minutes heavy shelling of Vale House commenced almost wiping out No.1 platoon and killing or wounding all the men who had just established a forward Head Quarters at this position.

On the left front were B Company. As soon as the leading platoons commenced moving forward, heavy machine gun fire and sniper fire opened up from the front. These were eventually cleared up but left the company about thirty strong. C Company who were in right support, moved up at zero plus 20 minutes and some of the leading men were involved in the fighting at Winzig. The left support company D, also moved up at zero plus 20 minutes and soon lost its officers and platoon sergeants to shell fire and snipers.

During the attack about 100 prisoners were taken by the Battalion. The troops were thinned out as too many men were in one area and they were being heavily shelled. On the 5th October 1917 the Battalion's location was again heavily shelled, on the 6th the outpost line was extended about 100 yards and on the 7th heavy shelling was again encountered. At the end of the period, 1st October to the 7th October the Battalion suffered heavily with 3 officers and 55 other ranks killed, 9 men were missing, 7 died of wounds and 183 men were wounded. Private Harvey has no known grave and is commemorated on the Tyne Cot Memorial.

Private **Edward (Ted) Peel**, 19255, 15th Battalion, Royal Warwickshire Regiment was killed in action at Ypres on the 5th October 1917. He was born in 1889, at Gildersome near Leeds and resided at 219 Sovereign Road. He was employed as a grocer's assistant prior to enlisting in April 1916. His Battalion had been involved in action on the 4th October and received a congratulatory message from General Plummer stating *"Please accept and convey to all troops engaged my hearty congratulations on success achieved today"*.

On the 5th October, C and D companies went forward to hold the line with A remaining in close support; the 16th Battalion Royal Warwickshire Regiment came up to take up a new support position. A, C and D companies were relieved under orders of the officer commanding 2nd Battalion King's Own Scottish Borderers and returned to a position known as Stirling Castle. B Company were seconded as a carrying party and during this 1 officer was wounded, 10 other ranks killed and 7 men were wounded. Private Peel is commemorated on the Tyne Cot Memorial.

Captain **Alfred Ernest Mander BA,** A Company, 4th Battalion, Duke of Wellington's (West Riding Regiment) was killed in action near Passchendaele Ridge age 38 on the 9th October 1917. He was the son of Alderman and Mrs. H. Mander, and resided with them at Spon House, Coventry. He was born on the 15th September 1879 at Spon End. He attended Bablake School in 1895 and then went on to Trinity College. He was employed as a Schoolmaster prior to enlisting on September the 14th 1914. He was commissioned as a Second Lieutenant to the Duke of Wellington Regiment on the 10th April 1915, formerly being a Sergeant in the 2nd South Midland Brigade, Royal Field Artillery. He proceeded to France in December 1915.

Captain Mander joined the 4th Battalion on the 28th December 1915 and was wounded near Thiepval on the 11th July 1916 in the Battle of the Somme. 'The Coventry Graphic' of July 21st 1916 contains details that he had been wounded and was now lying in the Duchess of Westminster Hospital at Le Troquet, Paris. He made a sufficient recovery and was able to rejoin his Battalion.

He rejoined on the 8th August 1916 as Training Officer and became the Officer Commanding A Company in June 1917. He must have been held back in reserve for the 3rd September 1916 attack on the Schwaben Redoubt attack as the 1/4th Battalion lost most of their officers. The 1/4th Battalion History states the Battalion were at the Belle Vue Spur on the 9th October and A Company were to move towards Yetta House. "*With A Company leading and B Company support they moved off in Artillery Formation, until they reached the swamps at Ravebeke.Here heavy machine gun and accurate sniping which affected the rest of the Battalion forced them to extend. Captain A. E. Mander was hit in the head by a sniper during the advance and died instantly His death to the Battalion was a great loss for not only was he a most conscientious officer but a general favourite with all ranks* ". He is commemorated on the Tyne Cot Memorial and more locally the Bablake School War Memorial.

His brother Second Lieutenant Percy George Mander also joined the Duke of Wellington's on the 8th November 1915, was sent to hospital sick on the 12th December 1915 and rejoined the Battalion on the 16th June 1916. He was wounded near Thiepval on the 17th August 1916 and survived the war.

The 2nd Battalion of the Royal Warwickshire Regiment would lose two men commemorated in the War Memorial Park between the 9th and 12th of October. Private Windridge on the 9th and Private Bates on the 12th October.

On the 7th October, at 11.30am the Battalion moved up to Zilebeeke Lake and had dinner on arrival. At 3.30pm they moved up to the line east of Polygon wood and held this line. At midnight on the 8th, Lieutenant Searle laid out tapes for the attack On the 9th October the Battalion were East of Polygon Wood, and at 5.30am D and C Companies attacked with the Honourable Artillery Company on the right. A company held the line on the left and B Company were in support. Twenty five minutes after zero hour green lights were seen along the objective line, signifying that this objective had been reached. At 6.20am one prisoner was captured and the enemy seen running away were fired upon continuously. At 6.50am more prisoners were bought in who had been found in a pill box.

At 7.10am a message was received that continuous machine gun fire was coming from a position known as Judge Copse, a platoon was quickly sent to mop up this position. At 7.30am it was noted that the left attacking company had lost direction, passed through Judge Copse and had mixed with the left company on the northern edge of a cemetery. Also B company had advanced in the direction of the cemetery and were with D and C companies.

During the course of the day, messages were received relating to the deaths of a number of officers and the positions of the companies. The 9th Devons were also called in to assist with clearing the enemy from a copse and the Battalion were relieved at 11.00pm on the 10th.   In operations from the 9th to the 11th October, 54 other ranks were killed, 188 wounded, 70 missing, 5 died of wounds and 2 men were diagnosed with shell shock. On the 12th October the remainder of the Battalion moved to rest at a camp.

Private **Matthew Lawrence Windridge,** 2805, 2nd Battalion, Royal Warwickshire Regiment was killed in action on 9th October 1917. He was born on the 25th September 1895, at 8 Radford Road and resided at 3 Hill Cross. Employed as a butcher he enlisted at the outbreak of war and is commemorated on the Tyne Cot Memorial.

Private **Frank Bates,** 265218, 2nd Battalion, Royal Warwickshire Regiment was died of wounds on the 12th October 1917. He was the brother of Mr H. Bates of 4/10 Cow Lane, Foleshill Coventry and was born on the 2nd March 1890 at 18 Junction Street. He resided at 45 Cromwell Street and was previously employed as a silk spinner before enlisting at the outbreak of war. Private Bates is buried in Godewaersvelde British Cemetery which contains 972 burials of the First World War. News of Frank's death was covered in *'The Coventry Graphic'* which stated *"News has been received that Private Frank Bates has died of wounds received in action. He was in the Territorials and was called up on the outbreak of war, going to France with the Royal Warwickshire Regiment. Aged 27 he was formerly employed at Courtaulds"*.

Private **Charles Raper,** 2nd Battalion, Duke of Wellington's (West Riding Regiment) formerly 076237 Army Service Corps died of wounds in Belgium aged 23 on the 10th October 1917. He was the son of John and Susan Raper, of 151 Bolingbroke Road, Stoke, Coventry and resided at this address. He was born in 1894, at Wheatley, Yorkshire and is buried in Dozinghem Military Cemetery.

Lance Corporal **Sydney James Riley,** G/18219, 7th Battalion, Queen's Own (Royal West Kent Regiment) formerly PS/10961 Royal Fusiliers, was killed in action in Belgium, aged 20 on the 12th October 1917. He was the son of Harry and Elizabeth Riley of 22 Kensington Road, Coventry and resided with his parents. Sydney was born on the 6th April 1897 at 88 Foleshill Road and employed as an assistant works manager in the textiles industry with Franks weaving factory, West Orchard, Coventry. He had worked there for five years and during this time he had passed all examinations at the Technical Institute and was becoming very useful in the trade. Sydney enlisted in March 1916 when he joined the Public School Battalion. Officially he is commemorated on the Tyne Cot Memorial although unofficial documentation implies he was buried in Poelcapelle. Sydney was a member of Well Street Sunday School and chapel and also prominent in the Young Men's guild.

Gunner **Leonard Warden**, 118983, D Battery, 108th Brigade, Royal Field Artillery was killed in action at Passchendaele on the 18th October 1917. He was born on the 1st July 1896 at Coventry and resided at 39 Holyhead Road. Leonard was employed as a coach painter and enlisted in November 1915. He has no known grave and is commemorated on the Tyne Cot Memorial and was one of 68 casualties recorded on the 18th October with the Royal Field Artillery.

A Victim of Passchendaele

Private **Albert Charles Thompson**, 28586, 15th Battalion, Royal Warwickshire Regiment was killed in action in France age 23 on the 26th October 1917. He was the son of Albert and Lucy Thompson, of 61 Gordon Street, Butts, Coventry and resided with his parents. He was born on the 23rd October 1893 and employed as a lithographic printer until enlisted in October 1915. He has no known grave and is commemorated on the Tyne Cot Memorial.

On the 25th October 1917 at 6.00pm the companies commenced moving to their assembly areas, C company in front of A company in immediate rear, D company in close support and B company in reserve. The dictate was for all companies being as close to one another as possible. At 7.00pm zero hour was fixed at 5.40am for the 26th and watches synchronised. The casualties on this day were reported as 5 killed and 17 wounded.

On the 26th at 12.30am all companies reported in the assembly area. Watches were resynchronised and the attack was carried out with companies in waves of one platoon. At the front, C company were leading, A company in immediate rear of C and D company in immediate rear of A. B company were in reserve. The ground on the left between C Company and the Reutelbeek was boggy and impassable, but so far as the ground permitted A company on a one platoon front were to come up as soon as possible on the left of C and make good a portion of the objectives.

At zero hour all companies got well away and casualties were few until C company reached the clearing to the north of the chateau where machine gun fire was encountered from the chateau causing considerable casualties, including all C company officers. D company co-operated with the 14th Battalion, Royal Warwickshire Regiment and with the aid of a Lewis gun team and a bombing party from B company succeeded in capturing the chateau, and the advance continued to the blue objective which was reached according to the programme. A, C and D companies commenced to consolidate with B Company in close support. About 8.00am the enemy were seen massing for a counter attack and at 8.15am the counter attack was easily repulsed by machine gun, Lewis gun and rifle fire.

At 10.00am the enemy massed again and continued to advance. Thirty minutes later communication with the Battalion's right could not be established. Dispositions were made and by 10.45am the Battalion's position had become critical owing to the enemy advancing and encircling the Battalion's right flank. In addition owing to the conditions of mud, all Lewis guns and brigade machine guns, and all but a few rifles were out of action. Casualties became very heavy and a withdrawal was attempted, engaging the enemy; the Battalion's original front line was successfully reached. Supports consisting of about 30 men from 2nd Battalion King's Own Scottish Borderers were called for and came about 12.30pm. Shelling was very intense and the condition indescribable, men sinking waist deep in the going.

On the 27th October the 15th Battalion Royal Warwickshire Regiment were relieved by the 1st Battalion Bedfordshire Regiment and withdrew to Bedford house. The total casualties for this attack were officers wounded 6, missing 1, other ranks killed 31, wounded 113 and missing 48.

Private **George William Caviar Gardner,** 78th Battalion, Canadian Infantry (Manitoba Regiment) died age 24 on the 30th October 1917. He was the son of George William and Emily Gardner. At the time of enlisting his address was Mowbray, Manitoba. He was born in Coventry on December 3rd 1891 and listed his sister, Mrs A. L. Jenkins, 1 Charterhouse Road, Coventry, as next of kin. Previously employed as a farmer, the *'Attestation Papers'* show he was 5' 9" tall, had a fair complexion, grey eyes and light brown hair. His religion was specified as Church of England and he was considered fit on January the 4th 1916.

On the 28th October the Battalion were conveyed by train to Ypres and from there marched to their destination. After a short stay here of several hours, they then moved forward to the point of assault and dug in near the village of Passchendaele. The strength was 28 officers and 637 men. Zero hour was at 6.00am and the successful tour for the battalion lasted until the 2nd November. Notes made in the *'War Diary'* show that a request was made to retain 20 captured machine guns as trophies of war and a complaint lodged that one of the six inch Howitzers had fired short throughout the operation. Private Gardner has no known grave, he is commemorated on the Menin Gate.

Private **Eric Charles Durrant Warner,** A Company, 7th Battalion, Royal Fusiliers formerly 7957 2/5th Battalion, Royal West Surrey Regiment was killed in action at Passchendaele age 20 on the 30th October 1917. He was born on the 17th January 1897, at Tidings Hill, Halstead, Essex. He was the youngest son of William Horne Warner and Elizabeth Warner and the third son to be killed. Eric resided with his parents at 145 Station Street East, Coventry and was employed as a clerk in the office of the Gloria Cycle Co. before enlisting in February 1917 with the Royal West Surreys. He was transferred to the 7th Royal Fusiliers after his arrival in France and originally posted as missing. News of his death appeared in *'The Coventry Graphic'* dated 7th December 1917. Eric is commemorated on the Tyne Cot Memorial and on the Triumph and Gloria Memorial. His brothers also have plaques in the War Memorial Park.

Corporal **William Pargeter,** 1st Battalion South Wales Borderers died on 10th November 1917 aged 30. He was the son of Edward and Elizabeth Pargeter and the husband of Beatrice Pargeter of 25 Godiva Street, Coventry. He was born in Staffordshire and enlisted in Brecon. He had been previously wounded three times and was posted as missing. His wife made an appeal for any information on his status in ' *The Coventry Graphic*'. William has no known grave and is commemorated on the Tyne Cot Memorial. Corporal Pargeter's number 9860 was issued in May/June 1908 giving him over nine years of service.

Over 4,700 Royal Dublin Fusiliers died in the Great War, however, there is only one casualty from the War Memorial Park associated with this regiment. Second Lieutenant **Bernard Michael Ward** was killed in Cambrai with the 11th Battalion on the 20th November 1917 aged 19. The Regiment had some success in a diversionary assault for the Cambrai offensive which hid the true place and scale of the attack.

Bernard was one of five children born to John (bicycle rim maker) and Mary Ward of Ballinrobe, County Mayo, Ireland. Born in Coventry on the 20th August 1898, he was the only one of their children not born in Ireland. Attending Wheatley Street Elementary School he entered Bablake and left five years later in July 1915.

In 1913 he gained a junior school certificate from Birmingham and in July 1915 was awarded a minor exhibition having his fees paid for three years at a technical institute or school of art. Prior to his enlistment Bernard was employed as a registrar's clerk at a motor works up to August 1916, a year later on the 1st August 1917 his name appeared as a temporary Second Lieutenant, Royal Dublin Fusiliers in *'The London Gazette'*. He is buried in Croisilles British Cemetery, near Arras and his name appears on the Bablake Memorial.

Private **Eardley Robert Preston Jeffrey,** G/205098, C Company, 7th Battalion, Royal Sussex Regiment formerly Royal Fusiliers was posted as missing and subsequently believed killed at Cambrai on the 30th November 1917. He was born on the 18th October 1889 at Bath and resided in Spencer Avenue, Earlsdon. Eardley was employed as a slot meter collector before enlisting in April 1915. He is commemorated on the Cambrai Memorial and also on the memorial in the council house to the two men who died from the Gas Department.

The 7th Battalion were one of the Service Battalions raised in August 1914. They trained at Colchester, Shornecliffe and Aldershot before going on to France on 31st May 1915, as part of the 36th Brigade, 12th Division. The Battle of Cambrai opened on the 20th November 1917 and the 7th Battalion took the full brunt of the German counter attack on 30th November, but losses were described as 'light'. Private Jeffrey being one of eight killed in action that day.

Private **Alfred Garnet Bentley,** PS/11198, 4th Battalion Royal Fusiliers (City of London Regiment) was killed in action age 39 on the 1st December 1917 in France. He was the son of Thomas and Emma Bentley of Liverpool and resided with his wife at 72 Broadway, Coventry. He was born on the 23rd May 1879 at Liverpool and was a teacher in an elementary school, enlisting in June 1916 in Coventry. Alfred is buried at Favreuil British Cemetery and commemorated in the Council House on the memorial to those who died from the Education department.

Private **George Albert Daniels,** 16854, 2nd/5th Battalion Royal Warwickshire Regiment was killed in action at La Vacquerie, near Cambrai age 25 on the 3rd December 1917. He was the son of Harry and Ellen Daniels of 30 Clements Street, Coventry and born on the 22nd February 1892. George was employed at the Post

Office in Coventry and had been for eleven years. His employment commenced at the age of fourteen as a messenger boy, afterwards he was appointed postman and at the time of enlistment he was a motor cycle mail carrier from Coventry to Arley via Radford, Keresley, Corley and Fillongley, an outward distance of ten miles which he covered twice daily.

George had the distinction of being the first postman to undertake the experiment and although he encountered many difficulties he always managed to surmount them and bring the mail safely to the various towns. 'The Coventry Graphic ' stated "When he was called up in February 1916 along with other members of the Post Office, his journey was done by horse and cart. George was a well known figure for the villagers for whom he always had a cheery word and smile".

On the 1st December the Battalion marched to Heudecourt and bivouacked in a valley just east of the villages. On the following day the Battalion moved to Gouzeacourt Wood via Fins-Metz-En-Coutre waiting there till 4.45pm and then moving to relieve the 2/8th Battalion Worcesters in the line north east of La Vacquerie. The dispositions being: One company B in trench and in touch with their unit on the left; two companies A and C in shell holes in front of trench ready to attack the trenches lost by the 2/6th Gloucesters; one company D in support; Battalion Headquarters and one company of the 2/8th Battalion Worcesters close by. Touch was established on the right flank between the Battalion's support company D, the support company of the 2/4th Gloucesters and the 2/5th Battalion. Part of the line was reorganised with new Lewis gun positions. Touch was also gained with the advanced company of the 2/4th Gloucesters in a location known as Vacant Alley.

The Battalion attack commenced at 7.30am on December the 3rd covering fire being arranged by the Lewis guns and rocket grenades on the left forward flank and by Lewis guns of the 2/4th Gloucesters in Vacant Alley. Very heavy opposition was encountered and the remnants of the two companies disappeared, one or two men only returning to the support company. At 8.20am the enemy placed an intense and accurate barrage on the Battalion's support company, D, and another across the southern edge of La Vacquerie and then lifting to a line drawn almost east and west through Battalion headquarters.

About 8.30 am the Battalion left company, B, was attacked by bombing parties on their right flank but they held their ground. About 8.45am on December 3rd the support company was also attacked on its right flank and they took up a position facing the attack along the road. This succeeded in keeping the enemy off, but few survivors remained. Both companies were ordered to withdraw, which they did about 6.00am on December the 4th.

George had been wounded three times and he had also been in hospital with septic poisoning. In a letter to the relatives his sergeant said *"I am heartily sorry to tell you that George was killed on December 3rd. I could not write before: I had not the heart to. He was more like a brother to me than one of my section and I found him a most willing man. I cannot say how sorry I am to lose him. I wish to send, on behalf of myself and the whole section our extreme sympathy in your terrible bereavement"*. Private Daniels has no grave and is commemorated on the Cambrai Memorial and a plaque in Coventry's main Post Office.

1918

Major **Harry Allen,** 8th Battalion Gloucestershire Regiment died of wounds received at Cambrai on the 16th January 1918. He was born on the 13th May 1870, at Newport Pagnell and resided in Queens Mary's Road. He was an employee of Courtaulds Ltd and enlisted in September 1914. *'The Coventry Graphic'* contained details of his promotion to Captain in the 9th Gloucesters on the 15th October 1915 and it also stated *"He was well-known locally and his promotion will bring gratification to his many friends".* Major Allen was buried in Rocquigny – Equancourt Road British Cemetery, Manancourt which was mainly used until March 1918 by the 21st and 48th Casualty clearing stations who were posted at Ypres.

Private **William Thomas Derbyshire,** PLY/2434(S) 1st Battalion Royal Marine Light Infantry was killed in action at Flesquieres, France on the 5th March 1918. He was born on the 15th March 1891 at Selby, Yorkshire and resided at 6 Stanley Street, Foleshill with his wife Edith (nee Gopsill). Prior to enlisting in September 1917 he was employed as a clerk and is buried in Rocquigny Equancourt Road, British Cemetery, Manancourt. This cemetery was begun in April 1917 and used until March 1918, mainly by two Casualty Clearing Stations the 21st and 48th. It was known by the Germans as Etricourt Old English Cemetery , the ground around the cemetery was lost to the Germans in their advance and not gained again until September 1918.

Sapper **Arthur Roland Lord,** 36831, 1st Field Squadron Battalion Royal Engineers was killed in action age 22 in France on the 10th March 1918. He was born in Coventry and at the time of his death his parents Mr A. W. and Mrs C. Lord resided at 198 Albert Road, Southsea, Portsmouth. He is commemorated in Vadencourt British Cemetery, Maissemy. This cemetery was used from September 1917 to March 1918 by the IX Corps Main Dressing Station. Arthur's grave was one of the original graves, more burials took place after the Armistice when scattered graves from the surrounding area were moved to Vadencourt.

Able Seaman **Walter John Farrell,** Bristol Z/3998, Hawke Battalion, BEF, Royal Navy Division, Royal Navy Volunteer Reserve died of wounds after suffering from the effects of shell gas age 25 on the 19th March 1918 in the 45th Casualty clearing station. He was the eldest son of John and Florence Farrell and resided with his parents at 20 East Street, Coventry. He was born in London on the 13th November 1892, his trade was blacksmith's

mate and he was a local athlete associated with the Godiva harriers. Walter enrolled on the 6th December 1915 and entered the RND at Portsmouth on the 15th June 1916 and was drafted to the BEF on the 9th October 1916. He then joined the Hawke Battalion on the 26th November 1916.

In 1917 he had several incidences of injuries to his legs and back and rejoined the Hawke Battalion on the 4th January 1918 until he was gassed on the 12th March, dying a week later on the 19th March 1918. He is buried in Achiet-Le-Grand Communal Cemetery Extension.

German Commander Ludendorff launched his offensive on the 21st March 1918. Russia withdrawal from the war enabled the movement of over 1,000,000 experienced men and 3,500 guns to the Western Front. Nature also came to the aid of the Germans as the 21st March 1918 was an unusually misty day and concealed the troop deployment. The attack codenamed Michael, was directed between Arras and La Fere with a heavy concentration around St. Quentin. It was known by the Allies that an attack was imminent but not the date or location.

Gunner **Richard Barnes**, 16224, C Battery. 70th Brigade, Royal Field Artillery was killed in action age 28 on 21st March 1918. He was the son of Mr. and Mrs. Richard Barnes of 37 Albion Street, Coventry and was born on the 15th August 1889 in Birmingham. Richard enlisted in September 1914 and prior to this was employed as an iron polisher. *'The Coventry Graphic'* stated *"A well known and respected Coventry man has paid for his devotion to his country. He was killed by a shell whilst in action on March 21st. For many years he was an employee of the Rover Co. and his commanding officer speaks with deep regret of the loss he sustained by his noble end. He joined up voluntarily in September 1914 and after about six months training went to France, where, with the exception of two short leaves he has been there since"*. Gunner Barnes is buried in Faubourg D'Amiens Cemetery, Arras.

Private **Herbert Lane**, 35097, 2/8th Battalion, Worcestershire Regiment was missing, presumed killed east of St. Quentin on the 21st March 1918. The City of Coventry Roll of the Fallen suggests he was 17 however the census records suggest he was 18 and died four days short of his 19th birthday. He was the son of Arthur Lane and resided with his father at 146 Bolingbroke Road, Coventry. Herbert was born in Coventry on the 25th March 1899 and enlisted in Coventry in 1916. He was employed as a miner at Binley Colliery. Herbert has no known grave and is

commemorated on the Pozières Memorial. Private Herbert Lane was killed at a young age and approximately 3% of the Worcestershire Regiment deaths were to men 18 years old and 1.3% of deaths were to "Men" 16 or 17 years of age.

Sergeant **Herbert Meredith Shaffir,** 2nd/7th Battalion, Royal Warwickshire Regiment died of wounds age 21 on the 21st March 1918. Herbert was the only son of Mrs. Mary Adele Shaffir, of 67 Radford Road, Coventry. He was born in 1897 in Coventry, initially educated at Radford Council School and won a scholarship to King Henry VIII where he was a pupil from 1907 to 1911. On leaving King Henry's he was employed as an assistant analytical chemist at Rudge-Whitworth Chemical Laboratory for eighteen months until enlisting in Coventry, November 1914. Herbert resided at 5 Trinity Terrace, Radford Road.

Herbert's work in the Battalion was recognized on more then one occasion. On the 19th July 1916 the *'Battalion War Diary'* referred to the communications work carried out by Signalling Sergeant Shaffir: *"The arrangement for communications from Battalion headquarters to the forward signal office was two separate lines and two lateral lines from the 2/6th forward signal office on the Battalion's left making four separate means of communication. From the forward signal office to the captured trenches, a party consisting of one NCO and six men went over with the 4th wave taking with them two telephones and two reels of cables and shutters. A second party was arranged to take over another reel and telephone in case the 1st failed to reach its objective. Unfortunately the instruments, cable and forward office were smashed up before this party got away.*

Direct communication from Battalion headquarters to forward signal office broke down at 5.55pm and communication was carried on by runners as well as over the lateral lines. At 6.30pm the forward signal office got in touch with our signalers in the German front line trench and the operator was shot through the head almost immediately but after a few words with another operator, again communication ceased. Several messages were received by runners from the German trenches in the course of the action. A lookout was kept for the shutters but it was reported afterwards that they were smashed on the way over. The whole of the signaling arrangements was organized and run by signal Sergeant H. Shaffir. The Brigadier General 182nd Infantry Brigade noted 'The signaling communications were extraordinarily good throughout the operations'.

Hebert had been home on leave in November 1916 and visited his former colleagues at the Rudge works. He had resisted pressures to return to work in scientific munitions although a desire for him to do so had been expressed by the War Office.

Sergeant Shaffir's work was again recognised for operations between December the 12th to 15th 1917 at Villers Plouich, north east of Peronne. He was awarded a parchment signed by the Major General Colin Mackenzie, Commander of the 61st (South Midland Division). The citation said *"in recognition of the act of gallantry that he performed on the 12th to 15th December 1917 at Villiers Plouich. The NCO is BN signal sergeant and with a reduced staff of six other ranks, on Welsh Ridge, never failed to keep up communication with the front line, although the lines were being continually cut by shell fire. On more then one occasion he went out alone to repair broken lines when nobody else was available. His conduct and example of devotion to duty was the highest order."*

Second 7th Warwicks Signallers at their War station.

From left to right. Back Row : - Signallers Emms, Overton, Wilkins, Burroughs, Sadler and Cole.
Kneeling:-Signallers Germain, Guest, Renton, Gilbert and Collins
Seated:- Signallers Read, Sergt Reading, Lance Corporal Shaffir and Bissel

On the 21st March the 2/7th Battalion were ordered to stand to and man battle stations. At 6.00am the order came through to move to trenches near the Battalion assembly position at Atilly Huts, close to St. Quentin where it was going to act as a counter attack Battalion. The march began at 7.15am and had been completed two hours later, the Battalion suffered 20 casualties en route. Sergeant Shaffir was shot in the head during the Battalions march and is buried in Ham Cemetery, Muille-

Villette. He is commemorated on his former school's war memorial and on the panels in Holy Trinity Church.

The *'Rudge Record'* covered news of his death in detail and printed the letters of condolence received by his mother; it also noted *"Just as when with us he made himself endeared to all with whom he came in contact, and the letters we annex will be read with deep sympathy, since they confirm the keen grief which is felt by all who knew him in more happy times".*

1/5th Northern General Hospital
Leicester
12th April 1918

To Mrs Shaffir,
Radford Road,
Coventry
Dear Madam,

Being myself in hospital, I have only just heard that your son " died of wounds" the same day he was hit. I can only tell you I am more than grieved to hear it, as his loss is a great blow to the Regiment, and none could touch him at his job. It has always been my hope to see him Signalling Officer of the Regiment, an appointment which would have been very popular. We shall all mourn him as a dear friend. He died as we all hope to die, if it has to be, doing his job as a soldier. Sympathising with you in your great sorrow, believe me to be

Yours Truly
Charles La Trobe (Capt and Adjt)
2/7th RWR

In the field 8th April 1918
Dear Mrs Shaffir,

You will know without words of mine the deepness of the sorrow and regret with which I have confirm that your son Herbert died of wounds on 21st March. You have been in my thoughts and prayers ever since Mrs Shaffir, for I know how dearly you loved your hero son. We who were with him out here loved him, for he was a man indeed, and in him I have lost a friend impossible to ever replace. He was as good, honourable, and true as he was brave, and his love for you was always declared to us who knew him best.

I was not actually with him when he was wounded, but my Corporal was with him. There is, unfortunately, no doubt as to his death, but my Corporal (who will write as soon as possible) states he was mercifully unconscious.

Corporal Carpenter and myself were his greatest friends out here-we loved him-his loss leaves us dazed and our hearts go out to you in sympathy. May God help you in your "hour"-mother of him we loved so much. His like we shall not see again

Heartfelt Sympathy.
Yours Sincerely
Sergeant Arthur Payne

Trooper **Cyril Maurice Garbutt,** 4917, 16th (The Queens) Lancers died on the 23rd March 1918 in the German advance. He was born in Arkley, Gloucestershire and resided in Headingley. He is commemorated on the Pozières Memorial and has no obvious connection with Coventry.

Private **Sydney Mornington Pickerill,** 2/7th Battalion Royal Warwickshire Regiment, was originally posted as missing and then subsequently as killed at St. Quentin aged 22. He was the son of Isaac (manager of a meat retail business) and Rose Pickerill, of 'Oak Mount', Windmill Lane, Berkswell. Born the 8th April, 1895, at Sutton Coldfield, he resided at 69, Shakespeare Street and worked for his father as a butcher's assistant. He studied at Bablake from 1908 to 1909 and previously attended Radford Elementary School. An only son, he enlisted in October 1914, in Coventry.

Having been at the front for two years his parents received notification in May 1918 that he had been wounded and an appeal was made by his parents via *'The Coventry Herald'* in January 1919, for any details of their son who was still posted amongst those missing.

On the 21st March, the Battalion were billeted at Germaine and ordered to man battle stations. In action on this day Sergeant Shaffir who has a plaque in the War Memorial Park was killed. On the 22nd March the mist was again heavy and at 9.00am verbal orders were received to move into the area of Holnon Wood. Four hours later orders were received to withdraw and fight a rearguard action. Shells were falling all around the Royal Warwickshire Regiment. The sight of masses of the enemy advancing, the superiority of enemy aero planes, the lack of artillery support, the useless trenches all sought to unsteady the troops but they were still the last to leave the line. The Battalion marched to Matigny and then to Offy, to cross the Somme and occupy trenches at a bridgehead. One hundred and twenty other ranks were picked up and joined the Battalion.

On the 23rd March the Battalion moved into assembly position in reserve and dug in. At 8.30am reports were received that the enemy were breaking through on the right; troops began withdrawing but they were assembled and send forward by the Commanding Officers. By 11.00am the enemy were gaining, their artillery and trench mortar fire becoming heavier and the retirement of the troops was becoming more obvious. Three hours later the left flank was opened by withdrawing King's Royal Rifles but quickly filled; the enemy artillery lengthened its range and kept the line under well- directed fire.

At 5.45pm as part of the rearguard action orders were received to destroy a footbridge and prolong the King's Royal Rifles line; troops not supporting the line were moved to Cazigny. During the night there was considerable enemy artillery and trench mortar activity on the front. By midnight 14 officers and 248 other ranks had been killed. Private Pickerill's official date of death is the 23ʳᵈ March 1918 and he is commemorated on the Pozières Memorial and on the Bablake School Memorial.

Corporal **William Henry Rowe,** Headquarters Company. 6th Battalion, Dorsetshire Regiment was killed in action age 33 on the 23ʳᵈ March 1918. He was the son of Mrs Mary Rowe, and the husband of Caroline Rowe, of 8 Court, 3 House, Grey Friars. He was born on the 24ᵗʰ April 1885 in Dublin and employed as a grinder at the Dunlop works, he was also known to be a reservist. William enlisted at the outbreak of war and is commemorated on the Arras Memorial.

Private **Norman Samuel Bausor** B company, 5th Battalion, Royal Berkshire Regiment formerly Berkshire Yeomanry died of wounds age 19 on 27ᵗʰ March 1918 near Albert. He was the son of John and Lydia Bausor of Duntroon, 6 Queen Victoria Road, Coventry. Norman was born on the 27ᵗʰ November 1898, attended King Henry VIII School between 1909 and 1914 and was employed as a butcher's assistant prior to enlisting in February 1917.

The 5ᵗʰ Battalion were not directly involved in the opening days of the German offensive but were moved by motor transport to the Somme area to meet the German advance. By March 26ᵗʰ, the Battalion had taken up their position on the west bank of the River Ancre kept in reserve, holding a line east of the village behind Aveluy Wood.

The Battalion's outpost line and front line were penetrated, with the assistance of low flying aircraft and they were forced to withdraw. On the 28ᵗʰ the Battalion managed to hold back a further German attack. On March the 29ᵗʰ the Battalion was relieved and marched several miles to the rear. The *'Battalion War Diary'* states *"during operations from the 25ᵗʰ to the 29ᵗʰ the total casualties were 1 officer and 10 other ranks killed, 1 officer died of wounds , 2 officers were wounded and 65 other ranks".* Norman Bausor was mortally wounded on March the 27th 1918 and is buried in Bouzincourt Ridge Cemetery, Albert. He is commemorated at King Henry VIII School and on a stained glass panel in St. John's Church.

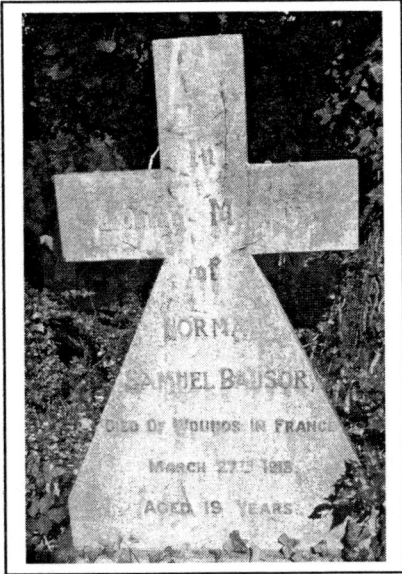

On Norman's death, his parents placed a personal memorial on the grave of his grandparents in London Road Cemetery, stating *'In loving memory of Norman Samuel Bausor, Died of wounds in France, March 27th 1918 Aged 19 years'*. The family headstone reveals that John Bausor, his father, died aged 66 on the 30th December 1921 and his mother, Lydia on the 24th April 1943 aged 82.

Rifleman **Arthur John Blackshaw**, B/203081, 3rd Battalion, Rifle Brigade (formerly R/17079 King's Royal Rifle Corps) was killed in action in France on the 27th March 1918. He was born on the 28th September 1896 in Little Church Street and resided with his parents at 72 King William Street. Prior to enlisting in November 1915 he was employed as a tool maker.

Arthur was 21 years of age and had been in France for over two years, joining the King's Royal Rifles on November 25th 1915. He was subsequently transferred to the Rifle brigade to which Regiment he was attached at the time of his death. His obituary printed in *'The Coventry Graphic'* stated "*He took a keen interest in all athletic sports, and while a scholar at Trinity schools, was very successful in swimming winning a bronze medal and two certificates. He was a keen enthusiast and supporter of the Coventry Fur and Feather Society, and ably assisted his father who is chairman of the society. He also took an active*

part as a member of the Coventry Chain Athletic Society and prior to enlistment he was employed at the Coventry Chain Co Ltd".

In a letter to his parents, the Captain of his company wrote " *I regret to have to write and tell you that your son Rifleman A. Blackshaw was instantly killed in action by shell fire in the great battle in which his Battalion did so well. Please accept my deepest sympathy with you in your sad loss. Your boy was also a good soldier and had he been spared would have been a great help to me at a time like this, when so many have gone. It may be a consolation to you to know that his death was absolutely instantaneous and that he knew nothing and did not suffer. If one is to be killed one cannot ask for anything better, fighting bravely one minute and then the end."*

The *'Battalion War Diary'* aligns with this account and reveals that on the morning of the 27th the enemy allowed the Battalion, 'a good rest', until 8.30am when they opened an intense bombardment on the village while swarms of aeroplanes circled overhead which forced the Battalion to vacate the place as quickly as possible and they took up position on a crest where they dug in. Arthur has no known grave and is commemorated on the Pozières Memorial.

Private **Kenneth John Taylor**, 4th Battalion Coldstream Guards was killed in action, at Boulincourt, age 25 on the 29th March 1918. He was the son of John Harrison Taylor and Clara Elizabeth Taylor of 50 Alfred Road, Coventry and resided with his parents at this address. Kenneth was born on the 13th April, 1892, at 5 Hales Street and employed as a fitter before enlisted in 1914. He is commemorated in Cabaret–Rouge British Cemetery, Souchez and the memorial in Coventry Cemetery to the men who fell from Triumph and Gloria works. Kenneth went to France with the 4th Battalion on the 15th August 1915.

Private **Fred Lord,** 1st Battalion, King's Own (Royal Lancaster Regiment) was killed in action at Arras aged 39 on the 2nd April 1918. He was the son of Fred and Selina Lord and husband of Clara Lord of 6 Winterton Road, Reddish, Stockport. Fred was born on the 20th June 1878 at Radford and resided at Manchester where he was employed as a master butcher. He also enlisted in Manchester in May 1917 and at the time of his death had served just short of a year. He is commemorated at Bailleul Road East Cemetery, St Laurent-Blangy.

Private **William Herbert,** 42463, 3rd Battalion Worcestershire Regiment, formerly 13079 Oxfordshire and Buckinghamshire Light Infantry, was killed in action at Steenwerck on the 10th April 1918 aged 28. William was born on the 11th December 1889 in Coventry and employed in the City as a cycle finisher. He enlisted in August 1914 and entered France with the 2nd Battalion, Oxfordshire and Buckinghamshire Light Infantry on the 7th August 1915 but was later transferred to the Worcestershire Regiment.

On the 9th April, an order reached the 3rd Battalion at 12.45pm that the line south of the River Lys was giving way and support was required. The men who were just about to be issued with dinner were ready to move off to Steenwerck by 1.30pm and form part of the 74th Brigade. The Germans were reported to be crossing the river at three main points and the 74th Brigade were required to drive back the enemy and establish a line covering these three crossings. The allotted segment for the 3rd Battalion was the section from L'Hallabeau to Erquinghem. A defensive line was established with A,B and C Companies holding the front line and D Company in reserve. At 7.00pm D Company were ordered to assist the Lancashire Fusiliers in driving out the enemy of Croix-du-Bac, this attack commencing at 2.00am on the 10th April.

At dawn the fighting recommenced, the Lancashire men being attacked from the rear. It was thought this was due to either the Lancashire men passing through the Germans when the village was stormed or a party of Germans making their way through the thinly held line in the night. The situation worsened when the Germans were reinforced at 10.00am and the 3rd Battalion were forced to adopt a new position which was held. The right flank of the Brigade was however broken by the enemy and the 3rd Battalion were forced to withdraw northward and the platoons lined a railway embankment facing south west towards Steenwerck.

As darkness fell the troops after almost twenty four hours of fighting tried to get some rest. Underneath the cover of darkness parties of the enemy had crept forward along the railway embankment, fierce fighting ensued and the attackers brought forward more troops establishing machine guns positions which were used to fire along the position of the 3rd Battalion. The platoons took shelter near the railway station and eventually fell back to the rear. Private William Herbert is buried at Croix Du-Bac British Cemetery, Steenwerck and has a special memorial B5. He was the brother of George Herbert of 33/11 Much Park street, Coventry.

Private **Albert Thornett**, 10th Battalion, Royal Warwickshire Regiment was killed in action at Wytschaete Ridge, Belgium aged 24 on the 10th April 1918. He lived with his parents, Albert and Elizabeth Thornett at 10 Drapers Field, Coventry.

Albert was also born at this address on the 27th March, 1894 and employed as a warehouseman until enlisted in Birmingham in February 1916.

On the 10th April the Battalion were based in the left sub sector in the Messines area and when the battle commenced the Battalion were holding the front line between the Wambeke and the Blauwepootbeek. There were front line companies on the right and left and a reserve line. The *'Battalion War Diary'* records *"No mans land was a mass of waterlogged shell holes and old trenches. The trench strength was 560 rifles and 16 Lewis guns"*. At 2.30am high explosives and gas opened on the Battalion, but decreased by 4.45am. In the following hours the enemy attacked and by 8.30am Battalion Headquarters were evacuated due to well-directed rifle and machine gun fire. Skirmishes took place throughout the day with the enemy reported in various locations close by. At 9.30pm the Battalion Headquarters was withdrawn again. Albert has no known grave and is commemorated on the Tyne Cot Memorial and on the Holy Trinity panels.

Captain **George Lionel Graham,** D Company, 2/7th Battalion Royal Warwickshire Regiment died in German hands on the 11th April 1918. He was 36 years old and born on the 31st October 1881, residing at Whitley and employed as a brewer with the Seven Stars wine merchant. George was a former pupil of King Henry VIII School and received his commission in April 1915 with the 11th Battalion, Royal Warwickshire Regiment.

On the 18th January 1918 Captain Graham joined the 2/7th Battalion and just over two months later on the 21st March 1918 the Battalion were heading for Attilly and received orders to man battle stations. By 6.30pm on the following day the enemy had advanced to within rifle range (600 yards) and the line opened fire with the result that his infantry immediately dropped. Realising that a wire obstacle and a switch belt of wire were on their left, the enemy threw out flanking troops. At the same time masses of infantry were observed working down the northern slopes towards the Battalion's right enveloping the Battalion's right flank.

The *'Battalion War Diary'* explains *"Lewis guns were worked out to that flank but considering that there were no troops on the right it was evidently only a matter of time before the Battalion's flank became enveloped. Heavy machine gun fire came from the exposed flanks causing heavy casualties in the wide shallow trenches. Units on the Battalion's left commenced to withdraw, and without any order men commenced going back from our trenches. The machine gun fire became much heavier and without orders the remainder of the Battalion retired under a very heavy enfilade machine gun fire which caused very heavy casualties. Captain G. L. Graham it is feared is mortally wounded".* From the 22nd March to midnight 23rd March the Battalion lost 248 other ranks and 14 officers.

Captain Graham had been captured by the Germans and was subsequently treated in a German hospital in Seboncourt for gunshot wounds to the chest and back, but died on the April 11th. On the 8th April 1918 he was reported as missing, in June as a prisoner of war and finally in August it was announced that he had died whilst a prisoner of war. His parents had previously lost another son, Captain Noel Graham who had died of wounds in November 1916 and the remaining brother Lieutenant Norris Graham, had been taken prisoner in 1916 whilst serving with the Royal Flying Corps. Captain George Lionel Graham is buried in Grand-Seraucourt British Cemetery to which his body had been moved after the war and he is commemorated on the Henry VIII School Memorial.

Private **Edgar Herbert Buckingham,** 2nd/7th Battalion, Royal Warwickshire Regiment was killed in action at Calonne near Merville, France on the 14th April 1918. He was born on the 27th May 1898 at Coventry and resided in the City. He attended Bablake School and prior to this he was educated at Spon Street Elementary. Edgar went on to become a confectioner, working for his father who was a baker and a shopkeeper. The 1901 census shows the family to have five servants, however three of these were occupied as bread makers. Herbert enlisted in May 1916 in Cheltenham, probably when he reached his 18th birthday.

On the 13th April 1918 the Battalion arrived at Hamet billet. The men breakfasted and rested. The Battalion strength was 16 officers and 536 other ranks. At 5.00am the British artillery opened a heavy bombardment on the enemy's line. By 1.35pm the enemy had worked his way up and by 2.50pm the enemy's machine guns had increased activity. The situation was good for the British troops as they were back in their old line and houses reoccupied, even though the enemy kept firing on the barrage lines and on Battalion's headquarters. The Battalion were due to be relieved by the 2/6th Battalion Royal Warwickshire Regiment. However, the relief proceeded very slowly, owing to an especially black night which resulted in the platoons getting lost in the darkness. On the 14th April the Battalion arrived at Hamet Billet; the men had breakfast and rested. The Battalion strength was sixteen officers and 536 other ranks. Killed in the period from the 11th April 1918 to 14th April 1918 were four officers and twenty eight other ranks. One hundred and forty six were reported as wounded, with sixty one missing.

One of the twenty eight other ranks was Private Buckingham, who was killed in action on the 14th April 1918, less then two years later after enlisting. The name of E. H. Buckingham is inscribed in a brass plaque in St. Barbara's Church, Ploegsteert Memorial, a plaque in the Methodist Central Hall and on his school's memorial.

Corporal **F. Leduc** was with the Belgian Army and employed by Siddeley Deasy Ltd. *'The Employee Quarterly'* covered details of his death: "*Corporal Leduc was badly wounded on April 17th last and died two days later. His friends and relatives, unfortunately were left in great anxiety and uncertainty as to his fate for a considerable time owing to a mistake at the hospital, resulting in him being buried under the wrong name. It was not until two months after his interment that his body was exhumed and identified as that of Corporal Leduc*".

His Regiment as a body was invested with the order of *'Chevalier de l'ordre de Leopold'* as they were called into action on the 3rd August 1914 and were one of the first Regiments in the firing line. Corporal Leduc also received the Croix de Guerre. *'The Employees Quarterly'* also stated:

"Employees will remember him as a fine-looking young man, splendid athlete and a good shot. He was formerly a member of the famous Aerschot Football and Athletic club of Antwerp, which met and defeated Aston Villa in 1913. He was a member of the famous company of the 9th Regiment of which only seven men were left after the Battle of Haecht. He was wounded after the retreat to Antwerp and came to England. He received an appointment under Mr F. R. Smith and remained with the company until he was called again to the front. Two days later before he was wounded he was awarded the Croix De Guerre for his pluck and daring.

The sympathy of the Siddeley Deasy employees is extended to his relatives and friends. His letters to the social secretary were always cheery and full of thanks for the gifts sent to him by the subscribers to the war relief fund, and may the writer use his words with regards to another brave lad who fell:
> " For freedom, right and country's might,
>   He marched where duty steered".

During research the match with Aston Villa could not be substantiated, the Aston Villa records do not allude to this fixture having taken place. Corporal Leduc is the only Belgian commemorated in the park and he enlisted in 1916.

1914 TO 1918

IN MEMORY OF

CPL. F. LEDUE

BELGIAN ARMY

DIED 1918

A discrepancy Corporal Leduc or Ledue

Driver **Harry Truslove**, 840762, C Battery, 307th Brigade, Royal Field Artillery was killed in action at Boutillerie, near Cagny aged 21 on the 23rd April 1918. He was the son of Harry and Mary Ann Truslove of 116 Nicholls Street, Coventry and enlisted in May 1915. Harry was born on the 14th November 1896 at 6 Vine Street. Prior to the war he was employed as a machinist. Driver Truslove is buried at Dive Copse British Cemetery, Sailly-Le-Sec. Plot III, Row D, Grave 1.

Gunner **John Ward,** 845308, D Battery, 162nd Brigade, Royal Field Artillery died of wounds in France on the 26th April 1918. John was the husband of L. Ward, of 7 Marsworth Street, Coventry and born on the 31st December 1887 at 8 Waterloo Street. He was employed as a capstan hand until enlisting in February 1915 and is buried in Arneke British Cemetery, Plot I, Row D,

Corporal **Reginald George Turrell,** 840399, 306th Brigade, Royal Field Artillery died of wounds received in Gonnehem, France on the 7th May 1918. He was born on the 9th March, 1897 at 13 Leicester Causeway and resided at 72 Bradford Street. Reginald was employed as a clerk prior to enlisting in January 1915 and is buried in Gonnehem British Cemetery, Row C, Grave 14.

The following two main are buried in Esquelbecq Military Cemetery, Private Harry Wainman and Sapper Aleck Sutton.

Private **Harry Wainman,** 70583, 9th Battalion, Royal Welch Fusiliers died of wounds in France age 26 on the 13th May 1918. Harry was the son of George Wainman of 115 Baughton Street, Birmingham and the husband of Martha Wainman of 59, High Street, Fenton, Stoke-on-Trent. A native of Birmingham he was employed by Siddeley Deasy Motors Limited and enlisted in Llanelly. From the 10th to 19th April the Battalion saw heavy action in the line in front of Greenwood and Oostaverne.

Sapper **Aleck Sutton,** 155608, 459th Field Company, Royal Engineers died in France aged 30 on the 21st May 1918. He was the son of Harry Sutton and husband of Annie Maud of 427 Foleshill Road, Coventry. Aleck was born on the 27th August 1887 at Bocking, Essex and enlisted in Warwick.

Private **Alfred Charles Baker,** 41820 C Company, 3rd Battalion, Worcestershire Regiment, formerly 6613 Royal Warwickshire Regiment, was killed in action in the Battle of Aisne, to the east of Soissons aged 20 on the 27th May 1918. Alfred was the son of William and Laura Ellen Baker of 5 Court, 3 House, Far Gosford Street, Coventry. Alfred was born on the 20th August 1898 and enlisted in Coventry in 1916.

Fortune did not favour Private Baker. He was drafted into the Worcesters just before he was killed. To make matters worse, the 3rd Battalion had had a bad time in Belgium and were sent down to the Aisne (France), to rest and recuperate. It had long been a quiet area with scenery to match. They 3rd Battalion left Belgium on 9th May 1918 for the perceived easier time in France. On the 27th May, the Germans launched a massive surprise attack, in the vicinity of Alfred's Battalion. He was killed that day with at least fifty two other 3rd Battalion men. The Germans had a stunning victory, wiping out all before them. The *'Regimental History'* presents a number of key factors. One being orders were not received to destroy the bridges which had made the communications so easy for the 8th Division and this allowed the enemy to advance unmolested.

The 3rd Battalion had been ordered to Concevreux, through field glasses advancing troops could be seen but the British guns did not fire as most of them were out of action. The German Infantry advanced and the battle was renewed at 3.00pm. The Worcesters held their ground but a breakthrough was made on the right and Major Traill decided the Battalion must retire. An optimal position had been reached by the Germans and half the Battalion were hit trying to obtain safety on slopes beyond the village.

Alfred has no known grave and is commemorated on the Soissons Memorial, but it is felt that he is buried in La Ville-aux-Bois Cemetery, under an "Unknown" headstone. This cemetery has the highest proportion of unknowns on the Western Front. Locally Private Baker is commemorated on the panels in Holy Trinity Church.

Private **Horace William Nelson,** 47625, 1st Battalion, Sherwood Foresters (Notts and Derby Regiment) was killed in action aged 28 on the 29th May 1918. Horace was the husband of Gladys Nelson and resided at 48 Highfield Road, Coventry. He was the son of Charles and Martha Nelson of 122 Harnall Lane East, Coventry and was born on the 22nd January 1891 at Burton-upon-Trent. His occupation was as a tailor and he enlisted in Sunderland at the outbreak of war. Horace is commemorated on the Soissons Memorial and in St. John's Church. His plaque states he was a drummer.

Private **Frederick Charles Maurice Jones,** 20296, A Company, 7th Battalion Queen's Own (Royal West Kent Regiment) formerly 231256 RASCMT was killed in action, near Albert aged 19 on the 18th June 1918. Frederick was the son of William Christopher and Georgina French Jones, of 37 Widdrington Road, Coventry. He was a native of West Boldon, Durham and was born there on the 28th November 1898. Frederick was employed as a fitter before enlisting in Warwick in October 1916 and is buried in Ribemont Communal Cemetery Extension (Somme), Plot III, Row A, Grave 9.

Pioneer **Frank Clifford Farrell,** 288994, No.1 Special Company, Royal Engineers was killed in action near Albert aged 28 on the 23rd June 1918. He was married to Emily Peggy Farrell, of 12 St. Nicholas Street, Coventry and was the son of Simpson Farrell and Ada Farrell. Frank was born on the 23rd June 1890 at Derby. A chemist, he was a member of the Pharmaceutical Society and the society records show he passed the minor examination (a rudimentary qualification for pharmacists' employed assistants) on January the 4th 1915 and gave his address as 55 Crewe Street, Derby. By 1917 this had changed to 14 Madeley Street, Derby. Notification of his death appeared in the society journal *'Chemist & Druggist'* on August the 17th 1918 as *"Pioneer Farrell passed the qualifying examination in January 1915, and was employed with Mr. S. H. Bird, Pharmacist, Coventry until he joined the Army at Coventry in September 1917. He leaves a widow and one child"*. Pioneer Farrell is commemorated on the Pozières Memorial.

Lance-Corporal **Victor Leslie Clarke,** 2/7th Battalion, Royal Warwickshire Regiment attached to the 182nd Trench Mortar Battery died of wounds on the 3rd July 1918 aged 24 as a result of wounds received on June 26th. He was the youngest of three serving sons of John (a gardener) and Mary Jane Clarke, of 66, Villa Terrace, Radford, Coventry. On the following page Victor is pictured on the right, Henry (middle) and Ernie Clarke (left). Henry lost a leg in the Battle of the Somme and Ernie survived the war.

Victor was born on 7th April 1894, went to Radford Elementary and then on to Bablake School. He was employed as an office boy before becoming an assembler with British Thompson Houston works. He joined the Royal Warwickshire Regiment in 1914. On the day of his death, Victor's Battalion were in reserve with a strength of 19 officers and 522 other ranks, resting at La Miquellerie. From the 25th June to the 1st July they spent six days in the line on the Right Sub-Sector Robecq Section. Despite excellent weather during this tour they had suffered 1 killed and 10 wounded. The Battalion then moved to rest and were based at La Miquellerie as Brigade reserve.

Victor is buried in Aire Communal Cemetery. At this time the 54th Casualty Clearing Station was in Aire and Victor probably received treatment there for his wounds. Victor's name appears on the Engleton Road Memorial and the Bablake School Memorial, it is known that Victor's mother was distraught at the death of one of her sons and paid for his plaque in the War Memorial Park.

The Clarke Brothers

Private **Donald Fraser,** 23861, 2nd/7th Battalion Royal Warwickshire Regiment was killed in action in France age 41 on the 20th August 1918. He was a native of Dunain, Inverness and born there on 1st May 1877. He was husband of Annie Fraser of 41 Poplar Road, Earlsdon, Coventry and employed as a tailor and cutter until enlisted in January 1916. Private Fraser is buried in Tannay British Cemetery, Thiennes, Plot V, Row E, Grave 12 and his name appears on the memorial in Earlsdon Working Men's club.

A Damaged Plaque

Private **Thomas Henry Barker,** 227029 1st Battalion, Royal Berkshire Regiment, formerly 2533 Royal Warwickshire Regiment, was killed in action in France aged 25 on the 21st August 1918. He was the son of Arthur and Amelia Barker of 8 Lord Street, Chapelfields, Coventry and was born on the 3rd February 1895. Thomas was employed as a moulder until enlisting in September 1914. *'The Coventry Graphic'* on the 8th October 1915, showed a *"fine example of patriotic service"* illustrating the Barker brothers. J. F. Barker was in the Royal Field Artillery (left) and T. H. Barker (right) at this point was in the 1/7th Battalion, Royal Warwickshire Regiment.

On the 17th August the 1st Battalion were at St. Amand. A Company bathed at Humbercamp in the morning and all officers and NCOs attended a lecture at La Breque at 5.00pm on co-operation between Tanks and Infantry. The following day orders were received that the Brigade would attack on the morning of the 21st with the 23rd Royal Fusiliers in front and the 1st Battalion, King's Royal Rifle Company in support. During the morning the Battalion took part in a tactical exercise in Cupertino with the Tanks. B, C and D Companies bathed at Humbercamp in the afternoon and in the evening the 37th Divisional Theatre was reserved for the Battalion for a special performance.

On Monday the 19th August 1918 from 2.00pm to 7.00pm the Brigade carried out practise attacks with tanks at La Rebeque Wood with preparations continuing for the forthcoming operations. On Tuesday at St. Amand, at 8.15 pm the Battalion left in lorries going via Pommier to Monchy where it debussed and marched to the jumping off positions in front of the Ayette - Bucquoy Road.

On Wednesday the 21st August 1918, the Battalion were in position by 1.30am. B and D Companies were to capture the 1st Objective. A and C Companies to pass through them and capture and consolidate the 2nd Objective. Six Tanks (Mark IV) were to assist in the attack. At 4.55am the attack commenced, the morning was very misty and the troops found it was difficult to keep direction. The Tanks especially were soon in trouble and were of little assistance to the Battalion. However all objectives were captured to time with little resistance except from isolated machine guns and the 3rd Division passed through to capture Courcelles and the railway beyond. Battalion headquarters were established at 7.00am. Twelve hours later, orders were received that the Brigade was to be relieved by 76th Infantry Brigade and would move to Quesnoy Farm.

The relief was finally completed at 6.40am the following day and the Battalion Headquarters and D Company reached Quesnoy Farm by 8.30am. The men slept and rested during the day and orders were given for salvaging to be carried out in the evening. However at about 7.00pm the BGC arrived at Battalion Headquarters and stated that the Battalion was to come under the orders of 6th Infantry Brigade and be prepared to carry out an attack on Ervillers the next morning. Private Barker died on the 21st August and is buried in Bienvillers Military Cemetery. He was a member of the Queen's Road Church and is commemorated on a stained glass memorial in the church.

Bienvillers Military Cemetery was begun in September 1915 by the 37th Division, carried on by other Divisions in the line until March 1917, reopened from March to September 1918, when the village was again near the front line, and completed in 1922-24 when a number of graves, mainly of 1916, were brought in from the battlefields of the Ancre. Its twenty-one plots show a remarkable alternation of original burials in Regimental or divisional groups, and groups of concentrated graves.

Sergeant **Sydney Harry Smith**, G/53674, 1st/19th Battalion, London Regiment, formerly 23033 Northants Regiment, died of wounds age 24 on the 24th August 1918. He was the son of Harry Daulby and Sarah Ann Smith of 28 Berkeley Road, Earlsdon, Coventry. A native of Northampton he was born in 1894 and also enlisted in the town. He is buried at Daours Communal Cemetery Extension, Plot VI, Row B, Grave 29. The plaque for Sergeant Smith could not be found but reference was made to a plaque for Sergeant S. Smith. Two men fit this category in the *'Roll of the Fallen'* and both have been included, the other being Sergeant Samuel Smith.

Private **Albert Bartlett,** 377, 18th Battalion, Australian Infantry, (Australian Imperial Forces) was killed in action at Mereacourt Wood age 23 on 28th August 1918. Albert was the son of Francis and Alice Barnett of 43 Aldbourne Road, Coventry and born in West Bromwich on the 22nd November 1895. He resided in Coventry until 1914 when he emigrated to Australia. In May 1915 he enlisted in the infantry and was occupied as a boundary rider when he was killed. Private Bartlett is buried in Assevillers New British Cemetery. Plot II, Row E, Grave 3.

'The Australian Archives' show that Private Bartlett embarked from Australia on the 25th June 1915 and proceeded to Gallipoli on the 16th August 1915. He fell ill and finally ended up in a hospital in Fulham, England suffering from rheumatism on the 27th October 1915. He then proceeded to France on the 24th March 1916 and was wounded in action on the 5th August 1916 when he was shot in the left arm and shoulder. This saw him return to England by the 10th August 1916. He recovered and returned to France on the 13th December 1916. On the 3rd May 1917 he was wounded for the second occasion in the right arm and embarked for England on the 19th May 1917 to recuperate at Weymouth. He then appears to have remained in the UK for some time as he suffered from Influenza and finally left for France again on the 22nd August 1918. Four days later he rejoined his unit and was killed two days after this reunion on the 28th August 1918.

Assevillers was taken by the French in the autumn of 1916, evacuated by the Fifth Army on the 26th March, 1918, and retaken by the 5th Australian Division on the 28th August, 1918. Assevillers New British Cemetery was made after the Armistice by the concentration of graves from the battlefields of the Somme and from other burial grounds. The following were among the burial grounds from which British graves were brought to Assevillers New British Cemetery:- Barleux German Cemetery in which ten Australian soldiers were buried by their comrades in

August and September 1918. Estress-Deniecourt German Cemetery, between Estrees and Fay, where two Australian soldiers were buried by the enemy. Plantation Cemetery, where one United Kingdom soldier was buried in February, 1917, and four Australians in August and September, 1918.

Private Bartlett's memorial plaque was sent to his mother in Coventry, and his original grave was found by the Grave Registrations Unit and his remains were re-interned on the 2nd December 1925.

Rifleman **Leonard Harris,** 315350, 5th Battalion, London Regiment (London Rifle Brigade), formerly 4149 South Staffordshire Regiment, died on the 28th August 1918. He was born and enlisted in Wolverhampton and is buried in Bac-Du-Sud British Cemetery. In August and September, when the Germans had been pushed back, the 45th and 46th Casualty Clearing Stations were posted to the neighbourhood. Bac-du-Sud British Cemetery contains 688 Commonwealth burials of the First World War. The name L. Harris appears on the memorial in the Central Methodist hall.

Private **Arthur Trickett,** 26204, 14th Battalion, Royal Warwickshire Regiment was killed in action at Vaulx, near Cambrai aged 19 on the 28th August 1918. He was initially posted as missing. Arthur was the son of Edward and Emily Trickett of 39 Poplar Road, Earlsdon, Coventry and he had a brother serving with the Army Service Corps. Arthur was born on the 2nd July 1899 in 10 Raglan Street and employed as a greengrocer until enlisting in August 1917.

The 14th Battalion were in operations in the region of Cambrai from the 21st August to the 31st August 1918. On the 25th the New Zealand Divison captured Grevillers and on the 27th August the 14th Battalion's Headquarters were moved just west of Favreuil, with companies B and D

holding strong points. Those killed from the 21st August to the 31st were 9 officers 120 other ranks and the capture included 4 officers, 273 other ranks, 9 heavy machine guns 23 light machine guns and 1 trench mortar.

Private Trickett is buried in Mory Abbey Military Cemetery, Mory. The family grave in London Road Cemetery reads "*He died to save his country*", his father Edward died 23rd November 1931 aged 62, his mother Emily died July 30th 1943 aged 72 and Arthur's sister Edith died on the 23rd February 1965.

Private **Arthur Welch**, 17028, 1st Battalion, Royal Warwickshire Regiment was killed in action in France aged 30 on the 31st August 1918. He was the son of Arthur and Hannah Welch of 21 Primrose Hill Street, Coventry and was born on the 11th September 1887 at Coventry. Arthur resided with his parents and was employed as a grinder until enlisting in March 1916. '*The Coventry Graphic*' informed its readers that "*His mother received official notification of his death. Private Welch joined up under the Darby scheme and had been at the front for two years. Previous to enlisting he was employed at the Triumph works*".

The '*Battalion War Diary*' notes on the 30th August 1918, the Battalion moved South East of Remy Wood and Village; "*Companies dribbled forward but the movement was observed and a heavy machine gun and artillery barrage was put down. B and C companies were disorganised and suffered severe casualties. Captain Arthur Joseph Adams was killed, the artillery were asked to shell the opposite ridge and hostile fire was considerably reduced*".

On the following day owing to reduced strength, A and C companies amalgamated, B and D also, which were then known as composite 1 and 2 companies. The companies then moved up to support the Duke of Wellington's together with 2nd Seaforth Highlanders in making an attack at 8.45pm on the 3rd objective from the previous day. The objective was not reached as the men on the way to 2nd objective had to cross a stream and swamp wading waist deep in mud. Owing to this delay the artillery barrage got too far ahead and this along with a shortage of men prevented the 3rd objective being taken. Private Welch is commemorated on the Vis-En-Artois Memorial.

Rifleman **Walter Herbert Hartopp,** G/44189, 1/21st Battalion, London Regiment (formerly 7th Battalion, Royal Warwickshire Regiment), was killed in action on the 1st September 1918. He was born on the 29th January 1900 in Coventry and was 18 years old. He resided at 11c, 3h. Cox Street and was employed as a fitter at the Siddeley Deasy works. He was also a reservist and is buried in Peronne Communal Cemetery Extension.

In a question in *'The Coventry Graphic'* :"*Which is the most patriotic street in Coventy ?*" the answer was judged by the percentage of families that had representatives with the forces. The record was awarded to Lower Wellington Street, Hillfields for no fewer then 22 houses or more then 50 per cent sent men to the colours. One of these men was H. W. Hartopp.

Private **Harry Holland,** 49811, 1st Battalion, Royal Irish Fusiliers formerly 6506 Oxfordshire and Buckinghamshire Light Infantry was killed in action on the 2nd September 1918. He was born in Birmingham and employed by Armstrong Siddeley Deasy Motors Ltd. With no known grave he is commemorated on the Ploegsteert Memorial.

Private **George Hopkins,** 266418, 2nd/6th Battalion, Royal Warwickshire Regiment was killed in action in France aged 24 on the 6th September 1918. George was born on the 12th September 1894 in Coventry and resided at 79 Mulliner Street. He was employed locally as a bottler until enlisting in April 1915.

Almost two years before his death *'The Coventry Graphic'* of November 24th 1916 showed the photos of the four sons of Mr and Mrs Hopkins, 79 Mulliner Street Coventry. The pictures reading from left to right are: top row, George Hopkins who was wounded in the head whilst serving with the Royal Warwickshire Regiment in France and had been awarded the "parchment" for gallant conduct and Private T. Hopkins who was at that point training in England; bottom row Lance Corporal "Jim" Hopkins who was in France with the Royal Warwickshire Regiment and Gunner Joe Hopkins who was serving in Salonica.

At dawn on the 6th September, C Company were established at Fort Rompu and had posts from a road junction to a river. D company were in the same position as at nightfall, their men along the Rue Bataille having been shelled heavily during the night. After a reconnaissance of the position at Fort Rompu it appeared that this was satisfactory and there was a good prospect of reaching the road junction and position known as H.8 Central although notes were made that the enemy machine guns were firing from South East.

A combined operation between C and D companies was therefore decided on to reach the objectives laid down the previous night. The details of the scheme were carefully worked out by the Officers Commanding C and D companies and time was given to ensure that all concerned were fully acquainted with the details.
The general idea was that C company should send up another platoon to assist in taking H.8 central and the copse and houses to the south which were held by the enemy. As soon as they reached this, they would send up a light signal which was to be answered by D Company. C company would then open fire in a southerly direction and D company would commence operations. B company and the artillery were ordered to fire North East from the road so keeping suspected enemy strong points in front under fire.

Two platoons successfully accomplished their task and a green verey light was sent up by them at about 11.30am. This was answered by a red verey light from No.15 platoon, then more platoons worked forward to the south west corner of the enclosure. These platoons were under covering fire from No.15 platoon, a Vickers gun and a trench mortar. No.13 platoon reinforced no.16 platoon who started bombing the enemy out of a post he held. As a result the enemy was seen running across the open in all directions from the enclosure and posts to south and East of it.

The two platoons of B company under Lieutenant Massey fired at the retreating enemy from the Rue Bataille. Numbers 13 and 16 platoons moved to the south east of the enclosure and opened fire with Lewis Guns. Number 15 platoon moved east along the railway and joined up on the left of Second Lieutenant Williams, and fifteen of the enemy under a sergeant Major surrendered to them. It is estimated that 120 to 150 enemy were seen to retreat and a great many were hit, one Lewis gun claiming as many as thirty. Our losses during this operation were very slight, being two men wounded. Great assistance was given by the fire of Vickers guns, four of which were attached to C and D companies, and the Trench Mortars.

By 1.00pm the Rue Bataille area was cleared and a line established as follows: In front of the close ground along the Rue Bataille running south west. B company on the right shortly afterwards slung their left forward and joined up with this new line. The platoon of C company after reaching H8 Central was fired at from the wood and houses to the North east but a patrol pushed through successfully and cleared the wood establishing a post during the morning. This cleared the left flank of the Battalion.

A Battalion to the left of the 2/6th Battalion had worked round the northern bend of the river and held the northern bank. This movement was completed by the evening of September 5th but this Battalion did not cross to the south of the river and in consequence the 2/6th Battalion's left flank had been unprotected during the day, there being a 1000 to 1500 yards of frontage between the 2/6th Battalion and the river, which should have been occupied by a Division on the left. Private Hopkins is commemorated in Anzac Cemetery, Sailly-sur-La-Lys

Private **Dennis Thorpe,** 43621, 2nd/7th Battalion Royal Warwickshire Regiment died of wounds in France age 18 on the 7th September 1918. He was the son of William and Sarah Thorpe of Kidlington, Oxon and born on the 21st September 1899 at Kidlington. He resided at 102 Bolingbroke Road and was employed as a fitter at Siddeley Deasy before enlisting in January 1918. Private Thorpe is buried in Aire Communal Cemetery, Plot IV, Row D, Grave 15.

On the 1st September 1918 the Brigade were at Estaires in support, the *'Battalion War Diaries'* notes from the 1st to 3rd there were no casualties, on the 4th 1 officer and 1 other rank wounded. By the 5th the Battalion had moved to the Sailly Sur La Lys Sector and a note made that twenty green cross shells fell and on the the 7th September one officer and four other ranks were wounded and two gassed.

Private **Thomas Percy Jackson** MM, 24869, 16th Battalion, Royal Warwickshire Regiment died of wounds age 32 on the 8th September 1918. He was the son of Henry Ainsworth and Harriet Jackson of 112 Earlsdon Avenue North, Coventry. Thomas was born on the 2nd December 1885 at Coventry, he resided near his parents at 47 Huntingdon Road and was employed as a journalist until enlisted in June 1917.

On the 3rd of the September, the Battalion moved forward again to the line for the final bound. During this advance enemy planes flew very low over the Battalion and enemy shot at them with 5.9 guns from close range and direct observation. The men were remarkably steady and only one casualty was sustained. The Battalion were relieved at 9.00pm. *'The Battalion War Diary'* states *"the fighting on the 2nd and 3rd especially was remarkable for the exceptional endurance displayed by the men, who after continuous fighting on the 2nd had no real settled rest for 14 days and had to advance some 5 miles across country carrying Lewis guns, panniers, picks and shovels"*. On the 5th and 6th September the Battalion rested, reorganised and bathed. In between the 7th and the 11th they undertook training under company arrangements and practice at advance guards. Also on the 11th September the following immediate awards were made in connection with recent operations, 22 MM's were awarded one of these being to T. Jackson. It was noted the strength of the Battalion on the 1st September was 31 officers and 817 other ranks and by the 30th was 24 officers and 606 other ranks. One of the 211 men killed or missing, Private Jackson is buried in Bagneux British Cemetery, Gezaincourt, Plot VI, Row F, Grave 25.

Gunner **Frederick George Page**, 944531, 49th Battery, 40th Brigade, Royal Field Artillery was killed in action aged 22 on the 16th September 1918. He was the son of Frederick and Selina Page of 13 Bond Street, Coventry and born on the 18th May 1896. Frederick also resided at 13 Bond Street and was employed as an Iron Turner at Siddeley Deasy enlisting in January 1915. He had four siblings Alfred who was born and died in 1898, Albert Ernest who was born in 1899 and died in 1917, Arthur was born in 1904 and finally Irene who was born in 1917.

Gunner Page is buried in Morchies Australian Cemetery. Frederick has two plaques in the park and his name appears on St. John's and the Holy Trinity memorials.

Private **Harold Hubert Harper,** 43250, 8th Battalion, Royal Berkshire Regiment was killed in action aged 21 on the 20th September 1918. Harold was the son of Joseph Harper and husband of Florence Elsie Harper of 26 Spencer Street, Coventry. He was aged 22 and born on the 11th July 1896 in Thomas Street and at one point resided at 36 Croft Road. Harold was employed at Siddeley Deasy as a tool fitter until enlisting in May 1918.

On the 18th September the Battalion were at Epinetie Wood, and the *'War Diaries'* note it was generally quiet. In the evening orders were received for an attack on Lempire. The objective was to form a line running from Yak Post Street, Patricks Avenue, Dose Trench, Lempire Post (N), Thistle Trench and St. Patricks Avenue as a defensive flank facing West.

Order of attack: C Company on the left were to form a defensive flank and occupy

Yak Post. B Company in the centre were to occupy Dose Trench and Lempire Post (N). A Company on the right were to occupy Thistle Trench and form junction with B Company. 1 platoon D Company were to occupy Enfer Wood. D Company (less 1 platoon) and 7th Royal West Kents were formed up in rear with orders to pass through to final objective

The following day at 8.15am the Battalion moved to the assembly positions. B, C and D Companies were in a trench south of the Ronssoy-Lempire Road. A Company were in a trench near the road east of the crossroads. Battalion Headquarters were located on the Western edge of Ronossoy. The enemy artillery was very active throughout the period of assembling causing A company a few casualties. Assembly reported complete at 10.40am with zero hour fixed at 11.00am.

A, B and C companies moved forward at zero and were close up with the barrage when it commenced to move forward. A company (less 1 platoon) remained in assembly position. 3 platoons of A company reported as being on their objectives (Thistle Trench) by 11.40am suffering few casualties during the advance. D company platoon reached Enfer Wood at 12.50pm. The situation was obscure until Captain M. Wykes MC went forward to reconnoitre the situation. He reported C company on their main objective and in Yak Post after a hot bombing fight. He then proceeded along Dose Trench and found it and also Lempire Post, unoccupied by the enemy or our troops. Returning via Lempire-Tombois Farm Road he found A and B companies held up by strong machine gun fire from Z copse. B company then proceeded to occupy their objective passing through C company and down Dose Trench. On reports being received of the enemy still being in Lempire, D company were ordered to mop up the village. This company returned and reported Lempire quite clear of the enemy.

Opposition on the right was very severe. C company pushed some men into Zebra Post during the evening. On the 20th September the Battalion were based at St. Emilie with the Battalion Headquarters moved to sunken road in front of Ronssoy. Private Harper has no known grave and is commemorated on the Vis-En-Artois Memorial.

Second Lieutenant **Joseph Arthur Edwards,** 16th Battalion, Royal Warwickshire Regiment was killed in action at Cambrai on the 27th September 1918. He was the husband of Nora Emily Edwards of 56 Stanway Road, Coventry and born on the 9th June 1891. A commercial traveller he enlisted in 1915 and was known locally as 'Arthur'.

At 1.00am on the 27th September the Battalion were in position. At 7.52am the 1st Bedfords moved forward towards their objective under heavy barrage to which the enemy replied immediately. Eight minutes later the Battalion went over and despite a hostile barrage advanced in perfect order. No definite news was received as to 1st Bedford Regiment being on objective, but reports from wounded pointed to having got there at 10.15am. Battalion Headquarters were moved forward to the sunken trench. The position was found to be very obscure; it appeared that only one of the initial objectives had been obtained, with the exception of B company who were further forward on the right. The left of the Battalion had almost reached the objective on the left but had to fall back as the 42nd Division on the left had failed to come up.

At 4.45pm a large enemy bombing party broke through the 13th Infantry Brigade front on the Battalion's right and worked round our right flank, leaving B company encircled and working up trenches towards Battalion Headquarters. Those on this position stood to and with rifle and machine gun fire drove the enemy back, the Company Sergeant Major of the 15th Trench mortar battery did particularly good work in making bomb stops in trenches.

At 6.30pm Captain Sewell MC Commanding B company was still holding out. The officer commanding B company skilfully withdrew his troops and conformed to general line, unfortunately being seriously wounded in the operation. Four hours later a supply tank was hit by a shell and burnt to pieces with three of its crew. The supply of bombs and small arms ammunition was very low. Second Lieutenant Edwards is buried in Gouzeaucourt New British Cemetery.

Private **Francis Joseph Ison,** 43083, 5th Battalion, Royal Berkshire Regiment was killed in action at Epehy aged 19 on the 27th September 1918. He was the son of Joseph Albert and Isabella Ison of 64 Fisher Road, Coventry and born on the 17th July 1898 at Wimbledon, Surrey. Employed as a clerk he resided at 54 Mount Street until enlisting in April 1918. Private Ison is commemorated in Villers Hill British Cemetery, Villers-Guislan

The Royal Berkshire were involved in operations from the 18th-30th September and prior to this from the 8th – 17th the Battalion were at Nurlu, France refitting and training for future operations.

Gunner **William Henry Wilcox Moy,** 840201, 56th Battery, 34th Brigade, Royal Field Artillery was killed in action at Beaumetz aged 22 on the 27th September 1918. William's father was also called William Henry and his mother was Amy Elizabeth; the family lived at 25 Broomfield Place, Coventry. William was born on the 28th August 1896 in Coventry and employed as a toolmaker, enlisting at the outbreak of war. Gunner Moy is buried at Ruyaulcourt Military Cemetery, Plot I, Row N, Grave 8.

Private **Joseph Vincent Jewsbury,** 48911, 7th Battalion, Leicestershire Regiment was killed in action aged 19 on the 28th September 1918. He was the son of Arthur and Emily Ann Jewsbury and resided with his parents at 138 Gulson Road, Coventy. Joseph was born on the 15th September 1899 at Measham and employed as a miller. He enlisted five months earlier in April 1918 and is buried in Gouzeaucourt New British Cemetery.

Private **Frank William Wells,** service number G/17145, was with the 13th Battalion, Royal Sussex Regiment. The G stood for 'general service' and replaced the GS sequence in November 1914. The 13th Battalion was one of three Battalions, the others being the 11th and 12th, raised by Colonel Claude Lowther of Herstmonceux in response to Lord Kitchener's call to arms. Their mascot was a Sussex sheep- hence the nickname 'Lowther's Lambs'. They were recruited mainly from the downland villages and coastal towns of East Sussex. They trained at Cooden Camp at Bexhill and at Witley Camp near Godalming. They went over to France as the 116th

(Southdown) brigade of the 39th Division in March 1916 and suffered heavy casualties at Aubers Ridge on 30th June 1916. The three Battalions fought at the third Battle of Ypres later in 1917 but the 11th and 13th in particular sustained very heavy losses in the struggle to stem the German offensive south of the Somme in March 1918. Both Battalions were practically wiped out and what remained of the 13th was finally destroyed at Ypres, in the German attack at Kemmel on 9th April 1918.

Frank Wells was captured in the spring of 1918, and *'The Coventry Graphic'* of July 19th 1918 cited it had been confirmed that he was a prisoner of war and had been missing officially since April 26th. He enlisted in September 1916 leaving the engineers office of the London & North Western and Midland Railways at Nuneaton.

Frank was born on the 7th September 1898 at Coventry and resided at 64 Arden Street. He was the son of Frank W. Wells, a railway barman, and Alice Wells, and brother of Arthur, who was two years younger. From Earlsdon Elementary he went to Bablake School. Before joining the colours, he was employed as a clerk and eventually died of his wounds in France, whilst a prisoner of war aged 21 on the 3rd October 1918. Along with other allied prisoners and German soldiers he is buried in Glageon Communal Cemetery Extension, the village being occupied by the Germans for practically the whole of the War. He is also commemorated in St. Barbara's Church and at Bablake School.

Private **Arthur Marshall Lewin Bull,** 34656, 2nd Battalion, Oxfordshire and Buckinghamshire Light Infantry died of wounds aged 19 on the 5th October 1918. He was the son of Richard and Frances Bull. Richard and Frances came to Coventry about 1905 with Richard working at the Standard, they rented 13 Arden Street. Arthur was their only child and born on the 19th June 1899 at Dartford, Kent. Arthur was employed as a planer until enlisting in July 1917 as Private T/R/8/24169 with the 52nd Battalion Hants Regiment. He was later transferred to the 2nd Battalion of the Oxfordshire and Buckinghamshire Light Infantry. Arthur is buried in Mont Huon Military Cemetery, Le Treport, Somme and commemorated locally on St. Barbara's Memorial. Arthur's father, Richard was older than his wife Frances and after Richard's death she remarried and became Frances Greenway residing in Broadway, Earlsdon.

Private **Ernest James Hall,** S/43592, 1st/5th Battalion, Seaforth Highlanders, formerly 5141094835, Army Service Corps and G/92023 Royal Fusiliers, was killed in action on the 13th October 1918. He died one week before his 20th birthday as he was born on the 20th October 1888 at Bretford, residing at 142 Cook Street. He was employed as a baker until enlisting in May 1915 and went to France in November 1915 with the Army Service Corps. Before being transferred to the Seaforth Highlanders he was in the London Regiment. *'The Regimental History'* reads *"The Final Allied Offensive -1918. After the 51st Highland division returned to the Cambrai area the 1/5th Seaforth took part in the attack on 12-13th October, the division's final major operation before the Armistice. The last battle of the war for the 1/5th Seaforth was the attack at Thun St. Martin. The final 16 days fighting had cost the battalion over 400 casualties".* Private Hall is buried in Avesnes Le-Sec Communal Cemetery Extension, Row B, Grave 10 and commemorated in St. John's Church.

Private **Walter Frank Francis,** 41343, 6th Battalion, Dorsetshire Regiment formerly 45055 Royal Army Medical Corps died of wounds on the 14th October 1918. Walter was born on the 17th November 1892 at Coventry and resided at 11 Croft Road. He was employed as a turner at the Triumph and Gloria works. He enlisted in November 1914. Private Francis died of wounds a few days after being injured on the 11th October 1918 and he is buried at Rocquigny-Equancourt Road British Cemetery, Manancourt. His name appears on the works memorial in Coventry Cemetery.

Private **David Clarke,** 23555, 1st Battalion, Coldstream Guards, formerly 2942 Household Battalion, was killed in action age 32 on the 16th October 1918. He was the son of David and Mary Ann Millar Clarke of Coventry and husband of Eleanor (nee Vosper) of 38 Gresham Street, Coventry. He was born on the 23rd January 1886 at 5 Leicester Street and worked as a plumber until enlisted in May 1917. Private Clarke is buried in Romeries Communal Cemetery Extension and a former employee of Siddeley Deasy.

Private **Albert Harold Sowter,** 41023, 6th Battalion, Dorsetshire Regiment was killed in action age 19 on the 16th October 1918. He was the son of Mrs M. Sowter who resided at the back of 44 Spon Street, Coventry. Albert was born on the 16th March 1899 in Coventry and resided at 44 Meadow Street, being employed as a turner at Siddeley Deasy. Albert enlisted in April 1918 and is commemorated on the Vis-En-Artois Memorial and locally in St. John's Church.

241

Lance Corporal **Joseph Newton Barber,** 41040. 1st Battalion Royal Dublin Fusiliers formerly 296758 Army Service Corps, died age 32 with pneumonia in Belgium whilst a prisoner of war on the 17th October 1918. Joseph was the son of George and Harriet Barber and husband of Mary Gertrude Barber of Beechwood, Westwood Road, Tile Hill, Coventry. He was born on the 26th March 1886 at 5c Cope Street and at some point previously resided at 56 Mickleton Road. Joseph was a wholesale grocer until enlisted in Coventry in February 1917 and is buried in La Louviere Town Cemetery, Belgium. A member of the Queen's Road Church he is commemorated on a stained glass memorial in the church.

No. 30 Casualty Clearing Station was at La Louviere from December 1918 to April 1919. They began the Commonwealth plot in the communal cemetery, and later, 11 Commonwealth burials made by the Germans elsewhere in the cemetery during the occupation were moved there.

Driver **Kenneth Merrick Powell,** 840547, B Battery, 306th Brigade, Royal Field Artillery was killed in action near Cambrai aged 20 on the 19th October 1918. Kenneth was the son of Arthur and Annie Mary Powell, of 33 Catherine Street, Coventry. An apprentice engine fitter, he enlisted in February 1915 whilst 15 as he was born on the 9th June 1899 at Hay, Breconshire. Kenneth is buried in St. Aubert British Cemetery, Plot II, Row C, Grave 3.

Private **Harold George Bonham,** 6645, 20th Battalion London Regiment, transferred to (409500) 883rd Area Employment Coy attached Officer Commanding Troops Office, Labour Corps formerly 23128 Somerset Light Infantry, died at Le Havre aged 27 on the 20th October 1918. Harold was the son of Alfred and Fannie Bonham of Bangor, Friars Road, Coventry. Harold was born on the 8th August 1891 at Coventry and also resided in Coventry attending Bablake School. He was on the Admin Staff in the Gas Department until enlisting in March 1916 and is buried at Ste. Marie Cemetery, Le Havre.

Second Lieutenant **Robert Logan,** 4th Battalion, King's Own Scottish Borderers died aged 25 on the 20th October 1918. He was the only son of James and Mary Dickinson Logan, of Birkhill, Earlston, Berwickshire. Robert was born in 1893 and after attending St. Mary's, Melrose and Morrison's Academy, Crieff he attended Watsonian College from 1909 to 1910. He was in the college XV and the XI of that season and on leaving entered the service of the Scottish Widows' Assurance Company, he continued to play for the Watsonian

XV. On joining the Forces he was mobilised as a Trooper and went to Salonika where he was invalided home with malaria. He was gazetted to the King's Own Scottish Borderers and did valuable training work as a bombing officer. Crossing to France he was killed in the fierce fighting around Landrecies and is buried in Caudry British Cemetery.

Private **Ernest John Hancocks**, 42895, D Company 1st/8th Battalion, Royal Warwickshire Regiment was killed in action aged 19 on the 23rd October 1918. He was the son of William and Kate Elizabeth Hancocks of Overtown, Appleby Magna, Burton upon Trent. Ernest was born on the 29th May 1899 at Coventry and resided at 191 Leicester Causeway, employed as a machinist.

On the evening of the 22nd October, the Battalion moved up to its forming up position along the railway near Pommereuil. On the 23rd the attack commenced at 1.20am, the Battalion moving in rear of the 9th Devons. The Battalion was used to help mop up Pommereuil if necessary or if this necessity did not arise to pass through the 7th Brigade and carry the intermediate objective which was the road. Owing to heavy fog the attacking units of the first wave became rather mixed up and the situation was obscure, Captain H. Mortimore MC who was commanding the Battalion went out and took command of the troops of all units and organised attacks on the enemy machine gun nests which had been missed by the first wave owing to the fog. The situation rapidly cleared and all objectives were gained. Private Hancocks is buried at Pommereuil British Cemetery. Row B, Grave 6

Private **Joseph Stew**, 43258, 8th Battalion, Royal Berkshire Regiment was killed in action aged 29 in France on the 23rd October 1918. He resided with his parents at 266 Hall Green, Foleshill, Coventry although he was born in 1883 at Coleshill and enlisted in Warwick.

The Battalion were at Le Cateau, France. Zero hour was 1:20am for the 18th Division. The barrage commenced and the enemy retaliation was quickly felt and was remarkably heavy, many shells falling on the line. The Battalion suffered about 15 casualties during its stay, including the Medical Officer, Captain W. H. Ferguson MC, RAMC. Although wounded this officer continued to attend to the wounded in a cool and heroic manner and while extricating wounded men from a blown in dug-out he was wounded a second time which necessitated his leaving the Battalion.

At 1:50am companies commenced to leave the cutting and form up about 100 yards in front. Order of companies was D company on the right, C company in the centre, B company on the left and A company in support. The Battalion had been ordered to capture and consolidate the 2nd objective of the 53rd Infantry Brigade, passing through the 10ᵗʰ Essex Regiment and 7ᵗʰ Royal West Kent Regiment from 1ˢᵗ objective.

An hour after this the Battalion moved forward keeping to the right flank of D company which was resting at a nearby wood, considerable difficulty was experienced in keeping touch with D Company although the moon had risen by this time making it easier to maintain direction. The first opposition was met at Richemont River, where a strong machine gun nest held up the left company. These guns had been missed by the 1ˢᵗ attack. Officer Commanding B company Second lieutenant J. Grant was killed here and most of his company Headquarters became casualties. On the right a little sniping from three Germans who had previously surrendered caused slight trouble.

The Battalion moved on behind the leading Battalion to just short of the 1ˢᵗ objective, the sunken road where the 10th Essex were found to be definitely held up by very heavy machine gun fire. Numerous attempts were made to rush this position both by the Essex and C Company without success. In addition heavy machine gun fire was coming from L'Eveque Wood and the right was also held up. Battalion Headquarters had, by this time, moved.

The position remained unchanged until dawn. As soon as it was light enough, it became evident that the attack on the left Brigade front was going well and the enemy in the sunken road apparently becoming uneasy, especially when tanks were seen moving on the far ridge to their flank, they began to retire. Captain M. Wykes MC, who had gone forward from Battalion Headquarters to reconnoitre, appreciating the situation moved the leading companies forward and the sunken road was rushed without much opposition. Over 30 light and heavy machine guns were taken in the road. The advance was then continued as far as the 2ⁿᵈ objective which was taken about 08.30 am. Owing to the fact that B company had been held up at Richemont River it became necessary to reinforce the line on the 2ⁿᵈ objective. A company was therefore moved up.

Company dispositions were as follows. C company from Fayt Farm with A company on their right and elements of B and D along the road, where touch was gained with the left Battalion (1ˢᵗ Worcesters) 25ᵗʰ Division. The 55ᵗʰ Brigade were soon in the action after passing through and machine gun fire was shortly afterwards heard from the direction of Bousies. Companies reorganised. B company was concentrated in the practice trenches. These positions were maintained during the night 23/24th October. The Battalion's capture in field guns were 11 machine guns over 20 definitely collected. 146 members of the Battalion died that month with many of these being casualties on the 23ʳᵈ. Private Stew is buried in Highland Cemetery, Le-Cateau.

Private **Thomas Kimberley,** 42394, 1st Battalion, Royal Warwickshire Regiment was killed in action at Verchain age 34 on the 24th October 1918. He was the son of Thomas and Rose Kimberley of Coventry and husband of Elizabeth (nee Townsend) residing at 7 Northfield Road, Coventry. Thomas was born on the 17th August 1881 in Gosford Street and employed as a cycle finisher until enlisting in May 1918. Thomas's employment was with Triumph and Gloria as his name appears on the works memorial.

On the 24th October, zero hour was 04.00am. The barrage was a little short to start with and there were a few casualties from our own side. The river Ecaillon was crossed without difficulty and the village of Verchain entered, large numbers of the enemy giving themselves up. At 05.00am the first objective was taken; A and C companies passed through B and D companies to the second objective which was on the high ground to the North East of Verchain. Opposition was encountered there in the form of a trench line and several machine guns rendered further advance impossible at this time. A and C companies consolidated on a line about 200 yards in rear of the objective having established touch on the left with 1st Somerset Light Infantry and on the right with 2nd Duke Of Wellington's Regiment. The Battalion was relieved at night by the King's Own Regiment and the companies went back to billets at Sauleoir. During the action the Battalion had about 95 casualties, captured 2 light trench mortars, 8 heavy machine guns, light machine guns and 150 prisoners approximately were taken. Private Kimberley is buried in Verchain British Cemetery, Verchain Maugre

Private **Arthur Robert Rotheram Moy,** M/288141, 37th Motor Transport, Motor Ambulance Convoy, Royal Army Service Corps died in France age 33 on the 25th October 1918. He was the son of James Thomas and Elizabeth and husband of Lilian Kate Moy of Roisel, 19 Spencer Avenue, Coventry. He was born on the 25th October 1885 at The Crescent, Holyhead Road and the family at some point also resided at 51 Broadway.

His father was a well known wholesale and retail grocer with a business in Smithford Street. Arthur completed his education at King Henry VIII School between 1898 and 1900, before helping manage the family business with his elder brother. He married Lillian Kate Snape the daughter of a local alderman and they had a daughter Marjorie. Like his father, Arthur was a leading member of Well Street Congregational Church in Coventry and was elected a deacon of the church just a few weeks before his death.

Arthur had attested his willingness to serve under the Derby scheme in December 1915 but was not called up until February 1917. He joined the Army Service Corps and after a period training at the Mechanical Transport Depot at Grove Park in

London, he was sent to France in April 1917. He was granted 18 days leave in July 1918 for the death of his father and returned to his unit in August. Arthur died of bronchopneumonia and is buried at Roisel Communal Cemetery extension. The British cemetery dates from the late 1918 when Roisel was an important Casualty clearing station centre, others graves were then concentrated there after the war.

Private **George Willliam Smith,** 43093, 5th Battalion, Royal Berkshire Regiment died of wounds age 19 on the 31st October 1918. An engineer's apprentice , he was the son of George and Maggie of 37 Drapers Fields, Coventry. He was born on the 30th August 1899 at Coventry and also enlisted in the City in April 1918. Private Smith is buried at Terlincthun British Cemetery, Wimille, Plot VI, Row F, Grave 4. His headstone reads *"Only those who have lost a loved one know the meaning of gone"*.

Private **William Henry Wilson,** 43401, 2nd/8th Battalion, Royal Warwickshire Regiment was killed in action in France on the 1st November 1918. He resided at Bilton Hall, Warwickshire and was employed by Siddeley Deasy Motors Limited. William is buried in Preseau Communal Cemetery Extension and enlisted in Coventry. By the time of William's death the 2/8th Battalion had been disbanded as no new reinforcements were available to maintain their effective strength. The majority of the men of the 2nd/ 8th Battalion went to join the 2nd/7th Battalion with approximately five percent going to the 2/6th Battalion.

Private **Leslie Thomas Jones,** 1/8th Battalion, Royal Warwickshire Regiment was killed in action at Landrecies, France aged 19 on the 4th November 1918. Landrecies was the scene of rear-guard fighting on the 25th August 1914, after the Battle of Mons, and from that date it remained in German hands until it was captured by the 25th Division on 4th November 1918. At 6.15am the 1/8th Battalion attacked and after a very severe fight secured the objective which was the line of the River Sambre at Landrecies, establishing a bridgehead there. The Battalion then received orders at 3.40pm to concentrate in another area and they moved in accordance with these orders.

Leslie was born on the 29th December 1898 in Queen Victoria Road, Coventry and resided at 33 Earlsdon Avenue South, Coventry with his parents Charles Arthur and Frances Jones. An electrical engineer, he enlisted in June 1918 in Warwick and had served only five months. He is buried in Landrecies British Cemetery. His name appears on the memorial in St. Barbara's Church and on the Bablake School Memorial.

Captain **Joseph Arthur Richards,** 1st/8th Battalion, Royal Warwickshire Regiment was also killed in action, at Landrecies on the 4th November 1918 aged 26. He was the son of James and Anne Richards of 45 Cartland Road, Stirchley, Birmingham and was a native of Tenterden, Kent and born on the 20th May 1892. He enlisted in 1915 and was previously employed as a Police Constable. He is buried in Landrecies British Cemetery. The local press stated That *"Joseph Arthur Richards was a young police officer of exceptional promise and received his commission in the field"* and he was known locally as Arthur.

Private **James Thomas Smith,** 58432, 10th Battalion Royal Warwickshire Regiment was killed in action in France on the 7th November 1918. He was born in 1898 in Coventry and resided at 129 Harnall Lane being employed by Siddeley Deasy Motors Limited. He enlisted in Coventry in May 1918 and is buried at Cross Roads Cemetery, Fontaine-Au-Bois.

Private **John Bartlett,** 266302, 10th Battalion, Royal Warwickshire Regiment was born on the 10th March 1898 at Hillfields and resided in the City being employed as a fitter. He lived at 14 King Richard Street with his mother until enlisting in December 1915 and died of wounds in France on 8th November 1918. Private Bartlett is buried in Awoingt British Cemetery, France, Plot II, Row G, Grave 16. His brother also has a plaque in the park, Private Henry Bartlett.

On the 8th November a previous attack was continued, C and D companies being in front with A and B companies in support. The advance was continued to the east of Malplaquet where the Battalion was held up by enemy machine gun fire. On the 11th November the Battalion attended divine service at 11.00am.

The last casualty on the Western Front to be commemorated in the War Memorial Park was Private **Reginald Thomas Beaufoy,** 1st Battalion, Norfolk Regiment. He was killed in action in the Sambre Area on the 8th November 1918 aged 20, having served five months. Reginald lived with his parents Mr. and Mrs. Thomas Beaufoy, of 'St. Keyne', Queen Mary's Road, Coventry, but was actually born in Lockhurst Lane on the 18th September 1898. He received part of his education at Bablake School and was employed as a grinder until enlisting in June 1918.

At 5.30am on November 5th the Norfolk Battalion led an attack with the 1st Bedford at Jolimetz in immediate support. The weather, which had been splendid, had now broken and the advance was made in a downpour. At first no opposition was met and by 7.30am, when the first objective had been gained well within the forest, the Bedford Battalion passed through to continue the attack. The 1st Norfolk re-formed at the crossroads at Le Godelot, ready to give assistance, which, however, was not required.

On the 6th the Battalion went on to La Haute Rue, near the eastern edge of the forest, for a further attack. At 5.30pm it was ready for an attack across the Sambre, which flows north-eastwards along the eastern edge of the forest. A bridge in front had been reported safe, but by 7.30pm it was found to have been blown up by the retreating enemy, as well as a footbridge.

Late that night a working party was detached to help in the reconstruction of the bridge at the lock. By 6.00am on the 7th work had to be abandoned owing to the hostile machine gun fire. At 7.30am the attack was launched across the river, with the railway running north to Maubeuge as its objective. The passage was made by a pontoon bridge constructed during the night by the Royal Engineers. The railway was reached and made good by the Cheshire Battalion and a platoon of B Company of the Norfolk Battalion.

About 4.30pm the Devonshire Battalion of the 95th Brigade passed through the Norfolk and Cheshire Battalions to continue the attack. Fontaine on the right, was taken but the Devonshire men were held up at St. Remi-Mal-bati on the left. At 5.30am on the 8th the Devonshire Battalion were attacking near Avesnes-Maubeuge road, and at 9.30am the 1st Norfolk were withdrawn to the railway, whence, on the 9th and 10th , they went back to rest and reorganise at Jolimetz on the west of the Mormal Forest.

Private Beaufoy lost his life in the fighting on the 8th and is buried in the south corner of Bachant Communal Cemetery, this cemetery contains only four burials from WW1. The same date of death applies to Private A. Dann in the East Yorkshire Regiment. The remaining two men buried in this cemetery also died on the same day, Driver Thomas Miller Driver T/3309 Army Service Corps and Driver Wilfred Arthur Tudor T/25963 Army Service Corps who both died on the 24th August 1914. A Bablake old boy his name appears on the school memorial.

Post Armistice

Corporal. **James Frederick Nelson,** M2/135613, G.H.Q Troops, Motor Transport Company, Royal Army Service Corps was accidentally killed in France on the 26th July 1919. He was born on the 3rd October, 1894 at Birmingham and resided at 165 Leicester Causeway employed as a turner. On the 3rd November 1916, *'The Coventry Graphic'* featured his wedding at St. Mark's Church, Coventry. The marriage between Lance Corporal J. F. Nelson and Miss Beatrice Sophia Lowe had been solemnised by special licence. He was the eldest son, whilst Beatrice was the third daughter of Mr and Mrs T. Lowe of 106 Cromwell Street. After the wedding the bridegroom returned to the front after a short leave. Corporal Nelson is buried at Terlincthun British Cemetery.

A Soldier's Wedding

The Unverified Plaques

Two plaques commemorate men of which little information is known, Private W. Mattocks and Private G. Peters. Neither of the men have any matches on the Commonwealth War Graves, *'Soldiers who died in the Great War'* or the *'City of Coventry: Roll of the Fallen'*. In addition no matches are shown in *'The Coventry Graphic'* or *'The Coventry Herald'*.

The Medal Index cards show a William N. Mattocks of the Army Service Corps but are unfortunately incomplete and *'The Coventry Herald'* dated 3rd November 1916 mentions a *"Private William R. Mattocks of the Royal Fusiliers, Public School Battalion, son of Mr. F. E. Mattocks, Kensington Road, Coventry has been wounded in the arm on the 7th October. He is now in Lord Derby's Hospital, Warrington and is making excellent progress. He was formerly a clerk in the offices of Messrs Browetts, Solicitors, Bailey lane, Coventry"*.

The Medal Index Cards show four matches for Private G. Peters, Royal Army Medical Corps. These are George William Peters 1827, George S. Peters 1887, George E. Peters 29319 and finally George Peters 102739.

In addition the name G. Peters appears on the Bablake School Memorial as one of those who served and *'The Wheatleyan'* mentions he was in the Royal Army Medical Corps but with no other supporting information.

Scant Details on Private Peters

Corporal Arthur Hutt VC

The last plaque to be unveiled at the War Memorial Park which references the Great War is the plaque dedicated to the memory of Corporal Arthur Hutt VC, Coventry's only Victoria Cross winner. The plaque on the 5 foot 6 inches memorial stone was revealed on the 17th April 1955 and records the official citation of the action in which Corporal Hutt won the VC.

The citation reads :

"On the 4th October 1917, the 48th Division were in the vicinity of St. Julien and the 7th Battalion had as their objective a location known as Tweed House. A Company captured their first objective but when they continued their advance, all the officers and non-commissioned officers in Private Hutt's platoon were hit. Private Hutt thereupon took command and led forward the platoon. He was held up at a strong point on his right, but immediately ran forward alone, shot the officer and three men in the post, and caused forty or fifty others to surrender. Presently, realising that he had pushed too far ahead, Hutt withdrew his party.

He personally covered the withdrawal, sniping the enemy and killing a number of them. Then he carried back a comrade, who had been badly wounded, and put him under shelter. After he had organised and consolidated his position, he learned that some wounded men still lay in the open, where they were likely to be taken prisoners. As no stretcher bearers were available, Hutt went out himself and carried in four men under heavy enemy fire".

Arthur was born on the 12th February 1889 at 1 Court 4 New Buildings, Coventry to Samuel Hutt and Jane Hutt (formerly Knibb). He attended Holy Trinity School and joined the 7th Battalion Royal Warwickshire Regiment as a Territorial in 1909 under Colonel Wyley and was in camp with his Battalion when war was declared on August 4th 1914. With his colleagues he was immediately mobilised, and after two and half days leave he went into training. Going overseas he fought at Armentieres, at Messines Ridge and at Gomercourt Wood. He also served in Belgium and Italy.

The news of *'Coventry's First VC'* was covered in *'The Coventry Graphic'* dated 30thNovember 1917: *"We are pleased to record that the Victoria Cross has been awarded to Corporal Arthur Hutt, son of Mr. Samuel Hutt, of 7 Gulson Road, Coventry. He is married and his home is at 8 Caludon Road, Stoke, Coventry. He was for many years employed at Courtald's artificial silk works, Coventry. A member of the 7th Battalion,*

252

Warwickshire Territorials, he was with the Battalion when it went to Rhyl camp just before the outbreak of war, and was never disbanded. Hutt went to France with the 1/7th Warwicks early in 1915, and served rather more then a year in the field. He was discharged, resumed his work at Courtald's and was called up again fourteen months ago. He has five brothers in the army, two being still in France, one is home wounded. Hutt is the first Coventry man to receive the VC. On behalf of the citizens of Coventry, the Mayor has forwarded a message of congratulation to Corporal Hutt". The message sent by telegram to Corporal Arthur Hutt 5428 A company Royal Warwickshire Regiment, British Expeditionary Force, France stated *"Heartiest congratulations from the citizens of Coventry on obtaining the VC. Alick Hill Mayor".*

'The Coventry Herald' also referenced the Mayor's telegram and added *"though he has been in the thick of the fighting, Corporal Hutt has never been wounded nor sick. Amongst his friends in Coventry Corporal Hutt is much esteemed. He has always been regarded as of a quiet, unassuming disposition, independence and trustworthiness being strongly marked in his character. He was promoted from the ranks of Private to Corporal quite recently."*

The patriotic Hutt family had already appeared in *'The Coventry Graphic'* at this point, and the corresponding article read *"Among the many fine military records held by local families none is more noteworthy that that of the brothers Hutt, sons of Mr S. Hutt of 7 Gulson road , Coventry. All are serving with the Royal Warwicks and two are at the front. Mr Hutt's sons together with a grandson, are shown , their names being (reading from the top downwards) Private A. Hutt. Private W. Hutt (in action), Private H. Hutt (grandson), Private William Hutt, Private A. Hutt (in action), Private B. Hutt and Private H. Hutt".*

Arthur Hutt's father, Samuel also tried to enlist but was told by the Recruiting officer that he had *'done his bit'* .

A month after the announcement of Arthur's VC the Mayor Alick Hill wrote to 'The Coventry Graphic' in December 1917:

To the Editor

Sir - It is intended that Corporal Hutt VC shall on return to his native city be accorded a welcome worthy of his valiant deeds. The citizens will, I am sure, heartily approve of this, and give it their warmest support. The committee having charge of the arrangements consider, however, that the citizens would desire to give him some tangible proof of their appreciation of his noble and heroic action, which has earned for him the greatest honour for valour which his King and Country can confer. It has accordingly been decided to establish a Fund, the proceeds of which shall be invested in War stock, and presented to him.

I have the greatest pleasure in stating that I have opened a Fund at Lloyds bank, and shall be glad to receive subscriptions, or they may be paid into the bank. In order that the Fund may be fully representative, individual subscriptions are to be limited to a guinea, but the smallest amount would be welcome. Subscriptions will be acknowledged in the public press. The Fund will be closed on December 31ˢᵗ. I earnestly appeal to the citizens to give their support to this Fund.

Yours Truly
Alick Hill , Mayor

In December 1917, Private Bertie Hutt Royal Warwickshire Regiment, brother of Corporal Arthur Hutt VC died of wounds received in France. He was 24 years of age, lived at 2c 5h Gulson Road and was born on the 11th November 1893, at Coventry. Before the outbreak of hostilities he was employed at Messrs Calcotts as a polisher being called up as a territorial and went to France in June 1916. He left a widow and two children and is buried in St. Sever Cemetery Extension, Rouen. At this point another brother Private Walter Hutt was lying seriously wounded at a hospital in the north of England.

On Saturday, 12th January 1918, Corporal Arthur Hutt VC came home and the people of Coventry turned out in their thousands to welcome him. Arthur was met at the railway station at 2.30pm by the Mayor and Mayoress and the Town Clerk and was driven through the town centre to the Council house, the procession being headed by a band including the cadets and the fire brigade. There was a large company in the council house and thousands of people waited outside. The Mayor welcomed Hutt and the Town Clerk read a copy of the address from the corporation which was to be illuminated and presented to the VC, together with a purse of money at a later date. Definite news of Arthur's arrival was not confirmed until the morning, although official circles suggested he would be home on leave.

Arthur's neighbours from Caludon Road also bought him a cigarette box inscribed with 'Corporal Hutt VC 4th Oct 1917' as a sign of recognition. The street was gaily decorated with flags and across the centre of the street was a sign *"Welcome home to our VC"*.

'The Coventry Graphic' stated *"Colonel Wyley having been connected with Hutt's regiment for 45 years spoke of his pride in this man and mentioned that the VC's father had given five sons to the army. After signing the council house visitors book, Hutt was carried shoulder high from the chamber. In the evening he attended a popular demonstration in the drill hall, where speeches were also made by Colonel Wyley, Captain Kaye and Councillor Wale. Mr Doyle on behalf of the directors of Courtalds Ltd by whom the Corporal was employed handed him war bonds to the value of £250"*.

In the course of a short speech Corporal Hutt said *"All I did was my duty to king and country. I saw that the officers and NCO's had been knocked out. The duty had got to be done by someone. It was the duty of the senior soldier to take command and so I took command of the platoon. I saw what was in front and I thought; " if someone does not do it, we shall be in Germany very soon and of course I carried on and did my duty"*.

Corporal Hutt leaving the station.

In February 1918 Arthur appeared on the front page of *'The Coventry Graphic'* promoting tank week.

The *'Coventry Graphic'* Cover

Arthur was demobilised in January 1919. At the dedication of the War Memorial in October 1927, Arthur was one of the key attendees supporting Mrs. Bench.

In 1937, 'The Coventry Standard' invited readers to relate some of their experiences during the Great War. Arthur Hutt participated in this project and revealed more about his role. The paper described Arthur as a " *A well knit, middle aged man of medium height who walked smartly into the office. There was nothing in his features to indicate he was a man of singular courage, save perhaps his firm set lower jaw and his alert manner. In fact he gave the impression he was of rather a mild disposition.*

Appearances however are sometimes deceptive and strangers passing him would hardly distinguish him from the other men who daily are to be seen in Coventry streets. Actually this man Corporal Hutt V.C, is one of the bravest of Coventry citizens and his daring exploits in the winter of 1917, when as the leader of a platoon in France he captured between 40 and 50 Germans and rescued a badly wounded man amid intensive fire, was one of the outstanding acts of individual initiative in the whole history of the Great War. His decorations include besides the VC the 1914-1915 star, the general service medal, and the Victory, the coronation and the Territorial Efficiency medals. Being of modest disposition Corporal Hutt was loth to speak of the daring deed which won for him the highest British decoration for valour and which made the 7th Battalion, particularly proud of him".

Arthur went on to explain the action which saw him awarded the VC but when asked what spurred him on to these deeds of bravery, he said *"I saw my wounded brother that morning. He was my youngest brother. I went to him and just got there as they were taking him away. The Germans I had captured afterwards carried him down on a stretcher. I lost two young brothers in the war, one was killed on the field and another died at Plymouth".*

This was Private Alfred Hutt, 2nd Battalion, Dorsetshire Regiment attached Labour Corps who died aged 27 on the 27th November 1918. He was born on the 13th January 1893 and the husband of Priscillia (nee Elkington) of 20 Howard Street, Coventry, prior to the outbreak of war he was employed as a fitter and is buried in London Road Cemetery. His headstone is shown and reads *'Gone but not forgotten'*.

Arthur died in April 1954. On his death an Arthur Hutt VC Memorial Fund was set up, chaired by the Mayor and with Mr. H. A. Satchwell as secretary. The committee estimated that the memorial of Cornish granite would cost £200 and a quote was accepted from Coventry stonemason Mr. J. H. Taylor. *'The Coventry Evening Telegraph'* of April 1955 printed details of the events which would take place on the 17th April 1955. A military parade would be held through the central streets of Coventry, to include various branches of the Old Comrades Association, a contingent from the Home Guard and the Regimental Band from the Royal Warwickshire Regiment. The parade would start after a short service at the War Memorial Park at 11.00am, the service being conducted by the Very Reverend R. T. Howard.

'The Coventry Evening Telegraph' dated 18th April 1955 revealed the success of the memorial service; *"Crowds lined the central streets as the parade passed by. Fluttering proudly were 28 standards of British legion branches and Old Comrades Associations representing as did the bemedalled men behind, service to the country in three wars, the Boer War and two World Wars".* In addition to members of Arthur's family, old comrades who were present at the action which won Arthur his VC attended as did three holders of the VC: Mr. Henry Tander, Mr. William Beesley and the Reverend Arthur Herbert Proctor.

When he unveiled the memorial Alderman Fennell told the gathering *"This is the proudest moment of my Lord Mayoralty – to have the great honour of unveiling this memorial to our fellow citizen. Arthur Hutt was the only citizen of Coventry ever to have been awarded the greatest honour for bravery and heroism when fighting for his country".*

The Dedication of Arthur Hutt VC Memorial

In June 1955 one final award was made to the Hutt family, when Field-Marshal Viscount Montgomery handed over replicas of the medals won by Arthur Hutt VC to his widow. Viscount Montgomery was Colonel of the Royal Warwickshire Regiment. The Regiment expressed a wish to give something personal to Arthur's widow and in presenting he told her *"Your husband was a very gallant soldier"*. Arthur's medals resides with his family.

Summary

To fund the purchase of Styechale Common and the building of a War Memorial the Citizens of Coventry were called upon twice to raise the required £34,000. The 249 men commemorated in the War Memorial Park make up less then ten percent of the Roll of the Fallen for Coventry, which stood at 2,600 names with later additions. There is little doubt that the costs of 25s for a plaque and a tree, determined by the War Memorial committee deterred many of the relatives and friends of the Fallen from taking up the offer. The contribution to the overall cost of the scheme seems to be minimal after the cost of the tree and plaque has been removed. Despite Mrs Eliza Bench representing *'sacrificial motherhood'* at the dedication of the memorial it was deemed unnecessary to provide her with plaques in memory of her sons, although appreciations were expressed to her *'on a very trying occasion'*.

The War Memorial Committee, reviewed several memorials and concluded that the overall cost for the memorial was estimated at £5,000 a cheaper memorial was considered by the Committee to be a *'laughing stock'*. Whilst the Committee deliberated, war memorials were being erected all over Coventry to the Fallen from different districts or works, sadly not all these memorials remain and others are kept in storage or inaccessible to the public. A memorial remains in Spencer Park where Coventry's original memorial once stood.

A War Memorial Park is not unique, but the combination of a park paid for by public subscription and with individual trees commemorating the Fallen appears to be a unique phenomenon. In one of his last public appearances prior to his death in 1928, the appearance of Field Marshall Earl Haig ensured that the Citizens of Coventry turned out to witness this historic occasion in their thousands. His tactics and strategies during the War are the subject of many debates, but the formation of the British Legion assured that he was welcomed by ex-service men and the Citizens of Coventry.

Unfortunately the traditions introduced after the dedication of the Memorial are no longer maintained, the Mayor no longer walks with relatives of the Fallen to open the 'Chamber of Silence' and the Chamber remains closed, only opening on Armistice Day.

It has been over ninety years since the start of the Great War and generations on the relatives and descendants of the Fallen have provided documents and photographs to compile this book. Documents kept by families of those commemorated in the War Memorial Park to ensure that they are 'Not Forgotten'.

The men commemorated in the War Memorial Park served in various 'Theatres of War' and represented Coventry in the Army, Navy and Royal Air Force. The details provided show some insight into the horrendous conditions and factors the men had to cope with on a daily basis. Corporal Arthur Hutt VC, was Coventry's only Victoria Cross winner and a plaque dedicated to his memory was placed in the park on his death.

During the Great War it is estimated that the Department of Munitions spent £40,500,000 in Coventry and the munitions work attracted employees from surrounding locations. The formation of the Friends of the War Memorial Park and the announcement of a lottery grant of £4,000,000 should be sufficient to ensure that the Park is used for its intended purpose and meets the expectations of the park visitors. The comments on the future of the Memorial from 1927 in *'The Coventry Herald'* remain today:

"The monument is the people's own tribute to their heroic fellow citizens, and that they should have frequent access to it. Though raised to the glory of the dead, it is no dead monument. It has a message for all time, and it will come home more deeply if the people not viewing it from a distance are able to move about it freely and intimately".

Appendix A

The Men of the War Memorial Park: Alphabetical Order

Name	Date of Death	Plaque
Private Frederick Cecil Abel	20th June 1918	O56
Pioneer Sidney Arthur Abel	26th June 1916	O56
Private John Adams	9th May 1915	P9
Major Harry Allen	16th January 1918	O32
Gunner William Walter Atkins	9th February 1917	O43
Private Alfred Charles Baker	27th May 1918	R16
Lance Corporal Joseph Newton Barber	17th October 1918	R11
2nd Lieutenant Kenneth Purcell Barford	27th March 1918	E3
Private Thomas Henry Barker	21st August 1918	J4
Gunner Richard Barnes	21st March 1918	F1
Sapper William Joseph Barnett	31st July 1917	O44
Lance Corporal Frederick Henry Barrett	4th May 1917	O38
Private Kenneth Barry	27th July 1916	J8
Private Albert Bartlett	28th August 1918	B4
Private Henry Bartlett	25th September 1915	R22
Private John Bartlett	8th November 1918	R22
Private Frank Bates	12th October 1917	L6
Sergeant Oliver Bates	6th August 1916	L11
Private Norman Samuel Bausor	27th March 1918	O29
Gunner Arthur Baxter	15th August 1917	R5
Private Reginald Thomas Beaufoy	8th November 1918	L10
Private George Bell	1st April 1917	R26
Private Alfred Garnett Bentley (2)	1st December 1917	4 & 5
Private Arthur Edwin Berry	4th October 1917	I3
Private Leonard Leslie Bicknell	2nd September 1917	G4
Rifleman Arthur John Blackshaw	27th March 1918	I6
Gunner Vincent Arthur Bloxham	18th September 1917	N5
Corporal John Blythe	25th September 1917	R14
Lance Corporal Walter Bodin	4th September 1916	O39
Private Harold George Bonham	20th October 1918	O19
Private Edgar Herbert Buckingham	14th April 1918	O51
Private Henry Buckland	2nd October 1917	O37
Private Arthur Lewin Bull	5th October 1918	R3
2nd Lieutenant Henry Acton Linton Bullock	14th July 1916	L7
Private Alfred Burrows	13th October 1914	K1
Private John Butler	24th June 1917	R9
Captain Alan Caldicott	7th December 1916	D5

Name	Date of Death	Plaque
Wireman Horace James Cantrill	1st March 1917	O15
Lieutenant Geoffrey George Edwin Cash	27th August 1916	O54
Private Arthur Checkley	23rd April 1917	E1
2nd Lieutenant Raymond Russell Cheshire	4th October 1917	D6
Private Alfred John Clarke	19th July 1916	P2
Private David Clarke	16th October 1918	P1
Lance Corporal Victor Leslie Clarke	3rd July 1918	M6
Private John Clews	9th April 1917	R10
Gunner Herbert Charles Collingbourne	4th January 1916	P14
Private William Frederick Cooke	17th March 1916	R30
Private William Herbert Cooke	1st October 1916	P16
Private Francis Daulman Cox	26th November 1916	Q11
Private Lawrence Cecil Cox	14th July 1916	P27
Lance Sergeant Henry Smith Craven	6th March 1916	J3
Private George Albert Daniels	3rd December 1917	O31
Sergeant Arthur Day	6th July 1916	Q3
Private William Thomas Derbyshire	5th March 1918	Q2
Sergeant Leonard Bennett Dufner	26th August 1918	M7
2nd Lieutenant Joseph Arthur Edwards	27th September 1918	M4
Private William Edwards	5th March 1917	D1
Private Percy Elliman	14th July 1916	M2
Private Horace Jesse Ellis	12th October 1917	P3
Private George Edward Everest	23rd January 1916	
Gunner William John Evetts	27th July 1917	O26
Pioneer Frank Clifford Farrell	23rd June 1918	R21
Able Seaman Walter John Farrell	19th March 1918	O34
Private Leonard Faulks	11th November 1916	P4
2nd Lieutenant Charles Fletcher	19th September 1918	O33
Sapper Percy John Francis	3rd July 1916	J1
Private Walter Frank Francis	14th October 1918	Q20
Private Hollister Clare Franklin	22nd January 1918	J2
Private Donald Fraser	20th August 1918	O71
Trooper Cyril Maurice Garbutt	23rd March 1918	Q12
Private George William Caviar Gardner	30th October 1917	O25
Private Frederick William Garner	10th February 1917	O61
2nd Lieutenant Jack Garside	18th November 1918	N9
Artificer Edward James Geater	10th September 1918	F2
Wheeler Reginald Frederick Henry Gibbens	29th March 1925	A9
Captain Francis Noel Graham	16th November 1916	R19
Captain George Lionel Graham	11th April 1918	R20
Private Frederick Grant	25th September 1915	O1

Name	Date of Death	Plaque
Private Herbert Henry Griffin	21st October 1918	I10
Private Thomas Edmund Griffin	14th March 1917	Q9
Private John Henry Gutteridge	27th August 1915	R4
Field Marshall Earl Haig	29th January 1928	J5
Private Ernest James Hall	13th October 1918	7
Private Ernest John Hancocks	23rd October 1918	L8
Private Harold Hubert Harper (2)	20th September 1918	Q26/O4
Lance Sergeant Herbert William Harper (2)	21st April 1917	O48/O49
Private Leonard Harris	28th August 1918	F4
Private Raymond Francis Harrow	27th July 1916	R24
Rifleman Wilfred Herbert Hartopp	1st September 1918	O22
Private Frank Harvey	4th October 1917	O28
Private John Harold William Hastings	19th October 1919	Q7
Private Frank Ellis Hattersley	15th July 1916	L5
Private William Herbert	10th April 1918	
Artificer James Moss Hewitt	31st May 1916	J9
Private Ernest Jacob Higton	6th August 1915	O2
Private Thomas Hogan	26th July 1916	E8
Private Harry Holland	2nd September 1918	O3
Private George Hopkins	6th September 1918	O59
Captain Frederick Julian Horner	15th April 1918	D4
Private Reginald Harold Hotton	15th October 1914	O9
2nd Lieutenant Evan Llewellyn Howells	23rd October 1918	O42
2nd Lieutenant William Arthur Imber	27th August 1917	A8
Corporal Alfred Ernest Ison	27th August 1915	P15
Captain Harold Jackson (2)	7th June 1917	3 & 6
Corporal John Jackson	29th June 1915	Q19
Private Lawrence Jackson	25th September 1917	P11
Private Thomas Percy Jackson	8th September 1918	A3
Gunner Charles Alfred James	29th September 1917	Q13
Private Eardley Robert Preston Jeffrey	30th November 1917	E7
Private Albert Jeffs	14th July 1916	M5
Gunner George Reginald Jenkins	14th March 1916	B1
Private Joseph Vincent Jewsbury	28th September 1918	G1
Private Arthur Johnson	1st November 1914	D3
Private Montague Johnson	1st September 1916	I2
Gunner 1st Class Charles John Jones	31st May 1916	G5
Private Frederick Charles Maurice Jones	18th June 1918	O30
Private Leslie Thomas Jones	4th November 1918	N6
Private Edward Arthur Kelly	16th March 1917	N8
Private Harry Edward Kimberley	22nd August 1917	O35

Name	Date of Death	Plaque
Private Thomas Kimberley	24th October 1918	Q16
Private John King	30th June 1917	F3
Private John King	7th July 1917	P6
Private Herbert Lane	21st March 1918	Q27
Rifleman Herbert Lawrenson	15th May 1915	O27
Corporal F Leduc	19th April 1918	Q1
2nd Lieutenant Robert Logan	20th October 1918	O47
Private Fred Lord	2nd April 1918	2
Sapper Arthur Roland Lord	10th March 1918	P13
2nd Lieutenant Alan Percy Charles Loveitt	25th July 1916	N3
Corporal Reginald Arthur Lucas	27th April 1918	N14
Private Ernest Lumbert	4th April 1916	R18
Private Alexander Ross MacDonald	15th September 1916	B3
Captain Arthur Ernest Mander	9th October 1917	O17
Sergeant Albert Ernest Mann	9th April 1917	N11
Private Charles Edward Mann	24th May 1916	O10
2nd Lieutenant Edward Mason	9th May 1915	A10
Driver Edward Ernest Mason	23rd July 1917	A11
Lieutenant Ernest Harold Masters	24th December 1918	Q24
Driver William Mattocks		G9
Petty Officer Edward Wallace Maxwell	1st January 1915	A5
Private Frederick Henry Mence	8th October 1915	P12
Sapper Royston Stephen Merrett	5th May 1917	L4
Gunner Alfred George Middleton	27th August 1916	P22
Private Thomas William Molloy	24th July 1917	O
Cadet Hubert Arthur Morley	27th October 1918	Q14
Private Arthur Robert Rotheram Moy	25th October 1918	L3
Gunner William Henry Wilcox Moy	27th September 1918	I9
Lance Corporal John Musson	5th May 1915	E9
Drummer Horace William Nelson	29th May 1918	P25
Corporal James Frederick Nelson	26th July 1919	R12
Private Edward Walter Newbold	28th April 1917	O24
2nd Lieutenant Theo Edward Newsome	25th September 1915	Q23
Gunner William Richard Northall	7th July 1917	G11
Rifleman George Odey	28th April 1917	O23
Private Herbert Henry Oswin	22nd November 1918	P26
Private Wilfred Albert Owen	25th January 1917	P8
Gunner Frederick George Page (2)	16th September 1918	P21/O21
Rifleman Hugh Conrad Pails	7th October 1916	M8
Corporal William Pargeter	10th November 1917	B2
Bombardier Henry Walter Parnell	20th August 1917	R2

Name	Date of Death	Plaque
Trooper William Ivens Patchett	14th November 1917	P7
Pioneer Herbert Joseph Payne	8th August 1915	L2
Private Thomas Speight Pearson	9th August 1916	Q8
Private Joseph Peddie	30th April 1916	O5
Private Edward Peel	5th October 1917	P5
Asst Paymaster Edward Leslie Peirson	9th July 1917	E6
Private G. Peters		N4
Rifleman George William Peters	8th October 1918	O57
Private Sydney Mornington Pickerill	23rd March 1918	J11
Private Charles Ponder	15th February 1915	O50
Driver Kenneth Merrick Powell	19th October 1918	E2
Gunner Horace Preedy	25th August 1917	N12
Lance Corporal Isaac Norman Price	13th October 1915	R23
Captain Percy Malin Pridmore MC	2nd September 1917	8
Private Ernest Peter Prior	28th October 1914	G2
Gunner George Nixon Punshon	22nd July 1917	O60
Private Eric Keppell Purnell	1st July 1916	F6
Sergeant George Frederick Randall	5th May 1917	A1
Leading Stoker James William Randall	11th February 1916	A2
Private Charles Raper	10th October 1917	A7
Private Bert Rawlins	25th April 1915	O52
Sergeant John Reddington	18th July 1916	Q15
Corporal Joseph Richards	26th January 1918	N1
Captain Joseph Arthur Richards	4th November 1918	G6
Private Henry Herbert Riley	11th April 1917	Q4
Lance Corporal Sydney James Riley	12th October 1917	I7
Lieutenant Ernest Charles Robinson	20th January 1919	Q8
Private Charles Wilfred Roe	7th March 1919	G7
Private Mark Welch Rollason	23rd October 1916	R27
Corporal William Henry Rowe	23rd March 1918	O53
Corporal Arthur Albert Rubley	13th February 1917	P10
Sergeant Herbert Meredith Shaffir	21st March 1918	R25
Lance Corporal Joseph Sharratt	4th May 1917	P18
Gunner Frederick Stanley Shepperd	2nd July 1916	B6
Private William Simmons	23rd June 1915	R28
2nd Lieutenant Frederick George Smith	8th February 1918	Q25
Private George William Smith	31st October 1918	R29
Private James Thomas Smith	7th November 1918	O7
Private Mark Henry Smith	16th May 1915	M1
Sergeant Samuel Arthur Smith	2nd August 1917	Q22
Sergeant Sydney Harry Smith	24th August 1918	Q22

Name	Date of Death	Plaque
Private Albert Harold Sowter	16th October 1918	O6
Gunner Arthur Ernest Sparkes	18th August 1917	R13
Sergeant Arthur Stagg	17th May 1915	N2
Private William Stagg	8th August 1915	N2
Gunner Sydney Reginald Stebbing	4th May 1915	G8
Private Joseph Stew	23rd October 1918	O40
Private George John Stokes	11th December 1914	E5
Private William Stonier	23rd June 1918	J7
Sapper Aleck Sutton	21st May 1918	G10
Private Frank Swingler	9th August 1915	1
Private Kenneth John Taylor	29th March 1918	P17
Private Albert Charles Thompson	26th October 1917	R8
Private Albert Thornett	10th April 1918	Q5
Trooper Dennis Thorpe	7th September 1918	O8
Lance Corporal Austin Timmins	16th August 1919	A6
Sergeant William Toms	3rd July 1916	L1
Private Wallace Towe	20th December 1915	E10
Private Andrew Thomas Townend	19th December 1914	I8
Private Arthur Trickett	28th August 1918	P24
Driver Harry Truslove	23rd April 1918	I4
Corporal Reginald George Turrell	7th May 1918	O55
Quartermaster Sergeant Arthur Richard Voice	13th March 1916	B5
Private George Wagstaffe	16th May 1915	O13
Private Harry Wainman	13th May 1918	O18
Private Cuthbert William Walker	30th August 1917	I1
2nd Lieutenant Bernard Michael Ward	20th November 1917	O41
Gunner John Ward	26th April 1918	R15
Gunner Leonard Warden	18th October 1917	E4
Private Ernest Edward Waring	14th July 1916	O11
Private Eric Charles Durrant Warner	30th October 1917	R7
Lance Corporal George Percy Warner	8th October 1915	R7
Private Stanley Thomas Warner	21st October 1916	R7
Private William Webb	19th July 1918	O16
Private Charles Clifford Webster	24th August 1916	J10
Private Arthur Welch	31st August 1918	N13
Private Frank William Wells	3rd October 1918	O36
Leading Stoker Rowland Whitehouse	8th February 1917	D2
Gunner Horace Rubert Whitmill	17th February 1921	Q18
Private James William Wilcox	14th July 1916	P19
Stoker Herbert Charles Wilkins	26th November 1914	R6
Private William Henry Wilson	1st November 1918	O14

Name	Date of Death	Plaque
Private Laurence Matthew Windridge	9th October 1917	M3
Private Charles Thomas Worrall	29th November 1916	O12
Private Leonard Joseph Worrall	10th July 1916	O46
Sergeant Arthur Tyne Wright	8th October 1918	9
Private Herbert George Wright	15th November 1916	R17
Lieutenant William Reginald Fitzthomas Wyley	19th September 1916	J6
Sergeant Thomas Yates MM	9th July 1916	O18

Appendix B

Maps of the Plaque Locations

The above map is subject to Copyright and not be reproduced without permission

Copyright Coventry City Council

The areas highlighted are shown enlarged on the following pages

Appendix B

Maps of the Plaque Locations

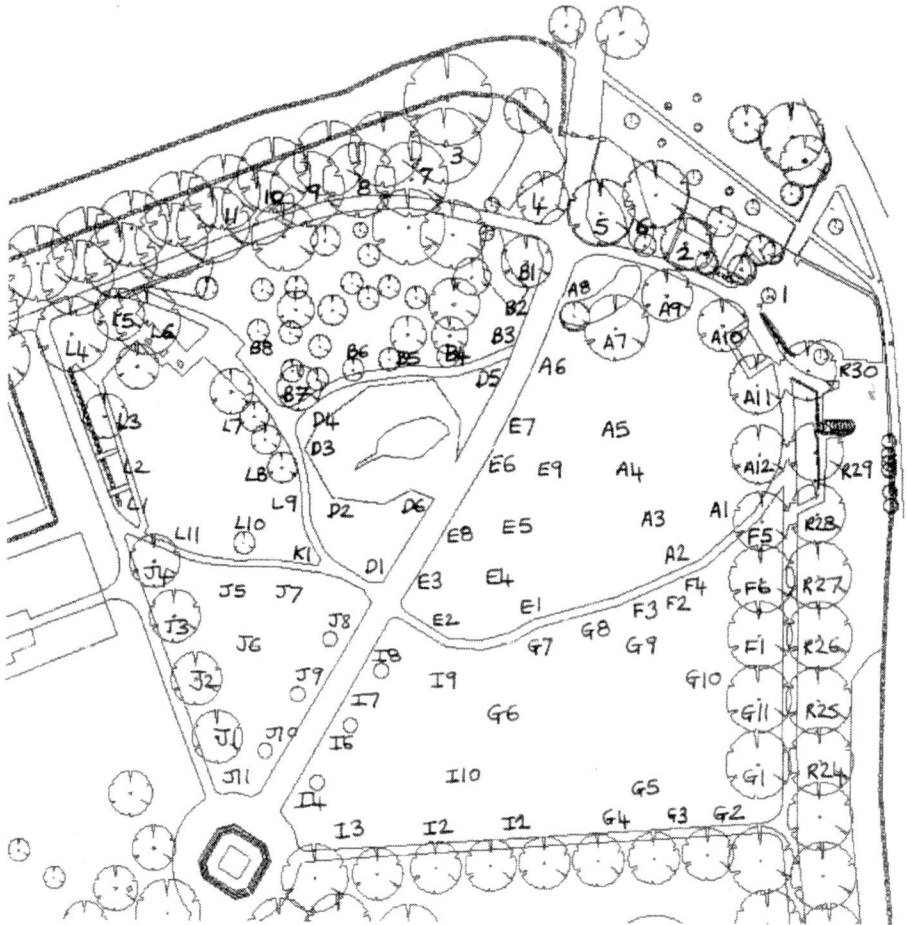

The above map is subject to Copyright and not be reproduced without permission

Copyright Coventry City Council

Appendix B

Maps of the Plaque Locations

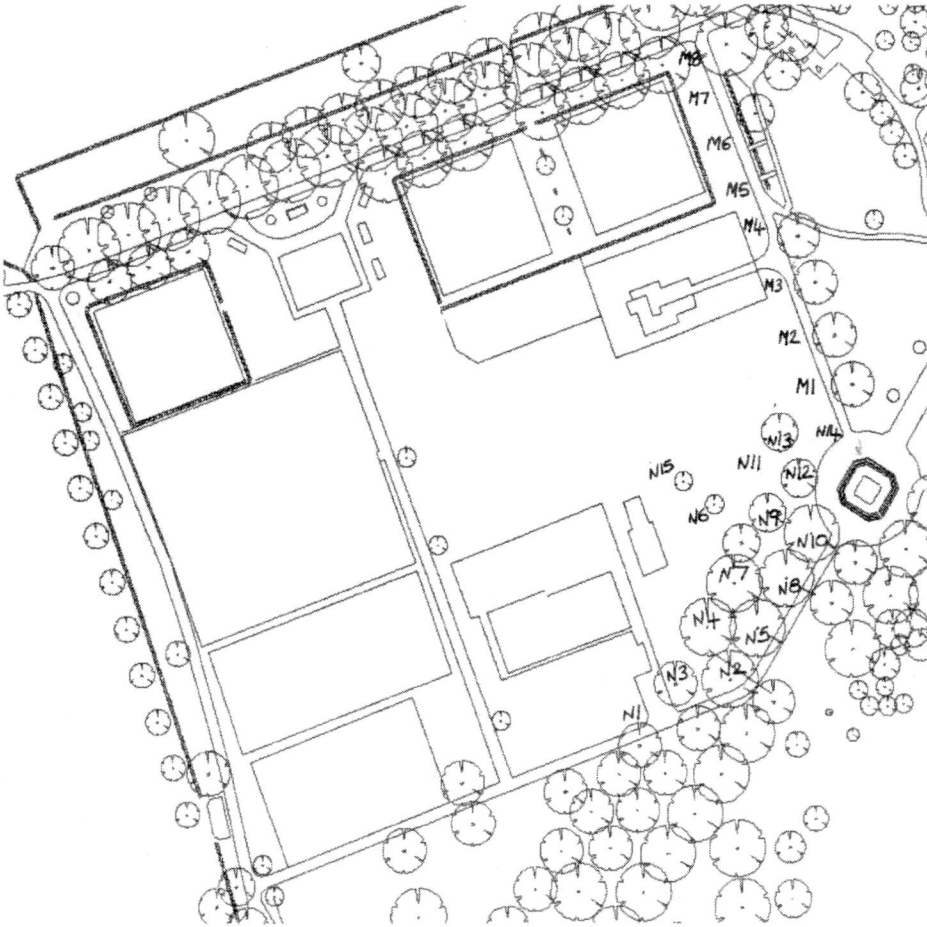

The above map is subject to Copyright and not be reproduced without permission

Copyright Coventry City Council

271

Appendix B

Maps of the Plaque Locations

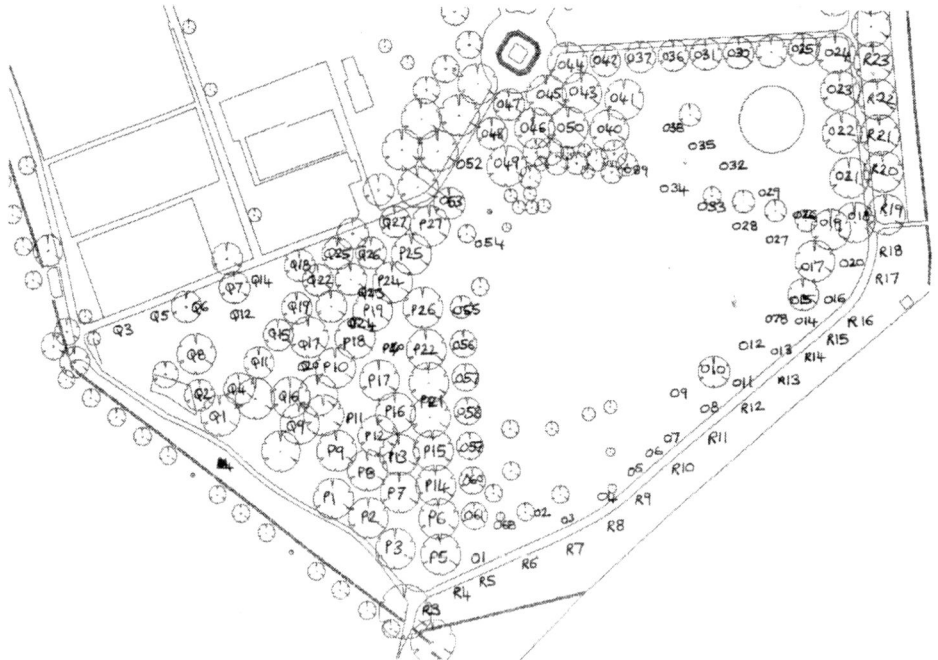

The above map is subject to Copyright and not be reproduced without permission

Copyright Coventry City Council

Appendix C
Cemeteries/Memorials Abroad

This section details where the Fallen are buried and commemorated outside of the UK. Exact location information, visiting information and historical information can be found on the Commonwealth War Grave Commission website www.cwgc.org or by phoning 01628 507200.

Belgium
Comines-Warneton, Hainaut

La Plus Douve Farm Cemetery	Private John Adams
Ploegsteert Memorial and Cemetery:	Private Edgar Hebert Buckingham
	Private Andrew Thomas Townend
	2nd Lieutenant Edward Mason
	Private Harry Holland
Rifle House Cemetery, Warneton	Private William Simmons

Heuvelland, West-Vlaanderen

Dranoutre Military Cemetery	Private Joseph Peddie

La Louviere, Hainaut

La Louviere Town Cemetery	Lance Corporal Joseph Newton Barber

Ieper, West-Vlaanderen

Bard Cottage Cemetery	Corporal John Jackson
	Private John King
Brandhoek New Military Cemetery:	Driver Edward Ernest Mason
Chester Farm Cemetery	Captain Harold Jackson
Duhallow A.D.S Cemetery	Gunner Horace Preedy
La Brique Military Cemetery	Gunner William John Evetts
The Huts Cemetery	Gunner Charles Alfred James
Ypres (Menin Gate) Memorial:	Private Ernest Peter Prior
	Sapper William Joseph Barnett
	Private Arthur Johnson
	Private Charles Ponder
	Private Bert Rawlins
	Private Frederick Grant
	Private Ernest Lumbert
	Private John King
	Private George William Caviar Gardner
	Private Eric Charles Durrant Warner
	Corporal William Pargeter
Vlamertinghe Military Cemetery	Gunner Arthur Ernest Sparkes
	Captain Percy Malin Pridmore MC

Nieuwpoort, West-Vlaanderen
Nieuport Memorial   Private John Butler

Poperinge, West-Vlaanderen
Dozinghem Military Cemetery: Private Charles Raper
Haringhe (Bandaghem) Military Cemetery
                                     2nd Lieutenant Charles Fletcher
Lijssenthoek Military Cemetery   Gunner George Nixon Punshon
                                     Private Leonard Leslie Bicknell

Zonnebeke, West-Vlaanderen
Tyne Cot Cemetery and Memorial: 2nd Lieutenant William Arthur Imber
                                     Captain Alfred Ernest Mander
                                     Bombardier Henry Walter Parnell
                                     Private Harry Edward Kimberley
                                     Private Cuthbert William Walker
                                     Private Arthur Edwin Berry
                                     2nd Lieutenant Raymond Russell Cheshire
                                     Private Frank Harvey
                                     Private Edward Peel
                                     Private Laurence Matthew Windridge
                                     Lance Corporal Sydney James Riley
                                     Gunner Leonard Warden
                                     Private Albert Charles Thompson
                                     Private Albert Thornett

East Africa
Dar Es Salaam War Cemetery   Captain Alan Caldicott

France
Aisne
Grand-Seraucourt British Cemetery   Captain George Lionel Graham
Soissons Memorial   Private Alfred Charles Baker
                                     Drummer Horace William Nelson
Vadencourt British Cemetery   Sapper Arthur Roland Lord

Nord
Anneux British Cemetery   Private Lawrence Jackson
Arneke British Cemetery   Gunner John Ward
Avesnes Le-Sec Communal Cemetery   Private Ernest James Hall
Awoingt British Cemetery   Private John Bartlett
Bachant Communal Cemetery: Private Reginald Thomas Beaufoy
Cambrai Memorial   Private Eardley Robert Preston Jeffrey

Private George Albert Daniels

Caudry British Cemetery — 2nd Lieutenant Robert Logan

Croix Du-Bac British Cemetery — Private William Herbert

Cross Roads Cemetery — Private James Thomas Smith

Esquelbecq Military Cemetery — Private Harry Wainman

Sapper Aleck Sutton

Estaires Communal Cemetery — Gunner William Richard Northall

Glageon Communal Cemetery: — Private Frank William Wells

Godewaersvelde British Cemetery — Private Frank Bates

Gouzeaucourt New British Cemetery — 2nd Lieutenant Joseph Arthur Edwards

Private Joseph Vincent Jewsbury

Hazebrouck Communal Cemetery — Private Thomas William Molloy

Gunner Sydney Reginald Stebbing

Lance Corporal John Musson

Highland Cemetery — Private Joseph Stew

Landrecies British Cemetery: — Private Leslie Thomas Jones

Captain Joseph Arthur Richards

Laventie Military Cemetery: — Sergeant William Toms

Lille Southern Cemetery — Lieutenant Ernest Charles Robinson

Meteren Military Cemetery: — Private Henry Buckland

Private Alfred Burrows

Outtersteene Communal Cemetery — Gunner Arthur Baxter

Ovillers communal Cemetery — 2nd Lieutenant Evan Llewellyn Howells

Pommereuil British Cemetery — Private Ernest John Hancocks

Preseau Communal Cemetery — Private William Henry Wilson

Romeries Communal Cemetery — Private David Clarke

St. Aubert British Cemetery — Driver Kenneth Merrick Powell

Tannay British Cemetery, Thiennes — Private Donald Fraser

Verchain British Cemetery — Private Thomas Kimberley

Villers Hill British Cemetery — Private Francis Joseph Ison

Pas de Calais

Achiet-Le-Grand Communal Cemetery — Able Seaman Walter John Farrell

Aire Communal Cemetery: — Lance Corporal Victor Leslie Clarke

Trooper Dennis Thorpe

Anzac Cemetery — Private George Hopkins

Arras Communal Cemetery and Memorial

Private Henry Herbert Riley

Private Arthur Checkley

Lance Corporal Joseph Sharratt

Sergeant George Frederick Randall

Corporal William Henry Rowe

Arras Flying Memorial	2nd Lieutenant Kenneth Purcell Barford
Bac-Du-Sud British Cemetery	Private Leonard Harris
Bailleul Road East Cemetery	Private Fred Lord
Bethune Town Cemetery	Private Mark Henry Smith
	Sergeant Arthur Stagg
Bienvillers Military Cemetery	Private Thomas Henry Barker
Cabaret–Rouge British Cemetery	Private Kenneth John Taylor
Calais Southern Cemetery	Sergeant Oliver Bates
Cambrin Military Cemetery	Private Thomas Edmund Griffin
Chili Trench Cemetery	Private Edward Walter Newbold
Cojeul British Cemetery	Private John Clews
Croisilles British Cemetery:	2nd Lieutenant Bernard Michael Ward
Duisans British Cemetery	Lieutenant Ernest Harold Masters
	Rifleman George Odey
Etaples Military Cemetery:	Private Francis Daulman Cox
	Lance Corporal Walter Bodin
Faubourg D'Amiens Cemetery	Gunner Richard Barnes
Favreuil British Cemetery	Private Alfred Garnett Bentley
Foncquevillers Military Cemetery	Private Frederick Henry Mence
	Private William Frederick Cooke
	Lance Corporal George Percy Warner
Gonnehem British Cemetery	Corporal Reginald George Turrell
Guards Cemetery, Cuinchy:	Corporal Alfred Ernest Ison
	Private John Henry Gutteridge
La Chaudiere Military Cemetery	Lance Sergeant Herbert William Harper
Le Touret Memorial:	Private George John Stokes
	Rifleman Herbert Lawrenson
	Private George Wagstaffe
Les Baraques Military Cemetery	Corporal John Blythe
Longuenesse (St. Omer) Cemetery:	Gunner Herbert Charles Collingbourne
Loos Memorial:	Lance Sergeant Henry Smith Craven
	Private Henry Bartlett
	2nd Lieutenant Theo Edward Newsome
	Lance Corporal Isaac Norman Price
	Private Alfred John Clarke
Morchies Australian Cemetery	Gunner Frederick George Page
Mory Abbey Military Cemetery	Private Arthur Trickett
Ruyaulcourt Military Cemetery	Gunner William Henry Wilcox Moy
Terlincthun British Cemetery	Private George William Smith
	Corporal James Frederick Nelson
Tilloy British Cemetery	Sergeant Samuel Arthur Smith
Vimy Memorial:	Private Alexander Ross MacDonald

	Sergeant Albert Ernest Mann
Vieille Chapelle, New Military Cemetery	
	Private Reginald Harold Hotton
Vis-En-Artois British Cemetery and Memorial	
	Private Arthur Welch
	Private Harold Hubert Harper
	Private Albert Harold Sowter
Wimereux Communal Cemetery:	Gunner Vincent Arthur Bloxham

Seine Maritime

| Mont Huon Military Cemetery | Private Arthur Lewin Bull |
| Ste. Marie Cemetery, Le Havre: | Private Harold George Bonham |

Somme

A.I.F Burial Ground	Lieutenant Geoffrey George Edwin Cash
Assevillers New British Cemetery	Private Albert Bartlett
Aveluy Communal Cemetery Extension:	Gunner Alfred George Middleton
	Lt William Reginald Fitzthomas Wyley
Bagneux British Cemetery	Private Thomas Percy Jackson
Beauval Communal Cemetery	Gunner George Reginald Jenkins
Bouzincourt Ridge Cemetery	Private Norman Samuel Bausor
Carnoy Military Cemetery	Gunner Frederick Stanley Shepperd
Citadel New Military Cemetery	Private George Edward Everest
Contalmaison Chateau Cemetery	Private Herbert George Wright
Contay British Cemetery	Captain Francis Noel Graham
Corbie Communal Cemetery	Private Charles Edward Mann
Daours Communal Cemetery	Sergeant Sydney Harry Smith
Dive Copse British Cemetery	Driver Harry Truslove
Epehy Wood Farm Cemetery	Private George Bell
Franvillers Communal Cemetery Extension:	
Ham Cemetery	Sergeant Herbert Meredith Shaffir
Heilly Station Cemetery, Mericourt-l'Abbe	
	Sergeant John Reddington
Hem Farm Military Cemetery	Private William Edwards
Louvencourt Military Cemetery	Pioneer Sidney Arthur Abel
Peronne Communal Cemetery	Rifleman Wilfred Herbert Hartopp
Pozières Cemetery and Memorial:	Private Sydney Mornington Pickerill
	Private Herbert Lane
	Trooper Cyril Maurice Garbutt
	Rifleman Arthur John Blackshaw
	Pioneer Frank Clifford Farrell
Quarry Cemetery	Sapper Percy John Francis

Regina Trench Cemetery   Private Stanley Thomas Warner

Ribemont Communal Cemetery Extension
           Private Frederick Charles Maurice Jones

Rocquigny –Equancourt Road Cemetery

           Major Harry Allen

           Private William Thomas Derbyshire

           Private Walter Frank Francis

Roisel Communal Cemetery   Private Arthur Robert Rotheram Moy

Thiepval Memorial: Private Kenneth Barry

           Rifleman Hugh Conrad Pails

           Private Eric Keppell Purnell

           Sergeant Arthur Day

           Private Frank Ellis Hattersley

           Sergeant Thomas Yates MM

           Private Leonard Joseph Worrall

           2nd Lt Henry Acton Linton Bullock

           Private Lawrence Cecil Cox

           Private Percy Elliman

           Private James William Wilcox

           Private Albert Jeffs

           Private Ernest Edward Waring

           2nd Lieutenant Alan Percy Charles Loveitt

           Private Thomas Speight Pearson

           Private Thomas Hogan

           Private Kenneth Barry

           Private Raymond Francis Harrow

           Private Montague Johnson

           Private William Herbert Cooke

           Rifleman Hugh Conrad Pails

           Private Mark Welch Rollason

           Private Leonard Faulks

           Private Charles Thomas Worrall

Warloy-Baillon Communal Cemetery   Private Charles Clifford Webster

Greece

Doiran Memorial   Sapper Royston Stephen Merrett

Struma Military Cemetery   Captain Frederick Julian Horner

Iraq

Basra Cemetery   Qtrmaster Sergeant Arthur Richard Voice

Basra Memorial   Private Frederick William Garner

           Sergeant Leonard Bennett Dufner

Amara War Cemetery   Private Wilfred Albert Owen

Corporal Arthur Albert Rubley
Private Edward Arthur Kelly

Italy
Giavera British Cemetery   Private Hollister Clare Franklin
Corporal Joseph Richards
Private William Stonier
Private Herbert Henry Griffin
Mazargues War Cemetery Extension Rifleman George William Peters
Montecchio Precalcino Cemetery Private Herbert Henry Oswin
Savona Memorial   Lance Corporal Frederick Henry Barrett

Gallipoli
Helles Memorial   Private Ernest Jacob Higton
Pioneer Herbert Joseph Payne
Private William Stagg
Sulva Bay   Private Frank Swingler

Malta
Pieta Military Cemetery   Private Wallace Towe

Palestine
Beersheba Military Cemetery   Trooper William Ivens Patchett

Persia
Tehran War Cemetery   Sergeant Arthur Tyne Wright

Appendix D

Cemeteries in the UK

This section details where the Fallen are buried and commemorated in the UK. Exact location information, visiting information and historical information can be found on the Commonwealth War Grave Commission website www.cwgc.org or by phoning 01628 507200.

Coventry

London Road Cemetery:

Private Horace Jesse Ellis
2nd Lieutenant Jack Garside
Wheeler Reginald Frederick Henry Gibbens
Private John Harold William Hastings
Private Charles Wilfred Roe
2nd Lieutenant Frederick George Smith
Lance Corporal Austin Timmins

Foleshill Congregational Ground — Gunner William Walter Atkins

Radford Cemetery — Gunner Horace Rubert Whitmill

Other UK

Bath (Locksbrook) Cemetery: — Cadet Hubert Arthur Morley

Belfast City Cemetery — Private William Webb

Chatham Naval Memorial: — Petty Officer Edward Wallace Maxwell
Asst Paymaster Edward Leslie Peirson

Haslar Royal Navy Cemetery, Gosport — Artificer Edward James Geater

Hollybrook Memorial — Corporal Reginald Arthur Lucas

Kensal Green (All Souls) Cemetery, — Private Frederick Cecil Abel

Plymouth Naval Memorial: — Leading Stoker James William Randall

Portsmouth Naval Memorial: — Wireman Horace James Cantrill
Gunner Charles John Jones
Artificer James Moss Hewitt
Leading Stoker Rowland Whitehouse
Stoker Herbert Charles Wilkins

Appendix E

Military Terminology

Able seaman: Merchant Navy seaman, certified to carry out routine duties at sea. This rank is higher than an Ordinary Seaman

Adjutant: Officer acting as an administrative assistant

Army: Commanded by a General with approximately 250,000 to 300,000 troops, sub-divided into 3 – 4 Corps

Bar: Small emblem on a military decoration showing a further award of this medal

Battalion: Army unit comprised of approximately 1,000 men, commanded by a Colonel or Lieutenant-Colonel; divided into four companies.

Brigade: Commanded by a Brigadier-General, comprised of approximately 4,000 – 5,000 troops sub-divided into 3-4 Battalions.

Captain: In the army, an officer who commands a company, troop, or battery; in the navy, an officer ranking above a Commander and below a Commodore

Casualty Clearing Station: The first stage on the route back from the front for the wounded, normally located about 1.5 miles from the front line.

Clasp: Metal bar or similar, clasped to the ribbon of a military decoration. Clasps were awarded according to the individual's deed or service. A Clasp could also be a further award of the same medal

Commander: The chief commissioned officer of a military unit whatever their rank

Company: Sub-unit of a Battalion, commanded by a Major or Captain comprised of approximately 200 men divided into four platoons.

Corporal: in the army, a non-commissioned rank below Sergeant and above Lance-Corporal.

Corps: A component of the army forming a unit comprised of approximately 80,000 men divided into 4 – 6 divisions, commanded by Lieutenant-General.

Derby Scheme: Named after Lord Edward Derby, all eligible males were asked to express their willingness to serve. The scheme lasted for 5 months from July 1915 to December 1915 and provided less then 350,000 troops.

Division: Largest tactical unit of the British Army (beneath Corps). Commanded by a Major-General, with approximately 15,000 – 20,000 troops split into 3 brigades.

Enfilading Fire: Fire which is directed from the side rather then the front

Gazetted: Officer's promotions and awards were posted in the London gazette.

Hindenburg line: A vast system of defence constructed during the winter of 1916-1917 under the guidance of General Paul von Hindenburg

Leading Seaman: A non-commissioned rank in the navy, above Able Seaman and Ordinary Seaman

Lieutenant: In the army, a commissioned officer below a Captain; in the navy, a commissioned officer below a Commander

Mentioned in Despatches: The award of a Mentioned in Despatches (MID) was the lowest form of recognition for services during the war, and was announced in the London Gazette

Merchant Navy: Term used for civilian seafaring personnel, the military used merchant ships and their crew during wartime

Minenwerfer: Translates into Mine Launcher, a class of short range mortars used to target obstacles including trenches and barbed wire

Non-Commissioned Officer: a position above private and below Officer

Ordinary Seaman: Lowest grade of crew member

Other Ranks: Soldiers, as opposed to Officers

Parados: Barricade at the rear of the trench to stop shrapnel getting into the trench.

Platoon: approximately 50 men, commanded by a Lieutenant or Second Lieutenant sub-divided into 4 sections

Rank: Level of authority held by an officer or soldier

Regiment: A large body of troops, organised under the command of a superior officer, and forming a definite unit of an army or military force; the specific name of the largest permanent unit of the cavalry, infantry, and foot-guards of the British Army.

Salient: A battlefield feature that projects into enemy territory. The salient was typically surrounded by the enemy on three sides making the salient vulnerable.

Section: Approximately 12 men commanded by a NCO

Sergeant: In the army, an NCO next in rank above a Corporal.

Sunken Road: A well worn road that over time had become sunken below its original level.

Yeoman of the Signals: Petty Officer who specialised in the handling and conducting of flag signals in the communications departments of a naval vessel.

Zero Hour: The time at which the military operations were planned to start

Appendix F

Military Abbreviations

Anzacs: Australian and New Zealand Armed Corps
ASC: Army Service Corps
BEF: British Expeditionary Force
BWM: British War Medal
CASC: Canadian Army Service Corps
CCS: Casualty Clearing Station
CEF: Canadian Expeditionary Force
CO: Commanding Officer
CSM: Company Sergeant Major
CWGC: Commonwealth War Grave Commission
DCLI: Duke of Cornwall's Light Infantry
DCM: Distinguished Conduct Medal
DOW: Died Of Wounds
DSO: Distinguished Service Order
GHQ: General Headquarters
GOC: General Officer Commanding
HAC: Honourable Artillery Company
HMT: His Majesty's Transport
KIA: Killed In Action
KOSB: King's Own Scottish Borderers
KRR: King's Royal Rifles
KSLI: King's Shropshire Light Infantry
MC: Military Cross
MGC: Machine Gun Corps
MIC: Medal Index Card
MID: Mentioned in Despatches
MM: Military Medal
MMGS: Motor Machine Gun Service
NCO: Non-Commissioned Officer
OBLI: Oxfordshire and Buckinghamshire Light Infantry
OR: Other Ranks
OTC: Officer Training Corps
POW: Prisoner Of War
RAMC: Royal Army Medical Corps
RAF: Royal Air Force
RAMC: Royal Army Medical Corps
RE: Royal Engineers

RFA: Royal Field Artillery
RFC: Royal Flying Corps
RGA: Royal Garrison Artillery
RHA: Royal Horse Artillery
RNAS: Royal Naval Air Service
RNVR: Royal Navy Volunteer Reserve
RWR: Royal Warwickshire Regiment
SWB: South Wales Borderers
TMB: Trench Mortar Battery
VC: Victoria Cross

Appendix G

War Memorials in Coventry

<u>Bablake School:</u> Memorial in the school hall showing the names of the 96 men who fell and the 700 who served.

<u>British Thompson Houston Memorial</u>: This memorial is dedicated to those who fell from the firm British Thompson Houston Company and can be found in the Royal Warwicks club, Tower Street, Coventry.

<u>Central Methodist Church</u>: This memorial can be found at the top of the staircase in the church and records the names from the congregation who fell during the Great War.

<u>Coventry Corporation Memorial</u>: Each department from Coventry Corporation had a memorial to those that served and those that fell. These are located throughout the Council House.

<u>Earlsdon Working Mens Club</u>: Now known as the Albany Club, shows the name of five Fallen members situated behind the bar.

<u>Holy Trinity Church</u>: This incorporates three panels showing the names of members of the congregation who fell.

<u>Iliffe Works Memorial</u>: The location of this memorial is not known, but a picture of it was found during research

<u>King Henry VIII:</u> A memorial mounted outside the school library to replace the original destroyed during the bombings of World War II. Shows the names of former pupils who fell.

<u>Post Office:</u> Wall-mounted in the main Post Office; bears the names of those who fell.

<u>Queen's Road Church:</u> Stained glass panels showing the names of the fallen from the congregation.

<u>Radford Memorial</u>: A free standing memorial next to St. Nicholas's church showing the names of 112 members of the Radford community who either fell or served during the Great War.

<u>St. Barbara's Church</u>: A brass plaque at the rear of the church, showing the names of members of the congregation who fell during the Great War. The majority of whom lived in the Earlsdon district.

<u>St. John's Church</u>: Stained glass panels that show the names of the fallen and located near to the old school in Hill Street in the City centre.

<u>St. Michael's Church</u>: A stone tablet with the names of the fallen inscribed, mounted in the front porch of the church in Stoke.

<u>Triumph and Gloria Memorial</u>: A free standing memorial in the grounds of Coventry Cemetery dedicated to the employees of the firm who died.

Appendix H

Ypres Salient Map

Late Addition

Additional information and picture of Private **Herbert Henry Griffin**, 2nd Battalion, Royal Warwickshire Regiment. A postcard sent to his wife in 1916 revealed he was fighting on the Austrian front to the north of Venice. A note written on the reverse of a postcard reads *'Friday 1st December 1916. Dear All, just a line to let you know I am alright. I wrote a letter yesterday but you needn't worry if I don't write for a day or two as I may not have the chance you understand, and please tell Mother if you have the chance XXXX Love Bert'*. The card had been censored by Sergeant Edwards.

Meet The Author

Trevor Harkin lives in Earlsdon, Coventry with his wife and two children. After leaving secondary school, he furthered his education at Coventry University initially achieving a Batchelor of Engineering and furthered this with an MBA in Management and an MSc in Automotive and Automotive Component Manufacture. He then wrote several articles on Knowledge Management and performance metrics which appeared in Engineering periodicals.

Having completed his studies, he began researching his family tree and found on his Mother's side that his Grandmother lost three uncles in the Great War and on his Father's side his Great grandfather served all the way through the war, although he never spoke about his experiences.

On a visit to Coventry's War Memorial Park he noticed the plaques dedicated to those who fell during WW1 and WW2 and set about researching the plaques and started a web page www.warmemorialpark.co.uk. Local appeals were made and relatives of the deceased came forward. Trevor has contributed articles to a local magazine 'The Earlsdon Echo' and a number of his articles have featured in local newspapers, 'The Coventry Telegraph' and 'Coventry Observer'.

Where time permits he has also assisted relatives of the Fallen and those who have expressed an interest in soldiers from Coventry. This is his second book, his first book 'Bablake School and the Great War' is also available

Index